LESSONS FOR
INTRODUCING
PLACE VALUE

GRADE 2

THE TEACHING ARITHMETIC SERIES

Teaching
ARITHMETIC

LESSONS FOR
INTRODUCING PLACE VALUE

▲▲▲▲▲

GRADE 2

MARYANN WICKETT
MARILYN BURNS

MATH SOLUTIONS
SAUSALITO, CALIFORNIA, USA

Math Solutions
150 Gate 5 Road
Sausalito, CA 94965
www.mathsolutions.com

Library of Congress Cataloging-in-Publication Data
Wickett, Maryann.
   Lessons for introducing place value : grade 2 / Maryann Wickett,
Marilyn Burns.
       p. cm. — (Teaching arithmetic)
Includes index.
   ISBN 0-941355-45-4 (alk. paper)
 1. Number concept—Study and teaching (Primary)   2. Place value
(Mathematics)—Study and teaching (Primary)   I. Burns, Marilyn, 1941–
II. Title. III. Series.
   QA141.15 .W49 2002
   372.7'2—dc21
                                                                    2002008151

ISBN-13: 978-0-941355-45-2

Editor: Toby Gordon
Production: Melissa L. Inglis
Cover & interior design: Leslie Bauman
Composition: Cape Cod Compositors, Inc.

Printed in the United States of America on acid-free paper
11   10   09   ML   7 8 9 10

A Message from Math Solutions

We at Math Solutions believe that teaching math well calls for increasing our understanding of the math we teach, seeking deeper insights into how children learn mathematics, and refining lessons to best promote students' learning.

Math Solutions shares classroom-tested lessons and teaching expertise from our faculty of professional development consultants as well as from other respected math educators. Our publications are part of the nationwide effort we've made since 1984 that now includes

- more than five hundred face-to-face professional development programs each year for teachers and administrators in districts across the country;
- annually publishing professional development books, now totaling more than seventy titles and spanning the teaching of all math topics in kindergarten through high school;
- videos for teachers and for parents that show math lessons taught in actual classrooms;
- on-site visits to schools to help refine teaching strategies and assess student learning; and
- free online support, including grade-level lessons, book reviews, inservice information, and district feedback, all in our *Math Solutions Online Newsletter*.

Also, we have expanded our own efforts and have collaborated with Scholastic Inc. to create a new intervention program titled Do The Math™ that supports at-risk and struggling students. Written with a team of Math Solutions consultants and based on the lessons from our Math Solutions Teaching Arithmetic series, Do The Math provides teachers with lessons carefully sequenced and paced to meet the needs of students who would benefit from intervention. To learn more about this program, please visit the Do The Math website at *www.scholastic.com/DoTheMath*.

For information about all of the products and services we have available, please visit our website at *www.mathsolutions.com*. You can also contact us to discuss math professional development needs by calling (800) 868-9092 or by sending an email to *info@mathsolutions.com*.

We're always eager for your feedback and interested in learning about your particular needs. We look forward to hearing from you.

CONTENTS

ASSESSMENTS   146

BLACKLINE MASTERS   159

INDEX   175

ACKNOWLEDGMENTS

Thank you to the students and the entire second-grade staff of Carrillo Elementary School, San Marcos Unified School District, San Marcos, California, who willingly opened their classrooms and freely gave their support, ideas, and feedback on the lessons in this book: Shamera Carlin, Betty Estrada, Janet Gilbertson, Barbara Rhodes, Ted Saulino, and Viki Stewart.

Thank you to the following teachers and their students for helping us to know more about second graders by understanding first and third graders: Eunice Hendrix-Martin, Carrillo Elementary School; Andrea Holmes, Carrillo Elementary School; Sally Wurts, Carrillo Elementary School; Elizabeth Sweeney, Community District 2, P.S. 11 and P.S. 33, New York City.

Thank you to Fred Wise, who has lived up to his last name. His instructional leadership and willingness to do what's best for kids have made a positive difference in the lives of all who have met him.

INTRODUCTION

"How do you read this number?" I asked Lori as I wrote *18* on a sheet of paper.

"Eighteen," Lori replied.

"How many ones are there in eighteen?" I asked.

"Eight," Lori answered.

"How many tens?" I continued.

"One," Lori said.

I pushed a pile of tiles toward Lori. "Please count out eighteen tiles," I said. Lori slowly counted out eighteen tiles, first carefully counting by ones, then recounting again by ones a bit more quickly.

"That's eighteen," Lori said.

I pointed to the numeral I had written and said, "Using the tiles, please show me what the eight means." Lori counted out eight tiles.

"There!" Lori said with a smile. "The eight means there are eight ones in eighteen."

"Using the tiles, please show me what the one means," I continued.

Lori removed one tile from the remaining tiles. "This tile is the ten," Lori explained, pointing to the one tile she removed from the pile. "There's one ten in eighteen and eight ones."

"What about the rest of the tiles?" I asked.

Lori shrugged, seemingly unconcerned about the nine remaining tiles.

The first two questions I asked Lori are typical of those students encounter in textbooks and on standardized tests. Lori's answers lead us to believe that she understands place value. But when asked to use her tiles to show her understanding, the evidence of her understanding crumbled. Lori's response of showing one tile to represent one ten with no concern about the nine remaining tiles indicates confusion.

What Does It Mean to Understand Place Value?

Most children at this age are familiar with numbers up to one hundred. They can count correctly, although some get confused when changing from one decade to the next—from twenty-nine to thirty or thirty-nine to forty, for example. They can write the numbers from 1 to 100, even though some from time to time still write individual digits backward or reverse the digits in numerals. They can compare numbers—fifty-six and thirty-seven, for example—and tell which is greater and which is less, even though they might not be able to explain why. Some children may be developing the understanding that a 3 in the ones place stands for three individual objects while a 3 in the tens place represents three groups of ten objects. An important notion most children have not thought about is how place value makes it possible to express all numbers with only the digits from 0 to 9.

The following three components are important indicators of children's understanding of place value. These are not separate or sequential aspects of place value but overlapping ideas that together contribute to children's overall understanding.

1. The Relationship Between Numbers and Groups of Tens and Ones—Children who have some understanding of the relationship between numbers and groups of tens and ones know that if they have three groups of ten objects and seven extras, they have thirty-seven objects altogether. Also, if they have forty-two objects, they know they can make four groups of ten and have two extras.

2. The Significance of the Positions of Digits in Numbers—When children have learned the significance of the placement of digits in numbers, they can explain the meaning of each digit. For example, when asked about the 3 and the 6 in 36, they know that the 6 stands for six individual units and the 3 stands for three groups of ten.

3. Solving Addition Problems—Children who understand place value can make use of the tens and ones structure of numbers to do addition, with and without regrouping. (Children who do not yet have a firm understanding of place value will rely on counting in some way.) In traditional instructional programs, place value is taught before addition as a prerequisite for learning to add with regrouping. Also, traditional instruction sees teaching of the standard algorithm—"carrying" or "regrouping"—as an important aspect of mathematics instruction in the primary grades. However, this unit takes the approach that integrating addition and regrouping with place value helps children see the relationship between the two ideas in a natural way. The unit doesn't "teach" students how to regroup but presents problems that require combining numbers to reach solutions. The emphasis isn't on procedures for adding but rather on the problem to be solved. From children's solutions, teachers can assess their ability to make use of the place value structure of our number system when working with numbers.

The Goals of Place Value Instruction

The goal of these lessons is to help children develop an understanding of the tens and ones structure of our number system and the ability to use their understanding when thinking about and working with numbers. At the end of second grade, students should be able to

▲ count large numbers of objects in two or more ways;
▲ recognize that regardless of the groupings used to count a group of objects, the total number in that group remains unchanged;
▲ relate large quantities of objects to their numerical representations;
▲ explain that digits have different values depending on their positions in numbers;
▲ understand that our place value system allows us to represent any number with just ten digits: 0, 1, 2, 3, 4, 5, 6, 7, 8, and 9;
▲ exchange ten ones for a ten and ten tens for a hundred;

▲ compare and explain the relative size of numbers to one hundred; and

▲ know that the same number can be represented with different but equivalent groupings; for example, twenty-three can be represented by two tens and three ones, one ten and thirteen ones, or twenty-three ones.

Traditionally students have demonstrated their knowledge of place value by simply stating the number in a particular place. For example, a student might be asked how many tens are in 436. A response of "three" might be considered as evidence the student knows there are three groups of ten in that number. A response of "three" actually shows that the student knows where the tens place is, not that he or she understands that the 3 indicates three groups of ten. Developing the understanding of what a digit means and the idea that the value of a digit within a number is dependent on its location in that number is a critical understanding for success with regrouping in addition and subtraction, and later on with multiplication and division.

What's in This Book?

The inspiration for this book was the Math By All Means unit *Place Value, Grades 1–2,* published in 1994. Since then, we have learned much about teaching place value to young children, from our individual teaching experiences, from our collaboration on revisiting the lessons from the original unit and working on the new lessons in this book, and from feedback from teachers who have used the initial unit in their classes. The changes in this book reflect what we've learned.

While place value is a frequent focus of mathematics instruction in all of the primary grades, we taught this collection of lessons to second graders. You may find, however, depending on your students, that some lessons may be appropriate for first or even third graders. We encourage you to use your best professional judgment when making choices about what is appropriate for your students.

The book includes practically all of the lessons and assessments from the initial unit, some reorganized and others with additions and edits. Five completely new lessons are included in this book, one of which includes a children's book, which did not appear in the earlier unit.

The Structure of the Lessons

In order to help you with planning and teaching the lessons in this book, each is organized into the following sections:

Overview To help you decide if the lesson is appropriate for your students, this is a nutshell description of the mathematical goals of the lesson and what the students will be doing.

Materials This section lists the special materials needed along with quantities. Not included in the list are regular classroom supplies such as pencils and paper. Worksheets that need to be duplicated are included in the Blackline Masters section at the back of the book.

Time Generally, the number of class periods is provided, sometimes with a range allowing for different-length periods. It is also indicated for some activities that they are meant to be repeated from time to time.

Teaching Directions   The directions are presented in a step-by-step lesson plan.

Teaching Notes   This section addresses the mathematics underlying the lesson and at times provides information about the prior experiences or knowledge students need.

The Lesson   This is a vignette that describes what actually occurred when the lesson was taught to one or more classes. While the vignette mirrors the plan described in the teaching directions, it elaborates with details that are valuable for preparing and teaching the lesson. Samples of student work are included.

Extensions   This section is included for some of the lessons and offers follow-up suggestions.

Questions and Discussion   Presented in a question-and-answer format, this section addresses issues that came up during the lesson and/or have been posed by other teachers.

While organized similarly, the lessons here vary in several ways. Some span one class period, others take longer, and some are suitable to repeat over and over, giving students a chance to revisit ideas and extend their learning. Some use manipulative materials, others ask students to draw pictures, and others ask students to rely on reasoning mentally. And while some lessons seem to be more suited for beginning experiences, at times it's beneficial for more experienced students to engage with them as well. An activity that seems simple can reinforce students' understanding or give them a fresh way to look at a familiar concept. Also, a lesson that initially seems too difficult or advanced can be ideal for introducing students to thinking in a new way.

How to Use This Book

Teaching the lessons described in the fifteen chapters requires at least twenty-five days of instruction, not including time for repeat experiences, as recommended for some lessons, or for the ideas for assessment suggested at the end of the book. While it's possible to spend a continuous stretch of five weeks or more on these lessons, we don't think that's the best decision. In our experience, children require time to absorb concepts, and we would rather spend a three-week period of time and then wait two months or so before returning for another three-week period, or arrange for three chunks of time, each two weeks long or so, spaced throughout the year. When students return to ideas after a break, they bring not only the learning they've done in other areas but also a fresh look that some distance can provide.

The three introductory lessons in the book build the foundation for developing understanding, and we suggest that you not skip these lessons. The other lessons are categorized to identify different aspects of place value. Experiences in each of the categories are beneficial for students, but no particular sequence of categories is best. However, the chapters within each category are placed in an order that reflects our experience teaching these lessons in several classes. A section on assessments at the end of the book, as well as a section titled "Linking Assessment to Instruction" found in several of the chapters, can help you think about making assessment an integral part of place value instruction.

Student participation is key to learning, and throughout the lessons in this book, students are expected to share their thinking. Students present their ideas in whole-class discussions, complete individual writing assignments, and talk in small groups, often preceded with a form of pair sharing called dyads. The use of dyads is based on the work of Dr. Julian Weissglass, a mathematics professor at the University of California at Santa Barbara. A dyad is an opportunity for all children to be listened to by another and for all children to listen. The following are the basic guidelines for using dyads:

1. Each person is given equal time to share and listen.
2. The listener does not interrupt the person who is talking. The listener also does not give advice, analyze, or break in with personal comments.
3. The listener does not share what the talker has said with anyone else. This confidentiality allows children to more fully explore their ideas without fear of being ridiculed or having their mistakes shared publicly.

It has been our experience that using these rules has given shy, less verbal children more opportunity to voice their ideas. In many cases, as these students gain confidence by sharing in a safe environment, they share more in class discussions, which often results in deeper thinking and understanding of the mathematics along with increased confidence. Using dyads frequently also helps keep more students engaged in the learning process.

Some children are more willing to share ideas than others. It's important, however, that all students learn to participate fully in our math classes. To facilitate this, we do the following:

▲ We make it a part of the classroom culture and our expectations that all students are capable and can think. They are expected to think and always do their best. Anything less is not acceptable.

▲ We support students by using our behavior as a model. We are constantly thinking about and exploring ideas with them. We do not expect them to believe that we know everything—we don't!

▲ To support students' thinking and development of strategies to use, we pose a question and then give students a few moments of quiet "think time," when all students are expected to focus their attention.

▲ After students have a few moments to form their own thoughts, we often use a form of pair sharing called dyads, as described earlier.

▲ Class discussions play a big role in our teaching. Before beginning a class discussion, we provide students the opportunity to think about the topic at hand, through think time, a written assignment, or a dyad. When students come to a class discussion prepared, the discussion is more lively and interesting and provides more opportunity for both the students and us to learn.

▲ In class discussions, students usually share strategies that they have used. We record these strategies on the chalkboard or some other highly visible place in the classroom, giving students a reference list of ideas.

As effective as this last strategy is, occasionally a student will still get stuck. In this instance, it often helps to ask a question such as the following:

"How might you begin?"

"What do you think the problem is asking you to do?"

"What would happen if . . . ?"

"Can you draw a picture that represents the problem or find a pattern?"

"Can you think of a smaller, similar problem?"

Our role as teachers is to be supportive and encouraging of all students. Listening carefully with a curious attitude about what children have to say is one way. Writing their responses on the board or a chart during class discussion is another way. Responding to their thinking with probing questions is another way still. When teachers demonstrate these behaviors, students know that they and their thinking are being valued. Sometimes this means putting aside any preconceived ideas and expectations of hoped-for responses. Being listened to and respected is highly motivating and longer lasting than quick words of praise. Quick words of praise can limit children and actually cause them not to try new ideas for fear of loss of praise or of disappointing the teacher. The focus should be on children expressing their thinking and reasoning processes, not just giving correct answers.

Throughout the lessons, we ask children to work with a partner. There are many ways to assign partners. Some teachers have children change partners every day, while others have their students keep the same partner throughout a unit of study. In some classrooms children choose their own partners, while in others partners may be assigned randomly, by drawing names as an example, or the teacher may assign children to be partners. Some teachers simply have students work with the person sitting beside or across from them. There are a variety of ways to do this and what works best with one group of children may not be the best way for another group.

It's likely you will choose to use these lessons along with other instructional materials or learning activities. It's important, however, to be consistent so that in all lessons you encourage students to make sense of ideas, communicate about their reasoning both orally and in writing, and apply their learning to problem-solving situations.

CHAPTER ONE
STARS IN ONE MINUTE

Overview

Children need many experiences counting quantities of objects and connecting their counting to our number system. *Stars in One Minute* provides children experience with thinking about ways to organize and count a large collection of objects. The students draw stars for one minute and count them in at least two ways. Extra bonuses of the lesson are that children get experience timing one minute and organizing their results into a class graph and interpreting the data.

Materials

▲ a clock with a sweep second hand or other timekeepers that measure one minute

▲ 3-by-3-inch sticky notes, 1 per child

▲ optional: *Draw Me a Star*, by Eric Carle (New York: Philomel Books, 1992)

Time

▲ four to five class periods

Teaching Directions

1. Begin the lesson by asking the children what they know about one minute. If you have a class clock with a sweep second hand, talk about how it measures one minute. Otherwise, you'll have to rely on your watch or bring to class some time-keepers that measure one minute for the children to use.

2. After all of the students have had a chance to tell their ideas about one minute, ask them to put their heads down and try to guess how long a minute is. Tell them that you'll say "Start" when you begin timing and "Stop" when one minute has passed. They should lift their heads when they think a minute has gone by. If they lift their heads before you've said "Stop," they should wait quietly.

3. Ask the children to predict how many stars they think you could draw on the board in one minute. Record their predictions on the board.

4. Have the students time one minute while you draw stars.

5. After you've drawn stars for one minute, ask the children to suggest ways to count the stars. Tell them you want to count them several different ways to be sure you've counted correctly. Because this lesson prepares the children for counting objects in different contexts, choose from their suggestions ways that involve grouping the objects into different-size groups, including twos, fives, and tens. If none of the children suggests grouping, make the suggestion yourself.

6. Count the stars several different ways, involving the children in helping you do so.

7. In another math period, discuss with the children the different kinds of stars they know how to draw. Draw a few on the board—a five-pointed star, an asterisk, a six-pointed star, an eight-pointed star. Have volunteers come to the board and show other kinds of stars that they know how to draw.

8. Tell the children that you'll time one minute while they draw stars. Before starting the minute, give students some time to choose one kind of star and practice drawing it on scratch paper.

9. Time one minute while the children make their stars. Have them count their stars in at least two ways and write about the methods they used. It's helpful to put a prompt on the board:

> *I counted by ___.*
> *I counted by ___.*
> *I drew ___ stars.*

10. When the children finish their work, check to see that they've counted their stars in at least two ways and figured the correct answer both times. If not, have them recheck and revise their work.

11. Each time a child brings you a correct paper, ask: "If you circled tens, how many circles would you have to make?" It's likely that not many, if any, chose to group their stars by tens. However, asking this question can help you assess their understanding.

12. On another day, have the children once again draw stars for one minute and count the stars in two ways. Distribute 3-by-3-inch sticky notes to the children, and have each one draw a sample star, write his or her name, and record the number of stars he or she drew. Ask the students to put their sticky notes on the chalkboard.

13. Talk with the children about how they might organize the notes into a graph so they can see the different kinds of stars they drew. (One nice thing about sticky notes is that you can move them easily to try out several suggestions.) Finally, select one way and put the notes on chart paper.

14. Ask the children to think about the information on the graph of sticky notes. Have children explain what the graph shows while you record their ideas on a chart. If you want, ask children to figure out the number of stars drawn in each category or by the children in the class altogether. These problems provide a sensible reason for children to use calculators.

15. Leave the graph posted on the wall for up to a week, giving children a chance to see and think about it. Then ask the children to look at the graph and think about sentences that would describe what they noticed. Call on children to give their ideas.

16. Post large chart paper and explain that you'd like to write about a dozen sentences about the graph. Ask students for sentences that describe the data on the graph. Record the sentences on the chart paper.

17. Give students the homework assignment for *Stars in One Minute*.

Teaching Notes

Draw Me a Star, by Eric Carle, begins with a young artist who draws a simple five-pointed star and then continues throughout his life to draw the sun, a tree, flowers, clouds, the moon, night, and finally as an old man, an eight-pointed star. The story captures children's imaginations, as do the bold and beautiful collages that illustrate the book. At the end of the book, Carle presents a step-by-step procedure for drawing an eight-pointed star. There is a suggestion for how to use this book as an extension activity at the end of this chapter.

Young children often count objects inaccurately. They may skip some objects in the group while counting others twice. As children begin to apply one-to-one correspondence, assigning one number to each object without skipping or double-counting any member of the group, their accuracy improves. Children of this age are often new masters of this skill. It is a huge leap for these young learners to recognize that not only can a 1 represent one object, but it can also represent one group of objects. For example, ten objects can be thought of as ten ones or one group of ten. Gaining this understanding is critical to making sense of our base ten number system.

Providing children with many opportunities to count large quantities of objects and relate the quantities to their numerical representations builds students' understanding of our base ten number system and its notation, particularly when they are asked to count the same group of objects in two or more ways. For younger or less experienced students, this means initially counting by ones. As students gain experience, they should be encouraged to count objects using specific-size groupings other than ones, for example, counting by twos. Also, children should be provided with opportunities to count the same number of objects using different-size groupings. In this lesson they might count the number of stars drawn in one minute by ones and then recount the same number of stars by twos, perhaps. Children come to realize through this kind of counting experience that the same number of objects counted using different grouping sizes will not change the total number of objects; that is, fifty-two objects is still fifty-two objects whether counted by ones, twos, fives, or tens.

The activities in this lesson support students as they grapple with these ideas, which are critical for computing accurately and efficiently. The recognition that 52 can be thought of as fifty-two ones or five tens and two ones or four tens and twelve ones builds the foundation for thinking about addition and subtraction of two-digit numbers.

This lesson has four parts, each requiring at least one math period. One year, I taught the lesson over four days, while another year, I spent more time, as described in the vignette. I chose to spend this additional time to allow the children to reflect on what we did before pushing further. Another year, I did the lesson in four days and it worked fine. When you teach this lesson, it's possible to collapse Days 4 and 5 into one day.

Note that the math periods for this lesson do not have to be consecutive. Sometimes, when children have time away from an activity, they're better able to reflect on what they've already done.

The Lesson

▲▲

DAY 1

I began the *Stars in One Minute* activity by asking the children what they knew about one minute.

"It takes sixty minutes to make an hour," Nick said.

"There are sixty seconds in a minute," Gwyn offered.

"We have ten minutes for recess," Jason said.

"The big hand on the clock is the minute hand," Katy said.

"The fast hand goes all the way around in one minute," Leslie said. Some of the children didn't know what she meant, and since our class clock didn't have a sweep second hand, I couldn't explain without showing them my watch. I decided it would be too disruptive to show my watch, as all the children would want to see it, so I continued calling on other children who were interested in contributing their ideas.

"My watch blinks every second," Timmy added. He was proud of the digital watch he had received for his birthday.

"Mine can be a stopwatch," Rudy said, "but I can't remember how to work it."

After all the children who wanted had told their ideas, I gave the next direction. "We're going to do an experiment that will give you an idea of how long a minute is," I said. "In a moment, I'll ask you to put your heads down. I'll say 'Start' and you'll keep your heads down until you think one minute has passed. I'll watch my watch and say 'Stop' when a minute is up. If you lift your head before I say 'Stop,' just wait quietly while I finish timing."

"Can I look at my watch and time too?" Nick asked. Several others with watches wanted to know if this was OK.

"You can either time along with me and see if we get to one minute at the same time," I said, "or put your head down and try to guess when a minute is up."

"Is it OK to count to sixty?" Sarah asked.

"Yes," I said, "you can do whatever you'd like to try to guess how long a minute takes."

"Why should I count to sixty?" Maria asked.

"Because there are sixty seconds in a minute," Sarah said, "and you go one, one thousand, two, one thousand, three, one thousand, like that."

"I don't get it," Maria said.

"I don't either," Colleen said.

Not all the children in the class could tell time or knew about seconds and minutes. I gave enough information so all could participate in the experiment. "You don't have to count as Sarah suggested," I said. "She thinks it will be helpful because she's learned that there are sixty seconds in one minute, and she has a way of counting that she thinks can help her keep track of seconds."

"But what do we do?" Maria asked.

"Try to guess how long one minute is," I said. "I'll say 'Start' and 'Stop,' and you have to try to feel how long a minute takes."

I got the children settled with their heads down, said, "Start," and began to time. When a minute had passed, I said, "Stop."

"We came out the same time," Nick said. He had decided to time on his watch.

"So that's how long one minute is," I said. "Now I want you to make a prediction about how many stars you think I could draw on the board in one minute."

"What kind of stars?" Tomo asked.

"Like this," I said, drawing a five-pointed star on the board.

Most of the children were interested in predicting. I wrote their guesses on the board, putting tally marks after each to show the number of children who made the same estimate. Their guesses ranged from fifteen to two hundred.

Counting the Stars

After one minute, I had filled the board with stars and asked the children for ways to count them. They had lots of suggestions.

"Erase them one by one," Katy said, "and draw them on the other side of the board, and the class can count as you do it."

"Just draw a circle around each star as you count it," Leslie said.

"Count by twos and draw circles around them," Rudy said.

"Even though they're not in good rows, they're kind of in rows," Andrew said, "so you can count the rows and then add up the numbers like we did with the zero to ninety-nine chart."

"Circle fives and count," Marina said.

"Color in each star and count," Grace said.

"I have another idea," Andrew said. "Count by twenties and circle them. You won't have to draw so many circles or add so many numbers that way."

"We don't have time to try all of your methods," I said. "Let me try some that I think you'll be able to use when you count your own stars. First I'll count by twos." I circled groups of two and had the children count by twos as I did so. They got stuck a few times; going from eighteen to twenty and then again from twenty-eight to thirty. Changing from one decade to the next is often hard for children. We counted fifty-nine stars.

"If you get stuck counting by twos," I said, "you can always use the zero to ninety-nine chart to help." I had them practice counting by twos, following my finger as I pointed to the numbers on the chart.

"Did anyone notice a pattern of the numbers I pointed to?" I asked.

"You skipped every other one," Marina said.

No one else volunteered an idea, so I continued by suggesting a different way to count.

"If I count the stars again, this time by fives," I said, "would I get fifty-nine again?"

"You can't count by fives," Teddy said. "It wouldn't come out right."

"What do you mean?" I asked.

"You would have some outside the circles," he answered.

"You mean like having this extra star outside the circle when I grouped by twos?" I asked. He nodded.

"That doesn't bother me," I said. "I can count the extras at the end. Watch and you'll see how. But will I still get fifty-nine stars?"

"You have to," Hassan said. "You have the same stars."

"Yeah," Andrew said, "it's the same."

"Well, it could be different," Colleen said. From my past experience doing this lesson with other classes, I've found that while it's obvious to some children that the number of stars will be the same no matter how I count them, others aren't sure.

I then circled groups of five, using another color, and the children counted. When we reached fifty-five, I counted the extras, "fifty-six, fifty-seven, fifty-eight, fifty-nine."

"I'm going to count one more way," I said, "to be sure that I've drawn fifty-nine stars. I'm going to count by tens. How many circles will I have to draw if I circle tens?"

A few children raised their hands—Andrew, Rudy, Leslie, Marina, Jonathan, and Hassan. Others didn't seem to have a clue. Although all the children could count

by tens, this didn't mean they understood the relationship between grouping by tens and written numerals or numerical quantities. The children counted along with me. Each time we reached ten, I stopped and circled ten stars, and then began counting again with one. After circling five groups of ten and seeing that there were nine extras, I invited the children to count the stars with me. Most joined in after I got started: "Ten, twenty, . . . fifty, fifty-one, fifty-two, . . . fifty-nine."

"I knew when I wrote fifty-nine, right after I counted by twos, that there would be five tens," I said. "It's easy for me because the first number tells how many tens there are and the other tells the extras." I offered this information to see if any of the children would comment or indicate confirmation by nodding or in some other way. I did not offer the information with the goal of having children learn about tens and ones. Rather, I offered the information with a light touch, conversationally, with no implied "this is important" tone, to make it available should any child find it useful. I planned to point out how tens and ones relate to numbers over and over throughout the year.

DAY 2

I began class by drawing a five-pointed star and an asterisk on the board and then asking volunteers to come to the board to draw different kinds of stars. I told the children that today I would time one minute while they drew stars. "First, think about the kind of star you're going to draw," I said.

"Do we have to draw just one kind of star?" Seth asked.

"Yes," I said, "I'd like you to choose one kind of star to draw. That way, we can do the experiment again another time, and you can see which kind of star is quicker for you to draw."

"Can't we do two stars?" Annie asked.

"I want you to choose just one kind," I said, repeating my directions.

"This isn't a contest to see who draws the most stars," I added. "It's not a race. It's an experiment, and we'll see what we can learn."

While timing one minute, I noticed that Timmy wasn't able to draw a star. Several times, he started a star and erased it, and he was getting frustrated and upset. I whispered to him that I'd teach him in just a little while and asked him to wait at the back table for me.

After one minute, I asked the children to count their stars in at least two different ways. I gave them each another sheet of paper and said, "Record the number of stars you drew and write about how you counted them. Remember, you've got to count in at least two different ways."

Some of the children were uncertain and uncomfortable with the task. I rushed about, helping children get settled and started. Mostly, I'd ask children to tell me one way to count the stars. Typically, they'd answer "by ones," "by twos," or "by fives." "That's a good way," I'd respond, "and be sure to show on your stars paper how you did it and then explain on the other sheet." (Figure 1–1 shows how one student recorded.)

Finally, I remembered Timmy waiting for me at the back table. He was sitting patiently. I brought him a clean sheet of paper, had him hold a pencil, and guided his hand to show him how to draw a five-pointed star. I did this four times, each time saying, "Up, down, left, right, connect." I thought that the combination of the movement with the words would help. He then tried one by himself but started down instead of up. I took his hand again and did three more. Then he did one right, followed by two more. "Keep practicing," I said, "and I'll be back in a minute."

I returned to supervising the rest of the

▲▲▲▲▲▲Figure 1–1 *Leslie grouped by 2s and 4s and drew 8 stars.*

class. Most students were settled into their work. Two were finished, or thought they were, and brought their papers to me. I accepted Marina's, stapling her star paper to her written description. She had written: *I counted by twos. I count by ones.* She had recorded *24* on her stars paper.

I then read Nick's paper, but I didn't accept it. It said: *I counted by 2s.* He had circled the stars in groups of two.

"You didn't record how many stars you drew," I said. "And you've only counted one way. You've got to count at least two ways so you have a check on your work." Nick groaned and returned to his seat.

I went to the back of the room. Timmy now had a sheet full of stars. "Would you like me to time one minute while you draw stars?" I asked. He nodded "yes." I gave him a fresh sheet of paper and started timing, watching the time as I read more children's work.

After reading several more papers, I realized how difficult this was for the children. It was the third week of October, and the children were still adjusting to new routines. They weren't yet comfortable with writing, and writing in math class was still new for them. With this task, I didn't insist on much revision. I decided to accept their work and try the activity again another time.

By the end of class, I had papers from almost all of the children. Four or five children were still working on theirs. About ten children were on the rug, reading silently. Others were at their desks reading. Figure 1–2 shows another student's response to this task.

DAY 3

A few days later, I again had the children draw stars and write about their methods of counting. Because they were already familiar with the activity, I felt they would be better able to describe their methods in writing, and I wanted to use this opportunity to help them become more comfortable with writing in math class. Also, I wanted to collect their data for a class graph.

I began class by telling the children that they were going to draw stars again. "Just as we did last time," I said, "I'll time one

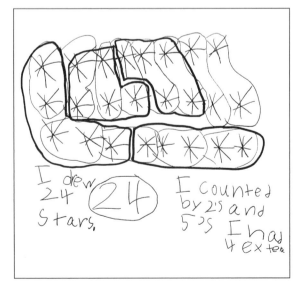

▲▲▲▲▲▲Figure 1–2 *Gwyn drew 24 asterisks and noticed there were 4 extras when she grouped by 5s.*

minute while you draw stars." The children were eager to do the activity again.

"There's something a little different I want to do this time," I said. I showed them a pad of 3-by-3-inch sticky notes.

"After you draw and count your stars," I continued, "and show me your paper about the two ways you counted them, I'll give you one of these sticky notes. On it, you are to write your name, draw a sample star to show which kind you did, record the number you got, and post it on the board."

For a few minutes, I let the children practice drawing the kind of stars they were planning to use for the activity. Then I called them to attention and began timing. After the minute was up, I reminded the children to count the stars they drew in two different ways. "That's so you'll have a check on your counting," I said.

This time, the children were much more willing and able to write about their counting methods. The lesson went very smoothly. By having students show me their papers before getting sticky notes, I was able to check their work. If they didn't show how they counted in at least two ways, or if they didn't record the number of stars they drew, I had them revise their papers.

The most frequent method they used was to count by grouping their stars into twos. (Of the twenty-four children present, eighteen used grouping by twos as one of their methods.) Counting by fives and counting by ones were also popular. None of the children chose to group by tens. This didn't surprise me, as my experience has been the same whenever I've taught this lesson. However, as each child brought me a paper to get a sticky note, I asked, "If you circled tens, how many circles would you have to make?" All but six children were able to answer correctly.

When all the children had completed the assignment, the notes were randomly arranged on the board. I counted twenty-four children in the class. "Let's check to make sure everyone's note is here," I said.

I counted the notes three ways: by twos, fives, and tens. Each time, I drew circles around the sticky note groups and had the students count. Before grouping by tens, I asked the class, "How many circles do you think I'll have to make?" About two-thirds of the children raised their hands. I asked the students to use a whisper voice to tell me how many circles. "Two," the students chorused.

I then asked the class for suggestions for organizing the notes. Sarah came up with the idea of sorting them by the kinds of stars. I did this, arranging the notes into a bar graph with five categories. There were five asterisks, thirteen five-pointed stars, four eight-pointed stars, one cross, and one different-looking five-pointed star, with only the outline drawn (see below).

We talked about the different number of stars in each row. Children were quick to report that there was one more asterisk than eight-pointed stars, and four more asterisks than crosses. But comparing the row of five-pointed stars (thirteen) and asterisks (five) was difficult for most of them. Figuring "how many more" is difficult for students of this age. The children offered a few different methods for figuring.

Jason said, "I know that eight plus five is thirteen, so it has to be eight."

Grace thought about it differently. "I know that ten plus three is thirteen and that ten take away five is five," she said, "so I did five plus three and got eight."

Teddy was more concrete in his approach. "I just saw where they lined up," he said, "and counted the extras." He came up to show the sticky notes he had counted.

Katy then noticed the numbers on the notes. "They're all different," she said, "and they're out of order."

I put the five notes in the asterisks row in numerical order. "That's going to be more difficult with the five-pointed stars," I said, "because there are more to rearrange."

"Can I do it?" Hassan asked. I agreed, and he came up to the front of the room. It was complicated to move all the notes, but with help from the rest of the class, Hassan finally accomplished the task.

The children enjoyed the activity. It especially appealed to Rudy's need for order. "When the notes were all over the board," he said, "it didn't look like anything. But now it's good."

The graph showed the different kinds of stars the children had drawn, with the notes in each category ordered by the number of stars. After class, I transferred the notes to a piece of chart paper so we could talk about the graph at a later time.

Stars in One Minute

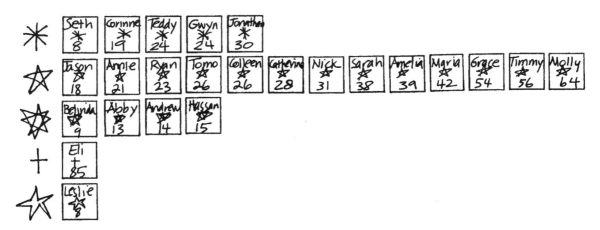

DAY 4

I waited a week before processing the *Stars in One Minute* graph. I did this for several reasons. One was to continue introducing other activities. Children enjoy having a variety of activities and a change of pace. Also, I've found that when a graph is posted for a while, children have the chance, if they're interested, to think about the data. Even if children don't focus on it, they become familiar with it and come to discussions fresh and interested.

Near the end of class one day, when about twenty minutes remained, I asked the children to look at the graph and think about sentences that would describe what they noticed. I had several of them give their ideas orally. Then I posted three 12-by-18-inch sheets of white paper and told the children that I'd like to write a dozen sentences about the graph.

"How many make a dozen?" I asked. About half the children raised their hands and I called on Jonathan. He knew it was twelve.

"I plan to write four sentences on each sheet of paper," I said. "Let's see if that will get us to twelve. How much is four plus four?" That was easy for most of the children.

"And how much is eight plus four more?" I continued. That was easy for fewer of them. I try to integrate numerical problems such as this one into lessons whenever possible. Not only does it give children a chance to think about numbers, but it brings numerical reasoning into situations on a regular basis.

"If I write four sentences on each paper," I said, "which number sentence will be at the top of the third sheet?" The students seemed interested in this question, and I waited until almost two-thirds of them had raised their hands. I could see that several were counting to themselves, pointing at the sheets as they did so.

I called on Grace and she answered, "Nine." I wrote a *9* at the top of the third sheet.

"As we write our sentences," I said, "we'll be able to check if that's the right place for nine." (I wonder what I would have done if Grace had answered incorrectly. I think I'd have asked her how she figured. And this reminds me that I accepted her answer without having her explain her reasoning. I didn't ask Jonathan to explain his answer to the number in a dozen because it is, I think, purely social knowledge. But Grace had to do some reasoning to come up with her response. It's hard to remember to ask all the time. We need to remind ourselves to do so.)

I wrote the sentences as the children offered them, recording in the language they used:

1. Most children did a 5-pointed star.

2. The most 5-pointed stars was Nick's, with 64.

3. The two stars with the least notes were the cross and the outline of the 5-pointed star.

4. There are two kinds of 5-pointed stars.

5. The student who made the most stars in the whole entire class was Eli, with 85 stars.

6. The 8-pointed row is the only row with three numbers in order. (There were four notes in the row with the numbers 9, 13, 14, and 15 on them.)

7. There are 24 notes altogether.

When Sarah made the observation that there were twenty-four sticky notes, I stopped and focused the class on the calculation. "Let's check," I said, and wrote down the number of notes in each row as I counted them:

5

13

4

1

1

Several children volunteered to solve the problem and came to the board to do so. Amelia did it by adding 13 and 5 to get 18, then adding 18 and 4 to get 22, and finally adding 22 and 2 to get 24. In a sense, she was counting on.

Teddy explained a different method. "I did four plus one is five," he said, "and another five makes ten. And I added that to the ten to get twenty." He was talking about the 1 in 13. "And then there is four more, so it's twenty-four."

Leslie had another way. "You go ten plus five is fifteen," she began, adding ten from the 13 to the 5. "Then four and one is five, so fifteen plus five is twenty. And then you have a three and a one left, and that makes four, so it's twenty plus four and that's twenty-four."

Timmy raised his hand. "I know because I counted," he said.

I then asked for another sentence to add to the chart. Tomo raised his hand. "There are ninety-five asterisks," he said, stumbling over the word *asterisks* and asking for help in pronouncing it. Tomo had been adding all the numbers in the asterisks row while the others were working on the total number of notes.

"How did you figure that out?" I asked, listing the numbers from the five sticky notes in the asterisks row:

8

19

24

24

30

As I wrote the numbers, I rounded off and estimated the sum to myself, adding 10, 20, 20, 20, and 30 to get 100. "I think that ninety-five is close," I said, "but I think it isn't large enough."

The children shifted their attention to this problem. Several reached for pencil and paper. I started to figure out loud and record to model for the class one way to do the adding. I added the tens first and got 80. Then I added the ones, combining 8 and 9 to get 17 and the two 4s to get 8 and then adding 17 and 8 to get 25. By the time I started to add 80 and 25, Tomo had changed his mind.

"It's one hundred five," he said. "I fixed it."

I continued with my work to verify his solution. Several others agreed. Only about seven children were involved with this calculation. For most, the numbers were too large, so I didn't dwell on it. I recorded Tomo's corrected sentence on the board.

8. There are 105 asterisks.

"Can I figure out how many stars there are altogether?" Andrew asked. This was just the kind of challenge that Andrew loved.

"We already did it," Jason called out. "It's twenty-four."

"No," Andrew said, "I'm going to figure out all the stars on all the notes." Jason was still confused, but some of the others caught on and also wanted to start working on the problem. Eli and Sean got up to get paper. I asked them to sit down and give me their attention.

"I'll write Andrew's suggestion," I said, "and put a blank for the number until we figure it out." I recorded on the list:

9. There are ____ stars on all the notes.

"We'll see what Andrew comes up with and then the rest of you can also try if you'd like," I said. "And we'll add more sentences to our chart tomorrow." I felt that the discussion had gone on long enough and wanted to change the pace. Also, I've learned that when I stretch an investigation over several days, children have time to think about it, and their participation often increases.

THE NEXT DAY

At the beginning of class, Andrew asked to make a report. "There are seven hundred fifteen stars altogether," he announced. I decided to have all who were interested check Andrew's answer with a calculator. Most had used calculators before, and they were available to the children at any time. But not many had shown much interest. This situation gave me a chance to encourage them to use calculators for a problem that they wanted to solve and could not really do any other way.

On the board, I recorded the numbers from each of the notes so there were five columns.

*	☆	✳	+	☆
8	18	9	85	8
19	21	13		
24	23	14		
24	26	15		
30	26	51		
105	28			
	31			
	38			
	39			
	42			
	54			
	56			
	64			
	466			

As children reported sums, I wrote them for each column so that the others could check. Some diligently worked on the problem; others made up problems of their own or just explored with the calculators. Some of the children using the calculators were fascinated by the M that appeared in the display and were experimenting with making it come and go; others didn't notice it or weren't interested. There are such differences among children!

Together we verified that Andrew had

found the correct total of 715 stars. A few more students had statements to make about the graph. They shared and their ideas were added to the list.

EXTENSIONS

1. A literature connection to this lesson can be made by reading aloud *Draw Me a Star*, by Eric Carle. Children enjoy the book. The illustrations are bold and the story invites students to predict what the author will draw next. The book provides directions for making one type of eight-pointed star, which intrigues a good number of children.

Have students repeat the experiment of drawing stars in one minute, only this time have them draw a different kind of star than the first time. As before, you can create a graph. Repeating the experiment and asking the students to draw a different type of star creates an interesting situation that invites them to compare to find out which type of star they can draw faster. Not only can students find out which star is faster to draw, but they can also compare to find out how many more stars of one type they could draw in one minute.

2. Lead a discussion with students asking them to predict the number of stars they could draw in two minutes based on what they know about the number of stars they can draw in one minute. Then time them for two minutes as they draw stars. Have the students count the stars they drew in at least two different ways. If appropriate for your students, ask them to compare their predictions to the actual counts.

HOMEWORK

Ask students to time one minute while one of their parents, or someone else at home, draws stars. Have them bring the data to class.

The next day distribute 3-by-3-inch sticky notes and have children record the number of stars drawn at home and put the notes on the chalkboard.

Talk with children about how to organize the notes into a graph. For this graph, rather than focusing on the types of stars the parents drew, consider ways to organize the data based on the numerical counts. Discuss with the children the conclusions they can draw from the graph.

Questions and Discussion

▲▲

▲ *What is the learning value of this lesson?*

Many children can count by tens, but this doesn't mean they understand the relationship between grouping by tens and written numerals or numerical quantities. Teaching children by telling them about this relationship doesn't help them construct their own understanding. Making sense of place value requires that children connect, for themselves, the meaning of the digits in the numbers to the structure of our place value system. They need many experiences counting large quantities of objects and relating the quantities to their numerical representations, as presented in this chapter.

▲ *How do you determine the appropriate use of calculators?*

Generally, calculators should be as available to children as paper, pencils, rulers, and other classroom supplies are. Calculators are tools used by adults to facilitate computation in everyday life. Before the calculator can be a useful tool, students must know what operation to use and what numbers to use, and they must also have some idea of the approximate answer in order to decide if the answer generated by the calculator is reasonable. Often, children and adults alike think if a calculator came up with the answer then it must be correct.

Andrew had figured the total number of stars drawn by the class. I encouraged the students to use calculators to check his work because the problem was beyond the ability of most of the students, but was still a problem in which they were interested. In this case, the use of a calculator allowed them to go beyond what they could have done on their own to make discoveries and conjectures they could not have made otherwise.

At times I ask the students not to use calculators, explaining to them that I am interested in knowing how they think about solving the problem on their own, but these times are the exception.

▲ *At one point in the lesson you modeled for the students how to solve an addition problem. You combined the tens first and then the ones. Won't this confuse the students?*

In the lesson, as one way of adding, I did model adding numbers by first adding the tens and then the ones. Many children do this naturally and it seems to make sense to them. Many things they are learning to do in school go from left to right. Reading and writing are important examples of this. Also, many children have little problem figuring the number of tens, holding that in their thinking, and then combining the ones, and finally putting both quantities together for the total.

Modeling as I did does not seem to confuse the students. We have many class discussions in which different computational strategies are shared and the way I shared is just one way of figuring the sum.

▲ Why didn't you require the students to group by tens when they counted their stars?

Although grouping by tens is an essential part of the numerical symbolism for our place value system, it seems unwieldy for young children to make groups of ten. It has been my experience that most children do not see grouping by tens as useful in this situation. They more naturally group by twos or fives or count by ones. I have seen many children who can circle groups of ten objects and tell the total, but still do not understand the tens and ones structure of our number system. For this reason, I think it is important not to impose counting by tens on students, but rather to take every opportunity to connect the tens and ones structure to the children's counting experiences and to written numerals.

CHAPTER TWO
THE 0–99 CHART

Overview

This lesson provides students with the opportunity to focus on an orderly arrangement of the numbers from zero to ninety-nine. Although most children at this age are familiar with numbers up to one hundred, few have thought about the tens and ones structure of our number system or examined patterns that emerge from looking at the numbers in an organized array. The activities in this lesson invite students to examine numbers in a variety of ways. Also, the lesson provides children with a context for developing familiarity with words such as *digit, horizontal, vertical, diagonal, row,* and *column.*

Materials

▲ wall chart with a 10-by-10 array of transparent plastic pockets
▲ 100 cards to fit in the plastic pockets, numbered from 0 to 99
▲ 0–99 chart, 1 per student (see Blackline Masters)
▲ *0–99 Patterns* worksheet, 1 or 2 per student (see Blackline Masters)

Time

▲ four to six class periods

Teaching Directions

1. Insert the number cards from 0 to 15 into the wall chart (see page 16). Explain to the children that you'll show other number cards and ask for volunteers to figure out where they belong on the chart. You may wish to have children volunteer individually or work in pairs to locate the position of the cards. Do not choose numbers sequentially.

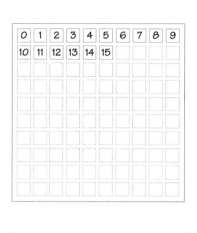

2. As children locate numbers on the chart, have them explain how they decided where to put them. If a child has difficulty explaining, choose a volunteer to help. To prompt students, say: "Convince the rest of the class that you've put the number in the proper place."

3. Continue having students add numbers to the chart over the next several days. Spreading the experience over a few class periods gives children time to reflect on the patterns that emerge in the chart. (To use a partially filled chart as a beginning assessment of children's abilities to add numbers with regrouping, see the assessment *Numbers on the 0–99 Chart* on page 149.)

4. Tell the children that you've thought of a rule that describes some of the numbers on the 0–99 chart, and they are to figure out which numbers fit the rule. Tell the students the rule: All the two-digit numbers on the chart that have both digits the same.

5. Have children guess numbers to fit your rule. If they guess correctly, turn the number card to its blank side. (**Note:** Children most likely won't know the meaning of the word *digit*. Don't tell them, however; let them figure it out from the context of the activity.)

6. When children have guessed all the numbers that fit the rule—11, 22, 33, 44, 55, 66, 77, 88, and 99—have children explain what they think the word *digit* means. Ask them to describe what the pattern looks like. Typically, children use phrases like "on a slant," "like a staircase," "on a diagonal," "from corner to corner," and so on.

7. Turn all the cards back so all of the numbers are showing and ask the children to think of rules that are different from yours. Distribute 0–99 charts for them to refer to. Choose a student to come up and whisper a rule to you but not announce it to the class. Instead, have the student call on others to guess numbers that might fit the rule. When a guess is correct, turn over the card. The class tries to figure out the rule from the correct guesses. When all the appropriate cards have been turned over, have students describe what the pattern looks like.

8. After the class has guessed the rules of two or three children, give each child a copy of the *0–99 Patterns* worksheet (see Blackline Masters). Each child writes his or her rule on the bottom half of the page and colors in the appropriate numbers on the chart at the top.

9. On the following days, you might want to ask more children to play *Guess My Rule* with the class. Also, use the student papers for the first extension activity on page 26.

Teaching Notes

Typically, children of this age are able to count from one to one hundred with little difficulty. Many children count rotely with little or no understanding of the structure of the base ten number system. Also, many children don't consider zero to be a number and have little idea of its meaning. Even some adults think of zero as a placeholder rather than a number representing a quantity.

Giving students the opportunity to place the numbers from zero to ninety-nine on a chart in an organized manner allows children the opportunity to see zero as a number. Initially as numbers are placed on the chart, especially with less experienced students, children will most likely either count from zero or a number already on the chart to locate where the new number should be placed. As students gain experience placing numbers and listening as others explain how they know their numbers are placed correctly, many will begin to make use of the structure of the base ten number system when placing numbers on the chart by recognizing that they can move down one row and it represents one ten. For children to recognize that one can represent both a single object or one group of something, in this case ten, represents a huge leap in understanding of place value as well as multiplicative thinking.

The Lesson

▲▲▲

DAY 1

For this lesson, I used a commercial hundred wall chart and prepared by inserting the numbers from 0 to 15 (see right).

My plan was to show children other number cards, one by one, and have them figure out where they belonged on the chart. (**Note:** In previous years when I haven't had a commercial chart, I've ruled a 10-by-10 grid onto a large sheet of chart paper and filled in the numbers from 0 to 15. Then I'd write a number on the board and have a child come up and point to the

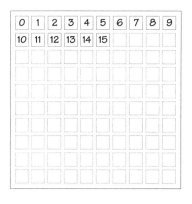

space on the grid where it belonged. This method worked fine, but I found the investment in a commercial chart to be valuable, as it allows me more flexibility in my lessons.) "When I hold up a number card," I said to the class, "raise your hand if you'd like to come up and put it on the chart where it belongs." I held up the number 25 and about half the students raised their hands.

I called on Jonathan. When he came up to place the card, others shouted advice. "Further up." "Over there." "Ooh, it's easy." "I know, I know." "No, higher." I wasn't able to quiet them entirely. Jonathan kept his calm—but barely—carefully counted on from fifteen, keeping track of the spaces with his finger, and inserted the card correctly.

I called the class to attention. "We need to talk before we continue," I said. I talked to them about the inappropriateness of their behavior and also told them what they should be doing when one of their class-mates was at the chart. "While someone else is thinking," I said, "you also should be thinking about where the number belongs. After someone places a card, you should raise your hand if you disagree."

To reinforce my directions, I asked who understood what they were supposed to be doing when someone else was at the chart. Several children raised their hands, and I had Gwyn explain.

"Remember," I concluded before return-ing to the activity, "you'll each have a turn."

I called on Catherine, and the class behaved well as she put up the card with 37. Catherine explained that she knew her card was correctly placed because she counted each box starting with twenty-five until she got to thirty-seven. Molly was next, and a few children called out. When Seth came up, however, the calling out escalated, and the atmosphere was more like a frantic TV quiz show than a class-room. I stopped the activity and talked again to the class, taking a different approach.

"I know you're excited," I said. "And I know you all have ideas about how to place the numbers. But you can't call out. Instead, try whispering to your partner when someone else is up at the chart."

I continued and called on Maria. The students were relatively quiet, although some of their comments were borderline whispers. When Katy came up, the calling out began again. Katy became completely flustered and broke out in tears. She jammed the number card into a slot and stormed to her seat.

"Uh oh," Hassan said. "Katy's crying." The class quieted, suddenly sober and repentant.

I talked with them about the risk of coming to the front of the room and trying to figure out where a number belonged— how it seemed easy from their seats, but that being up at the front of the room was a different experience. I told them about the importance of taking risks to try out their thinking. I told them that they could help one another by giving each person time to think.

It took the calamity with Katy for the class to calm down. I'm amazed that even with thirty years of teaching experience, I still have times when all my managerial skills seem to vanish in a classroom situa-tion. However, the thirty years of experience also help me keep my sights and not give up. The activity was valuable and enjoyable to the children. I was sorry Katy was hurt, but I'd have to wait until later to think about how I might have dealt with the class differently.

I continued and the lesson went well. The excitement was still high, and I had to remind several children not to talk. But the improvement was enormous, and I was able to focus on the students' methods for placing numbers instead of on the behavior of the rest of the class. I noted which chil-dren located spaces by looking at patterns—locating the sevens column and the thirties row, for example—and which children had to start with a number already on the chart and count spaces to decide where their number belonged.

DAY 2

The next day, I began class by having children put additional numbers on the 0–99 chart. After considering the incident with Katy from the previous day, I changed my method and led the activity in silence, trying to diffuse the students' energy. I explained to the children how we'd work.

"I'm going to draw a star on the board. I call it the 'Silent Star' and no one is allowed to talk until I erase it. Even I'm not allowed to talk, so we'll do everything in silence. I'll hold a card up and point at someone to come up and put it on the chart. You won't need to raise your hands, because I'm going to have everyone at the back three tables take a turn today."

The children listened attentively to my directions.

"Get the last of your wiggles out," I said, "and when I draw the star, we'll all be silent."

This worked perfectly. I suspected it would, as I've used the technique for years. It's especially well suited for an activity such as this one when I want each child to focus. The silence removes interference and allows children to think in their own ways without being interrupted by others' ideas.

I drew the star on the board and had each of the twelve children at the back three tables place a number. All except for Annie placed theirs correctly. She placed 68 in the correct column, but in the seventies row. I pointed to the 8 in 68 and ran my finger up and down the column on the chart, nodding affirmatively. Then I pointed to the 6 in 68. Annie immediately removed the card and moved it up a row.

After the twelve children had taken their turns, I erased the star. There was a chorus of sighs as they allowed themselves to relax.

I asked the students to talk about the patterns they noticed. Some children had continued to count to locate the spaces for their numbers, but more were seeing and noticing patterns in the array.

Filling in the Chart

I continued with the 0–99 chart for part of each class over the next several days, using the "Silent Star" method, until the chart was completely filled in. Although I found the "Silent Star" method to be effective, it eliminated letting children convince others why their location was correct. But I was able to see how children approached the problem by watching them at the chart.

Before beginning each day, I asked the class to figure how many numbers were on the chart already. The children counted the cards in each row and I recorded, winding up with a column of ten numbers. I then talked with them about shortcut ways to add the column.

Even though adding a column of ten numbers was beyond the ability of a good part of the class, I took the opportunity to demonstrate different ways to think about numbers. I showed the children how I combined numbers to make tens, how I looked for doubles to add, and how I added other combinations that I know. I did this all with a light touch, wanting the children to watch me think out loud and perhaps add to their own store of strategies for reasoning numerically.

A Class Discussion

One day, after everyone in the class had a turn placing a number card, only two empty spaces remained on the chart.

"How many numbers are on the chart now?" I asked.

The question sparked several children's thinking, and they presented different ways to think about the problem.

Hassan said, "I know. One hundred take away two is ninety-eight."

Molly said, "You can go ninety-eight, then ninety-nine, one hundred."

Andrew said, "If you take ninety-eight and add two, you get one hundred, so it has to be ninety-eight."

"But it only goes up to ninety-nine," Maria said.

"Yeah, there's no one hundred," Timmy added.

Some of the children still weren't convinced that there were one hundred pockets on the chart. This didn't worry me. Earlier in my teaching career, I would have pushed to have all children agree on answers. I've come to realize that I can get all the children to respond correctly that there are one hundred numbers on the chart and only ninety-eight on it now, but I can't necessarily get them to believe it or explain why it makes sense. Their understanding comes from their internal processes of constructing. At this time, I noted the children who were having difficulty locating numbers and those who were confused, so I could work with them to find out more about their thinking.

DAY 3

About a week after I had taught Day 1 of this lesson, I focused the children on the 0–99 chart in a new way. I told the children I had a game of *Guess My Rule* to play. The children had previous experience with the game.

"We'll play this game backward," I said. "I'll tell you the rule and you guess the numbers that fit it. My rule is 'All the two-digit numbers on the chart that have both digits the same.' "

"What does *digit* mean?" Sarah asked.

"Does anyone know that word?" I asked the class. A few children made attempts to define it, but no one knew the meaning of the word.

"Try guessing numbers for my pattern," I said, "and see if you can figure out what digits are from the guesses." A few children raised their hands. I called on Timmy.

"Twenty," he said.

"No," I answered, "that doesn't fit my rule."

"Six," Abby guessed.

"No," I responded, "my number has two digits."

"Ooh, I know," Tomo said. "Ninety-nine."

"Yes," I said, "that's one of my numbers because both of its digits are the same." I removed the card with 99 on it and inserted it so the blank side was showing.

"Ninety-eight," Catherine guessed next.

"No," I responded, "that doesn't fit my rule. Both digits aren't the same."

By now, more than half of the class wanted to give a number. The children were excited. I took a moment to quiet them and called on Molly.

"It's easy," she said. "I guess twenty-two."

"Things are always easy when you know them," I responded, turning the 22 card over to its blank side.

I continued calling on children until I had turned over all the numbers with both digits the same. (In retrospect, I would rather have had some squares of lightly tinted transparency to cover the numbers as they were guessed. Some children were confused when number cards were turned over. Also, an overhead transparency of the 0–99 chart could be used. Correctly guessed numbers could be circled.)

"Who can explain what *digit* means?" I asked. Only a few children raised their hands.

"Talk with your partner and see if the two of you can figure out how to explain what digits are," I said. Rather than call on one of the children when only a few seemed to have an idea, I decided to have all of them think about my question.

After a minute or so, I called the class back to attention. "Does anyone have an idea you'd like to report?" I asked. Now about half the children raised their hands. I called on Seth.

"It's like the numbers in a number," he said. "It's just another name."

Katy had something to add. "Some numbers have one digit and some have two."

"Some can have three," Andrew said, "like two hundred forty-five or something."

"A digit is like a part of a number," Grace said.

I called on a few more children and then changed the direction of the conversation. "Look at the pattern of the blank cards, the ones I turned over because they had both digits the same," I said. "How can you describe the pattern of the blank cards?"

"It goes down on a slant," Molly said.

"It's like stair steps," Teddy said.

"It's a diagonal," Rudy said. We had talked about diagonals of squares in the previous unit, and Rudy had remembered the word.

"It kind of goes from the corner to the other corner," Maria said.

Using Children's Rules

There were no other ideas, and I turned over the cards so that all the numbers were showing again. "Does anyone have a rule that's different from mine?" I asked. I distributed 0–99 charts for children to refer to. Several children raised their hands.

"This time we'll play the game the usual way," I continued. "Don't tell your rule. Call on children to guess numbers, and tell them if their guess fits your rule or not. I'll turn the numbers over for the correct guesses."

I called on Hassan and he came up to the front of the room. I had him whisper his rule to me so I could provide a backup check on his responses to the others'

guesses. Hassan called on children to guess numbers and I turned over the number cards for the correct guesses. When I had turned 10, 30, and 40, some predicted a pattern and figured out Hassan's rule. They soon guessed all the numbers that fit it. Finally, I had Hassan tell his rule. "They're numbers with a zero behind it," he said.

"How would you describe the pattern of Hassan's numbers?" I asked.

"It's just a straight line," Seth said.

"It's all the numbers down one side except for the top one," Leslie said.

"It looks like a flag pole without a flag," Annie said.

"Why do you think that Hassan didn't include zero?" I asked. Hassan looked a bit anxious when I asked this question.

"Because all of his numbers have two numbers," Teddy said.

"You mean two digits," Andrew said, always precise.

"That's it," Hassan said, looking relieved.

"I have a rule to try," Leslie said. Several other children indicated that they also had ideas.

"I'd like to hear all of your ideas," I said. "Here's how. First, I'll give each of you a chance to think of a rule." I showed the children the papers I had prepared with a 0–99 chart reproduced on the top half and lines for writing on the bottom. (See the *0–99 Patterns* worksheet in the Blackline Masters.)

"After you think of a rule that interests you," I said, "color in all the numbers that fit the rule. Then write the rule below the chart and describe the pattern."

"Can we do our rules with the class?" Leslie asked, a bit disappointed that she wasn't getting her turn right then.

"Some of you will get to share your rule with the class if you like," I said. This seemed to satisfy Leslie and the others.

I distributed the sheets and the children got to work. All were engaged and most finished their patterns. Several started a second pattern. Three needed to work on their papers later in the day to complete them.

DAY 4

I began class by playing *Guess My Rule* with some of the rules the children had written. I planned to have several children come to the front of the room and have others guess their rules. Instead of taking the time to have the class guess the numbers, I decided to have children show the numbers that fit their pattern and have others guess the rule and describe the pattern. In this way, I put the emphasis on the verbalization of the rules and the description of the patterns.

"This time, we'll do the activity a little differently," I said. "I'll show you the numbers someone has colored, and you'll guess the rule. Sometimes, people have different ways to describe the same rules, and we'll see if this happens."

The children were eager and interested. I started with Grace's rule. I had Grace come to the front of the room, and I gave her the paper she had done for reference. She had colored in all the numbers with a 6. (See Figure 2–1.)

I turned the numbers over on the chart and asked the class to guess the rule. Some children seemed confused when the number cards were turned over, so I made sure they had 0–99 charts so they could refer to all of the numbers. However, I found that most of the children who were confused didn't find the charts helpful.

I'm not surprised or particularly concerned when children are confused. Rather, it gives me information about how children are thinking at a particular time. At this

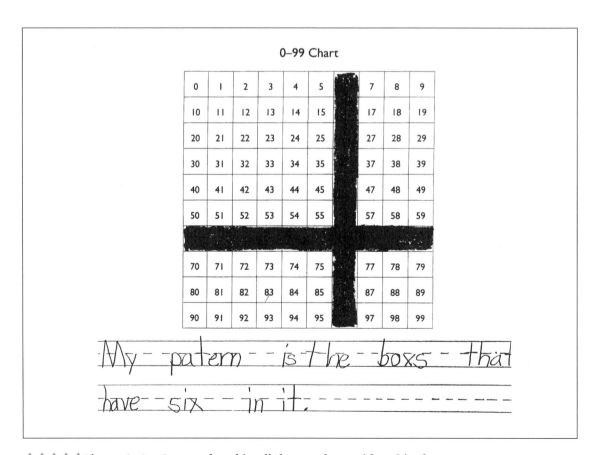

▲▲▲▲▲Figure 2–1 *Grace colored in all the numbers with a 6 in them.*

time, while some of the children were ready and interested in guessing the rule for Grace's pattern, others would benefit from merely guessing the numbers on the cards I had turned over. I planned for the class to have a good deal more experience with the 0–99 chart, however, and I'd have opportunities to watch for changes in individual children's understanding of the structure of numbers on the chart.

I asked for volunteers to guess Grace's rule and called on Sarah.

"The numbers are the sixties," she said.

"That's not it," Grace said. "I colored sixteen, and that's not in the sixties."

"But you colored in all the sixties," Sarah pointed out.

"It's not my rule," Grace insisted. She called on Nick.

"You did the sixties and the ones that end in six, too," he said.

Grace looked at me. "That's sort of it, but not how I said it," she said.

"See if anyone has another way to say the rule," I said, "and then you can read the way you wrote it."

Grace called on Amelia. "They have to have a six in them," she said.

"That's more like it," Grace said, and she read her rule: *My patern is the boxs that have six in it.*

I thanked Grace and asked her to return to her seat. Then I asked the children to describe what her pattern looked like. I was interested in terminology that would describe the position of the numbers that had been colored. I called on Tomo to give the first description.

"It looks like a pogo stick," he said. Tomo's description seemed to spark a flurry of imaginative remarks that the children found interesting. Although the discussion wasn't leading in the direction I had hoped, I recorded all their comments on the board.

"It looks like a cross," Marina said.

"It looks like a lowercase *t*," Seth offered.

"This is kind of a Halloween idea," Maria said. "It's like the sign on graves in cemeteries."

"That's a cross," Marina said, reiterating her contribution.

"I agree," I said, "but Maria expressed the idea in different words." I recorded Maria's idea. (I take all opportunities to model writing for them.)

As I continued to record their ideas, more and more children raised their hands. When I called on Timmy, he began to get out of his seat to come up to the board and show what he meant. "Just use words, Timmy," I said. "Try to explain your idea."

"See, there are four spaces," he said, "and one is bigger." Timmy was referring to the areas on the 0–99 chart that weren't part of Grace's rule.

Then I listed some other words for them to use to describe the pattern of Grace's numbers: *row, column, top, bottom, middle, horizontal (across), vertical (up and down),* and *diagonal.*

"I find these words helpful for describing patterns on the zero to ninety-nine chart," I said. "We used some of them yesterday. Can someone describe Grace's pattern using at least one of these words?" I asked.

Colleen's hand shot up. "I have one, but it's like the others," she said, referring to the ones the other children had offered.

I replied, "Right now, I'd like only descriptions that use at least one of the words I wrote."

I called on Nick. "There's one row and one column," he said.

Next I called on Katy. "One goes across and one goes down, and they're not really in the middle, but kind of."

Only two hands were up now. Clearly, the children were more comfortable with their own words and more interested in their own ideas. However, I continued pushing to give them more experience with the new words and took two more suggestions.

"There's an up-and-down line and an across line," Gwyn said.

"One goes from top to bottom," Teddy said.

"Let me show you another rule," I said. "This one is Jason's rule." Jason had colored in all the forties and fifties. Jason came to the front of the room and I rearranged the number cards on the chart so that all the numbers in the rows of forties and fifties were turned to their blank sides. (See Figure 2–2.)

I called on Hassan first.

"All the numbers with fours and fives in them," he said. Others nodded. Jason shook his head to indicate that Hassan's guess wasn't correct.

"I notice that Jason didn't color the number fourteen," I said, "or fifteen or twenty-five. Those have a four or five in them."

"Oh yeah," Hassan said.

Amelia raised her hand. "I think it's just the forties and fifties," she said.

Jason confirmed her guess by nodding, looking a little disappointed that he hadn't stumped the class for a longer time. As I had done with Grace's rule, I asked the children to describe the pattern made by the numbers in Jason's rule and I recorded their ideas on the board. Again, their descriptions were imaginative.

"It looks like a row of marching ants all carrying something on their backs," Rudy said.

"It looks like a belt," Jonathan said.

"It's a wide stripe," Grace contributed.

"How about descriptions that use at least one of the words that I recorded?" I requested. I got a few more volunteers this time, but I still wasn't engaging all the children.

"It's a double row," Marina said.

"It goes across in the middle," Gwyn said.

"It's horizontal," Andrew said, "unless you turn it, and then it's vertical."

Next I had Leslie try her rule on the

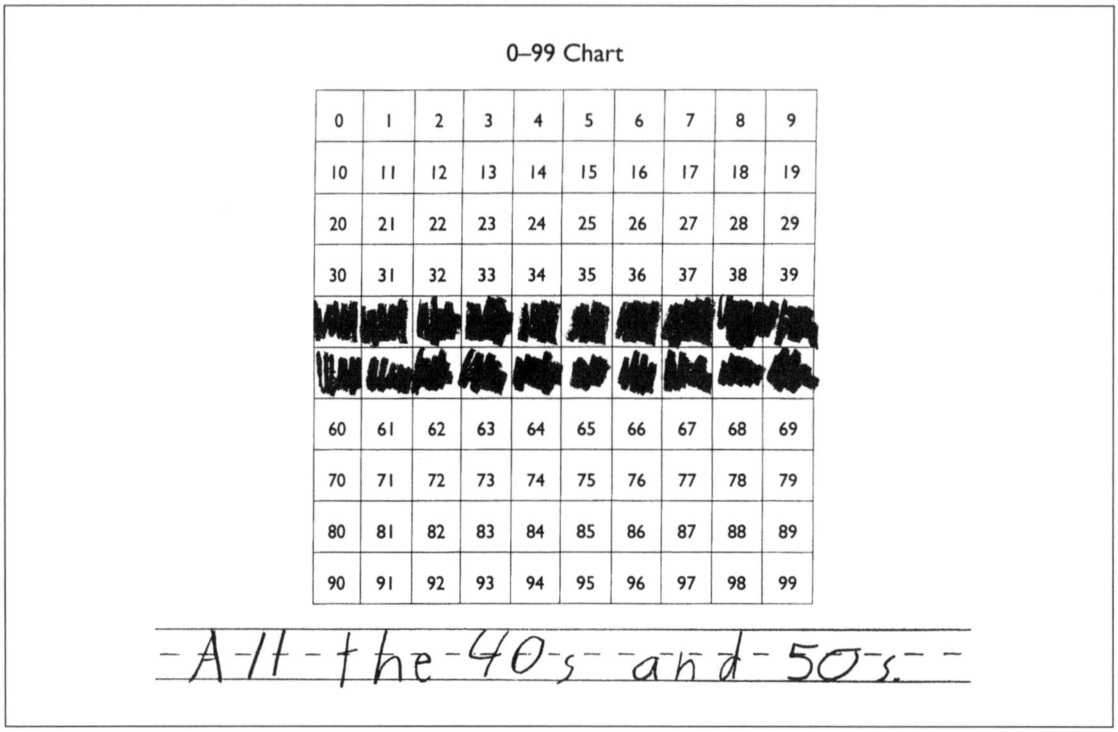

Figure 2–2 *Jason's pattern made a double row on the chart.*

class. She had colored in just four numbers—3, 12, 21, and 30. She had written: *All the ones that equal 3.* (See Figure 2–3.)

I had Leslie come to the front of the room, and I turned all the blank cards back to their numbered sides.

"Leslie colored in just four numbers," I said, and the children watched as I turned over the four cards that fit Leslie's rule. The children tried guessing.

"The numbers go three, two, one, zero," Nick said, reading the ones digits down the diagonal. Leslie shook her head to indicate Nick wasn't right.

"It goes zero, one, two, three," Maria said, reading the ones digits from the bottom. Leslie shook her head.

"They're little numbers in the corner," Timmy guessed. Again, Leslie shook her head.

For each guess, I commented that it could have been Leslie's rule, but it wasn't the way she wrote it. Leslie was thrilled to be stumping the class. Finally, I asked her to read her rule, and she did so in an unusually strong and confident voice with a big grin. "I did math problems," she said to preface her rule, and then read, "All the ones that equal three." The children were impressed, but perplexed.

"Explain what you mean by 'equal three,'" I said.

"Like, one plus two is three and three plus zero is three," she said.

"How about describing how the pattern looks?" I asked the class.

Marina raised her hand. "It's a teeny diagonal," she said.

"It's a short staircase," Jonathan said.

"It cuts across the corner," Timmy said.

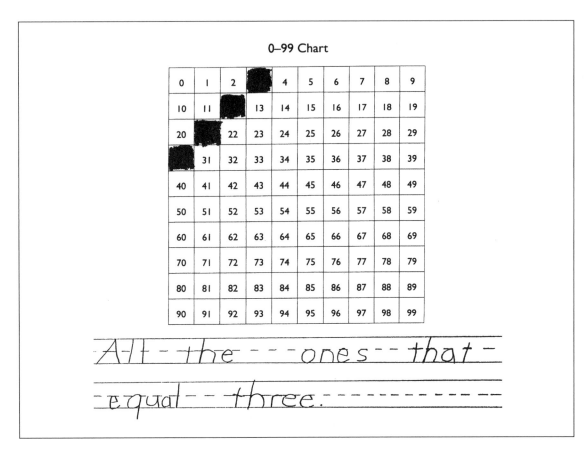

▲▲▲▲▲▲Figure 2–3 *Only 4 numbers fit Leslie's rule.*

I told the children that they would have other chances to investigate the rest of their patterns.

EXTENSIONS

1. Gather the 0–99 chart patterns the students completed during Day 3 of the lesson. Number the top and bottom of each child's pattern with the same number and cut each paper in half. Staple all the 0–99 charts into one booklet and all the descriptions of their patterns into another. Put a construction paper cover on each, labeling one *0–99 Patterns* and the other *Answers to 0–99 Patterns.* This activity can be presented as an individual or whole-group activity. Either way, you may find it helpful to have multiple copies of the booklets. You can either photocopy the students' work before making it into booklets so you have several booklets that are the same, or you can take the students' work and divide it into a couple of smaller booklets so that the booklets are different.

Choose one of the student's patterns to model the activity for the class. Show the children the 0–99 chart you've chosen and have them give you suggestions for what the rule might be. Record what you think the rule might be on the board. Next show the children the student's rule and ask them to compare it with what you've written on the board. Show the students the booklets and explain that they must first choose a 0–99 pattern, then figure out the rule, and finally write it on their paper. Tell the students to check their answer by looking in the second book, *Answers to 0–99 Patterns.* If there is disagreement, then the student should talk with the person who made the rule. Encourage students to do this for at least five patterns. Also, students may create new patterns and put them in a folder to be added to the class supply of patterns. Figure 2–4 shows some student patterns that were included in a booklet.

2. Number puzzles are another way to reinforce and extend children's experience with the 0–99 chart. Each child writes the numbers from 0 to 99 on a blank 10-by-10 grid, glues the chart onto tagboard, and cuts the chart apart into seven to twelve pieces. Students then try to piece together one another's puzzles. Both making a puzzle and solving others' puzzles help deepen children's familiarity with the orderliness of the numbers on the 0–99 chart.

Show the students how to make the puzzle by completing a partially filled-in 0–99 chart. Next, spread glue all over the back of the 0–99 chart so that the chart will stay glued onto the tagboard when it is later cut into seven to twelve puzzle pieces. Remind students that they must have you check the numbers on their charts before gluing them to tagboard. When the glue has dried, cut the chart into seven to twelve pieces, cutting only along the lines. Write your name or initials on the back of each piece so the pieces can be identified if they should get lost or misplaced. Also, write on an envelope your name and the total number of puzzle pieces and then place the pieces inside. A shoebox makes a great storage container for the puzzles.

Explain to the students that they will each make a puzzle as you have shown them and that they will have the opportunity to solve one another's puzzles. When they have solved a puzzle, they should put their name on the back of the envelope to show they have completed that puzzle and then return it to the shoebox.

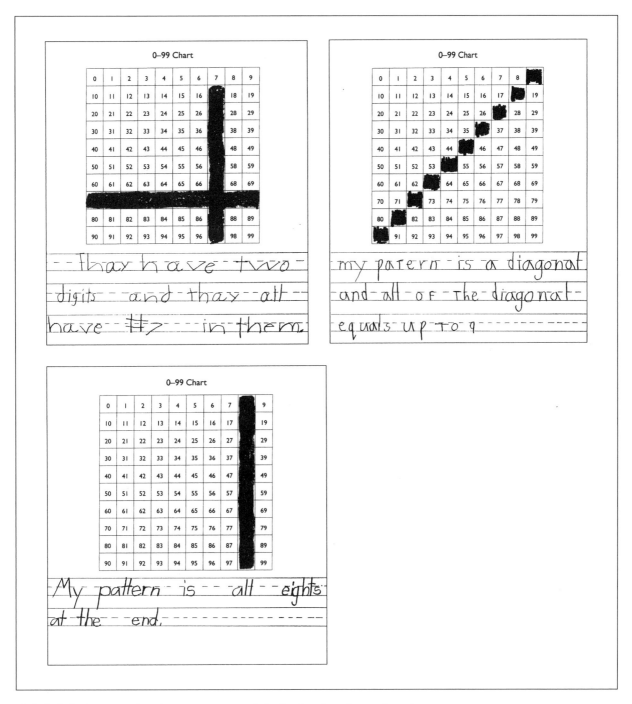

▲▲▲▲▲▲Figure 2–4 *There was a good deal of variety in students' patterns.*

HOMEWORK

When students have completed their 0–99 puzzles, they can take them home to put together with their parents or someone else at home. Also, children in class can fill in another 10-by-10 grid with the num-bers from 0 to 99 and glue the grid onto tagboard. They can take it home and, with their parents, cut it into ten to twelve pieces to make another puzzle for the class puzzle box. Remind students to write their name or initials on the back of each puzzle piece. Give each student a letter-size envelope to hold the new puzzle.

The next day, have students report about their experience sharing their number puzzle and making a new one at home.

You may wish to send a letter home to explain the puzzle activity to the parents.

Dear Parent,

Your child made the number puzzle by writing the numbers from 0 to 99 on a 10-by-10 grid and cutting it into pieces. Putting the puzzle together encourages children to look for patterns in the order of numbers. Work with your child to assemble the puzzle.

Your child also has an uncut 0–99 chart. Ask him or her to point out to you patterns in the numbers on the chart. Then, working together, cut the chart into 10 to 12 puzzle pieces, cutting only on the lines. Initial the back of each piece, put it in the envelope, and send it back with your child for our class puzzle box.

Questions and Discussion

▲▲▲

▲ *Why do you use a 0–99 chart rather than a 1–100 chart?*

There are a few reasons I prefer to use the 0–99 chart. The first is that all numbers in the same decade (twenties, thirties, forties, etc.) are on the same row of the chart.

Because the 0–99 chart includes zero, it gives zero the same status as other numbers; that is, that it is a number. I am reminded of how important it is to build meaning for zero when I hear adults state zero isn't really a number, just a placeholder.

Some people are not sure that zero is an even number. A 0–99 chart makes it easy to see that zero fits the pattern of all even numbers.

▲ *Why did you feel it important to have the students figure out the meaning of* **digits?** *Why not just tell them?*

The context of the activity was an excellent opportunity for the students to use their logic skills as well as the clues embedded in the activity to figure out the meaning of the word *digit* for themselves. When students have the opportunity to figure something out in this way, several things happen: the students gain confidence in their ability to be independent learners capable of finding things out for themselves, the students will most likely remember the meaning of the word *digit* longer than if someone had just told them the definition, and this kind of opportunity keeps students engaged.

Once students have been introduced to vocabulary words that will be used within a unit of study, I have found it helpful to list them on a large sheet of chart paper along with a short definition, key word, picture, or some other clue to help them remember the word. This is useful, as it encourages children to use the mathematical language presented to them in class discussions. Also, when students need words for their written work, the words are already posted. This improves spelling and increases the likelihood the students will make the listed words their own.

▲ *In the lesson, you stated that adding a column of ten numbers was beyond the ability of many of your students. What is your purpose in doing something too hard?*

Children learn from imitating behaviors they observe. By calculating aloud to demonstrate strategies for adding numbers, teachers can model for children ways to think mathematically. The lesson provided me the opportunity to think aloud as I grouped numbers to make tens, looked for doubles to add, and added other combinations that I knew.

▲ *At various times during the lesson, you had students talk about their thinking with a neighbor. Why?*

Taking time during a lesson to have children talk with their partners gives them one way to explore an idea. It gives students the chance to think before listening to a class discussion. Also, talking in pairs provides the opportunity for more children to verbalize their ideas and practice careful listening skills, and it keeps the students actively engaged in thinking about and learning the mathematics.

▲ *Why is it that you are not particularly surprised or concerned when students are confused?*

Partial understanding and confusion are natural to the learning process and if accepted as such, can provide motivation for students to persist and explore an activity more fully, thus deepening their learning. To accommodate differences in children's learning, lessons should allow children to think about mathematical ideas in their own ways and on their own timetables. An important goal is to provide students time and opportunities to construct their own understanding.

CHAPTER THREE
THE BIG YELLOW WORM

Overview

This lesson provides students with a second opportunity to create a 0–99 chart while at the same time giving them a chance to make a 1–100 chart. Students begin by making predictions about where the hundredth 3-by-3-inch sticky note would be if one hundred notes were laid side by side beginning at the door of the classroom. Using sentence strips and sticky notes, students work to create a continuous strip that is one hundred notes long—"the big yellow worm," as one class called it. Students work in pairs or small groups to count the notes by twos, by fives, and by tens. Then the strip of one hundred is cut into ten lengths of ten. By arranging and posting the ten strips of ten, one beneath the other, and labeling the notes, a 0–99 chart is created. A 1–100 chart can also be created by writing the numbers from 1 to 100 underneath the notes on the sentence strips.

Materials

▲ 13 24-by-3 inch sentence strips
▲ 3-by-3-inch sticky notes, 1 package of 100 to use and 1 to show students (Yellow notes were used in this vignette, but any color will do.)

Time

▲ two class periods to create the chart, plus several additional days for labeling and discussion

Teaching Directions

1. Before the lesson, attach sticky notes to two sentence strips and half of another for a total of twenty notes. Eight notes fit on a sentence strip. Place the sticky edges of each note running along the same edge of the sentence strip. Tape the sticky edges of the notes to the sentence strip to prevent the notes from falling off as children handle the strips. Underneath the notes, on the sentence strips, number from 1 to 20 using a light-colored marker or pencil so that the children can't read the numbers through the notes. Also, clip a pile of eight notes to each of the remaining sentence strips.

2. Show the students a full pad of one hundred sticky notes and ask where they think the hundredth note would be if they were laid side by side beginning at the door (or some other spot in the classroom). Repeat this question several times during the lesson as students gain more information. Remind children it is OK to adjust their estimate as new information is gathered.

3. Show the students a strip with eight notes on it. Ask students to estimate the number of notes on the strip. Together, count them by twos, marking each group of two as they are counted.

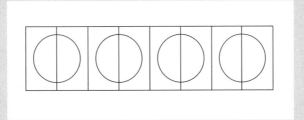

4. Ask if there would still be eight if they counted by fives. Count and mark the group of five, then count on the three remaining notes to verify there are still eight notes even though they were counted by fives.

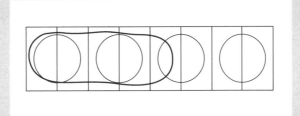

5. Ask students how many strips would be needed for twenty notes if each strip holds eight. Have the students explain their reasoning. Verify with the strips. Talk with the children about how many tens there are in twenty.

6. Lay the strips with the twenty notes on the floor to show how far twenty notes are from the door (or from the spot you initially designated). Invite the children to revise their estimates of how far one hundred would reach.

7. Have students work together in twos or threes to make nine additional strips with eight notes on each. You will have one strip left. Set this one aside. Give each group a sentence strip with the pile of notes attached. Remind students to put all of the sticky edges along the same edge of the sentence strip. As students complete their strips, tape the sticky edges to prevent the notes from falling off. This work period goes quickly.

8. Ask the class how many notes they attached altogether to the nine sentence strips. Have students explain their strategies for figuring out the answer. Record their strategies on the board. If appropriate, ask students how many more notes are needed to make one hundred.

9. Before class the next day, tape all the strips together into one long strip. Tape the two and a half strips with the original twenty sticky notes to the beginning of the strip. Divide and mark the strip in sections of ten each, marking the first note in each section with a green marker and the tenth in each section with a red marker. There will be two extra notes.

10. Explain to the students how you marked sections with green and red markers. Model for the first section how to count and mark the notes in twos, fives, and tens.

11. Lay out the strip and assign students to sections. Have them work in eight groups, each counting the number of squares on a section first by twos, then by fives, and then by tens. Students working together should agree on the count. Collect the data from each group of students and record on a chart:

	2s	5s	10s	altogether

12. Add the information from the first section of ten notes to the chart. Then ask the children how many notes there are on the entire long worm. Record their strategies for figuring. Use the remaining sentence strip to add notes to make one hundred.

13. Cut a strip of twenty. Discuss the number of tens on the strip. Post. Begin numbering the squares starting with zero and stopping at nine. Ask what number will be on the last note on that section of the strip. Continue numbering to the end of the section of strip. Cut the strip into two tens.

14. Cut the remaining strip into strips of ten and post to form a 10-by-10 square. Ask students what number the last square in the third row will be and why.

15. Complete the numbering of the 0–99 chart in this way over several days. To create a 1–100 chart, underneath each note, write the numbers from 1 to 100.

Teaching Notes

The lesson *The 0–99 Chart* is an excellent prerequisite to *The Big Yellow Worm.* Ideas and understandings introduced in *The 0–99 Chart* are expanded and developed further in this lesson. While it may not be necessary for all classes to do both lessons, multiple experiences with the same idea provide additional opportunities for learning and deepening understanding.

Creating a chart such as this provides children with additional experiences counting a large number of objects by twos, fives, and tens. It also provides students with a very concrete experience to verify that there are actually one hundred boxes on a 0–99 chart, a difficult idea for some children to grasp at this age.

How you proceed with numbering the 0–99 chart can offer students a rich variety of experiences. Some classes, for example, may need to focus on the idea that there really are one hundred boxes on a 0–99 chart, while other classes may benefit from searching for patterns as numbers are added to the chart and making predictions based on those patterns. Another class still may benefit from guessing what a particular missing number could be. The direction you take will depend on the needs and interests of your particular class.

The Lesson

▲▲

DAY 1

I held up a pad of 3-by-3-inch sticky notes and asked the students, "If I laid one hundred of these notes on the floor beginning at the door to our classroom, where do you think the one hundredth note would be?"

"In the next classroom," Jaime said.

"Over by the corner," Michelle guessed.

"Maybe halfway across the room by where Roger is sitting," Camille suggested.

"I think maybe by the bookcase," Annie said.

"Before class, I attached some notes to some sentence strips," I explained as I held up a strip with eight notes on it.

"It looks like a yellow worm!" Sunjai said. The class giggled.

"It looks like a tatterpillar," Michael said.

"You mean a caterpillar," Valerie corrected him.

"Looks like a worm to me," Roger said.

To redirect the conversation, I asked, "Who would like to guess how many notes are on my worm?" The students giggled as I used Sunjai's idea to increase their interest.

I allowed all who wanted to share their guess to do so. I listed their guesses on the board using tally marks next to each to show how many children guessed each number.

"Let's count," Alex said.

"How would you like to count, Alex?" I asked.

"By twos," Alex replied.

"Help me count," I said to the class. "As we count, I'll mark with a circle groups of two to help us keep track of the notes we've already counted." The students counted out loud by twos as I circled groups of two. They found there were four groups of two, or eight notes on the strip, or worm as they continued to call it.

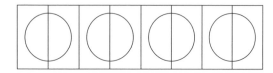

"What if I counted by five? Would there still be eight notes on the worm?"

"I don't think so," Valerie said. Several others shook their heads "no" also.

"Maybe," Jaime said with hesitation.

"There would be," Annie said. "I think if we count by fives, there'll be one group of five and three extras."

"There would have to be eight still because it's the same group of notes," Kerri said.

"Yeah, you're not changing the number or anything, you're just changing how you count them. It should be the same," Christopher said.

"Let's count and find out," I said. Together we counted by fives as I marked a group of five on the strip. We counted on from five to verify there were eight altogether.

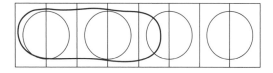

"If I can fit eight notes on one strip, how many strips will I need for twenty notes?" I asked.

"Three," Melissa said.

"How many would fit on three strips?" I asked her.

"Eight and eight is sixteen, then seventeen, eighteen, nineteen, twenty, twenty-one, twenty-two, twenty-three, twenty-four. Twenty-four," Melissa explained.

"I think two," Ned said. "Two and some extra, because eight and eight is sixteen, then you'd need some extra for the seventeen, eighteen, nineteen, and twenty."

"Two and a half! That's what you need," Morgan announced. "You need enough of a strip for four more, and four is half of eight, so that would be two and a half." Several others nodded, indicating their agreement.

I placed the original strip on the chalkboard tray, then put an additional strip of notes beside it and asked the students how many notes there were in all. They responded with sixteen. I added the third strip, which was half covered with the four remaining notes, to make twenty.

"Let's count by twos to be certain there are twenty," I suggested. I marked each group of two as the students counted aloud. "What if we counted by fives—do you still think there would be twenty squares on my worm?" Some students said no, but most said yes. We counted by fives as I marked each group and found there were indeed twenty squares.

"We've figured out the number of squares on my worm in several ways," I said, "and we always seem to find there are twenty squares. How many tens do you think there are in twenty? Think in your heads for just a moment before you answer." Some students seemed to have an answer right away, while others used their fingers and needed a moment to figure it out. "Show me with you fingers how many tens in twenty." I said. Most students held up two fingers.

"Can I explain why?" Melissa asked. I nodded. "You count ten and twenty—that's two tens!"

"I think two tens, too, but for another reason," Michelle shared. "It takes two fives to make a group of ten. There are four groups of five circled on the strip, so there must be two groups of ten."

"Does anyone else have an idea you would like to share?" I asked. No one did.

"Let's lay the worms on the floor and see how far away from the door they go," I said as I laid them on the floor. "Remember, you can change your guess about where the hundredth square will be as we gain new information."

"I'm changing my guess," Jose said.

"Me too," others said as they started discussing their new guesses with their neighbors.

"You can change your guesses in your heads," I said in order to move the lesson forward.

"I'm going to assign you a partner to work with on the next part of the lesson," I explained. "Your task is to work together with your partner to make a worm strip with eight sticky notes on it. When you put your notes on the sentence strips, be sure to put all of the sticky edges along the same edge." I modeled this for the students. "When you are finished, bring your worm to me so I can tape the sticky edges to keep the notes from falling off," I continued as I handed each pair of students a sentence strip with a stack of eight notes clipped to one end.

As the students worked, I circulated through the room, reminding them to put their notes together so there weren't any gaps and to put the sticky edge at the top of the strip. One group was singing, "Yellow worm, yellow worm, Much better than a

Jell-O worm!" As students finished I taped the top edge of their strips so the notes wouldn't fall off. The students followed directions and worked well together. They were done with the task quickly. As they finished I gathered them on the rug.

"Together you completed nine strips each with eight notes. How many notes is that?" I asked. This problem was difficult for the students. "How could we write this using a number sentence?" I asked.

"You could write eight + nine," Jaime suggested.

"Tell me more," I replied.

"The eight means eight notes and the nine means nine worms," Jaime explained. It was clear Jaime was having difficulty making sense of what I was really asking.

"My question is how many notes," I said. I held up one strip. "On one strip, how many notes are there?" I asked. Jaime responded that there were eight. I held up a second strip alongside the first. "Now how many notes?" I asked.

"Sixteen," Jaime said.

"What number sentence tells our story so far?" I asked.

"Oh, I think I see," Jaime said. "The number sentence is eight + eight, not eight + nine." Several others wanted to share, so I decided to leave Jaime for a moment to consider what we had discussed so far. I called on Michelle.

"You could do eight + eight + eight + eight, like that for nine times since there are nine strips," Michelle suggested.

I recorded Michelle's idea on the board:

$8 + 8 + 8 + 8 + 8 + 8 + 8 + 8 + 8$

I thought of it going up and down, not sideways," Michelle said.

I recorded her idea again, this time as follows:

8

8

8

8

$$
\begin{array}{r}
8 \\
8 \\
8 \\
8 \\
+\underline{8}
\end{array}
$$

"That's it," Michelle said.

"I think you could put eights together," Ned suggested. "You could put two eights together, and that would be sixteen. Sixteen plus sixteen plus sixteen plus sixteen plus eight."

I recorded Ned's idea on the board:

$$
\begin{array}{ll}
2 & 8s = 16 \\
2 & 8s = 16 \\
2 & 8s = 16 \\
2 & 8s = 16 \\
& +\underline{8}
\end{array}
$$

"Would anyone else like to share?" I asked. No one had anything else to add. "About how many tens do you think this would be?" I asked, pointing to the ideas the students had shared.

"Maybe thirty," Valerie shared. She had no explanation about why she thought this.

"At least four," Jose said. "Each of the sixteens has one ten, and there are four sixteens, so I think at least four."

"Maybe five," Camille said. "There's six extras for each sixteen, so they should make enough to have at least one more, so that would be five."

"There are nine eights," Roger noticed. "Eight is a little less than ten, so I think there maybe are eight tens."

"I think maybe seven tens," Ned offered. "Two sixteens is enough for three tens because sixteen plus sixteen is thirty-two. There are four sixteens, so that would be six tens, and then the extras and the last eight, so that's seven. . . . or maybe even eight tens." The students sat quietly thinking.

"Tomorrow you'll work together with a partner and we'll figure out how many," I said as I concluded the lesson for the day.

DAY 2

Before class began, I taped the nine strips of sticky notes into one long strip. At the beginning of the strip, I taped the two and a half strips with the original twenty notes and the numbers from 1 to 20 written underneath. I then marked off the notes into groups of ten, using a green marker to mark the first note in each group and a red marker to indicate the last note in each group of ten.

I gathered the students on the rug. Once they settled, I held up the strip to show them I had taped it together and to give them a sense of how long it was.

"Wow!" Brian exclaimed with big eyes. "It's like a really huge, gigantic yellow worm now!" The others giggled.

"It's supposed to have one hundred notes on it," I said, "but I haven't counted yet. I am going to ask for your help in counting." I held up the beginning of the worm. "I've divided the worm in sections. I put a green mark to tell you where your section begins and a red mark to tell you where your section ends."

"That's smart," Michelle said. "Green means go and red means stop!"

"Working with your partner, you'll need to figure out how many groups of two there are in your section, how many fives, how many tens, and how many notes there are altogether." I modeled, using the first section of ten notes to show them how to count and mark the notes by twos, fives, and tens. "You need to agree on the data," I continued. "When you have your information and you both agree, come see me. I'll record your information on this chart." I drew a chart on the board (see top of next page).

I laid the continuous strip on the floor. As I assigned a section of the strip to a pair of students, I asked them to move carefully from their seats to their section to avoid stepping on the strip or bothering those

	2s	5s	10s	altogether

already working. Because I had modeled for the students how to mark and count the notes on the first section, there were few questions. The students got to work quickly and cooperatively. As partners finished, they came to me to give me the information for the chart. I asked if they agreed before accepting their data, then I asked them to sit down and read for a few moments until the other groups were finished. When the chart was complete, I began a discussion.

	2s	5s	10s	altogether
	5	2	1	10
	5	2	1	10
	6	2	1	10
	5	2	1	10
	5	2	1	10
	5	2	1	10
	5	2	1	10
	5	2	1	10

"What do you notice about the information on the chart?" I asked the class. The students were quiet. Then a few hands went up. "Talk with your table group about what you notice." One thing I was hoping they would notice is that the information from the third pair, Kerri and Camille, didn't make sense. After a few moments I asked for the students' attention. I called on Michael.

"All the numbers in the fives column are the same," Michael shared.

"What does the five mean at the top of the column?" I asked.

"It means groups of five," Michael replied.

"All the sections had the same amount of squares," Amanda said.

"How many notes did each section have?" I asked.

"Uhm, ten, I think," Amanda replied.

"Yeah, they all had ten," Sunjai agreed.

"I think they all had the same on everything except our group. Camille and I had six instead of five in the first column," Kerri noticed.

"That seems strange," Roger said. "If Kerri and Camille had as many groups of five as the other tables, I think they should have had the same number of twos."

"Kerri must have counted it wrong," Camille blurted. "She was in charge of twos."

"Remember you and your partner were supposed to have worked together and agreed on the information before you shared it with me to post it on the chart," I told Camille, who tended to be pushy and quick to blame, as was Kerri. "Rather than blame Kerri for what was the responsibility of both of you, I think you should go back to your section and recount to see if you can figure out what happened. Mistakes are a natural part of living and learning and something that we all make, especially when we are doing something for the first time." Perhaps I should have handled this a different way, by asking the pair to recount their twos before I put their data on the chart; however, they said they agreed on the information. Mistakes happen and I think it is important to handle them so that they are learning opportunities rather than embarrassments. In this case, it was both partners' responsibility to make sure they agreed on their data, so the decision to report there were six groups of twos was a shared responsibility. Opportunities like this prepare students for dealing with similar situations that will confront them later on. I waited the few moments it took the girls to check their work.

"We made a mistake," Kerri said. "There really were five groups of two and we both checked and we agree this time." Camille nodded her agreement. I changed the information on the chart.

"Thanks for taking a moment to check your work," I said. "It'll help us make sense of all the information on the chart."

"It's all the same now," Alex said.

I hadn't assigned students to count the first section of ten on the worm, as I had used it to model how to circle groups of two, five, and ten. "I need to add the information from my section of the worm, plus one leftover group of two from the end of the worm," I said as I added my information to the chart. "How many notes are there on the entire long worm?" I asked.

"Ninety-two," Maggie said. "I just counted by tens and then added the extra two."

I recorded:

10, 20, 30, 40, 50, 60, 70, 80, 90

90 + 2 = 92

"I think it's ninety-two too," Alex said.

"Convince me," I said.

"Well, you can take two tens and that makes twenty," Alex explained. "There are eight tens you can do that with, so that would be like four twenties. I know that two plus two plus two plus two is eight, so twenty plus twenty plus twenty plus twenty is eighty. Then there was one more group of ten, so that makes ninety, and then two more extras, so that's ninety-two." I recorded as Alex explained:

2 10s = 20

8 10s = 4 20s

2 + 2 + 2 + 2 = 8

20 + 20 + 20 + 20 = 80

80 + 10 = 90

90 + 2 = 92

No one else had any other ideas to offer.

"How many more squares do we need to add to make one hundred?" I asked. I waited until over half the students had their hands raised. I called on Ned.

"Eight," Ned said.

"Tell me more," I said.

"I thought, 'Ninety-two plus how much is one hundred?' " Ned explained. "Then I used my fingers to keep track and counted ninety-three, ninety-four, ninety-five, ninety-six, ninety-seven, ninety-eight, ninety-nine, one hundred. I had eight fingers up, so it had to be eight."

I recorded Ned's thinking on the board:

92 + □ = 100

93, 94, 95, 96, 97, 98, 99, 100

92 + 8 = 100

"I think eight too, but I did it differently," Jose said. "I got rid of the nine in ninety. I know that two plus eight is ten, so I added back in the ninety with the ten, and it was one hundred." I recorded Jose's idea on the board:

92 – 90 = 2

2 + 8 = 10

90 + 10 = 100

No one had anything further to say. I agreed that we needed to add eight more squares and added them.

I then took a pair of scissors and cut off the first section of twenty notes, the ones I had already numbered from 1 to 20 on the strip under the notes.

"How many notes on this worm?" I asked.

"Ten, "eighteen," "twenty," "twenty-one," and "nineteen," were some of the responses.

"Let's count to find out," I suggested. When we reached ten, I interrupted the class and said, "That's one ten. Let's start again from one to count the rest." We counted ten more. This confirmed for the children that there were twenty in all on the strip.

"We know there are twenty squares. Think in your brain about what number the last one will be if I start numbering beginning with zero," I said as I began to number the squares starting with zero so the students could easily see what I was doing. I stopped at nine and asked, "What number will be here?" I was pointing to the last square.

"Eighteen," Valerie said.

"Nineteen," Roger responded.

"Twenty-one," Michael added.

"Twenty," Amanda said.

"When I made this strip, I wrote a number on the strip underneath each note. I began with one. What number do you think is under the last square?" I asked.

"Twenty," was the response.

"I have started numbering on top of the notes beginning with zero rather than one," I said, "and I stopped with number nine. What number do you think is under nine?"

"Ten," the class chorused.

"Let's check by looking under the nine," I said as I lifted the 9 to verify there was indeed a 10 under it.

"I'll keep numbering and you watch." I continued to number as the children watched.

"Nineteen!" they called out as I labeled the last square with a 19.

"How many squares are there?" I asked.

Most said twenty although a few said nineteen. We counted the squares by twos to confirm that there were indeed twenty and looked under the 19 to find there was a 20 there. "How many groups of ten in twenty?" I asked.

"Two," the class chorused.

"I am going to cut the strip into tens," I said, holding up the strip of twenty we had been working with. "How many tens, or pieces, will I have?"

"Two," Kerri said. "Ten and ten more would be twenty." The others nodded their agreement. I cut the strip into two tens, pinned the 0–9 strip on the wall, and then

the 10–19 strip beneath it. I pinned them high enough so that I could post eight additional strips of ten underneath, which would eventually create a 0–99 chart.

"There were one hundred squares on our worm. I cut off two strips of ten. How many are left?" I asked.

"Seventy?" Valerie answered with a shrug.

"Eighty," Jose said. "It has to be eighty because if you count from eighty and add ten, that's ninety, and ten more is one hundred. That's twenty and then eighty more to make one hundred."

I recorded Jose's idea:

80 + 10 = 90

90 + 10 = 100

20 + 80 = 100

Annie shared next. "I just thought, 'Twenty plus how many more makes one hundred?' Then I counted from twenty to one hundred and got eighty. I started at twenty, then thirty, forty, fifty . . . like that," Annie explained as she counted by tens and held up one finger each time she added another ten. I recorded Annie's thinking on the board:

20 + □ = 100

start at 20: 30, 40, 50, 60, 70, 80, 90, 100

20 + 80 = 100

"How many tens are there in eighty?" I asked the class. "Show me with your fingers." Most students held up eight fingers. "Let's check," I said. "Let's count by tens together and I'll record as we count to be sure there are eight tens in eighty." As the students counted by tens, I recorded on the board to verify there were eight tens in eighty. I cut the rest of the worm into tens and pinned the strips to the wall to create ten rows of ten notes.

"How many tens in one hundred?" I asked.

"Ten!" chorused the class.

"I numbered the first two rows before," I said. "What if I wanted to put a number on this note?" I asked, pointing to the last note in the third row. "What number do you suppose should go there? Put your thumb up when you know." I was able to observe the children as they thought about this. A few were quick to put their thumbs up, while many pointed as they silently counted the squares one by one to determine the number that should go on the square I had indicated. A few seemed lost and were looking at the ceiling or out the window or playing with their fingers. When most students had their thumbs up, I called on Amanda.

"It would be thirty," she said. "There's ten in each row, so ten, twenty, thirty."

"I think maybe twenty-seven," Roger said. "The last number on the first row is nine. There are three rows, so three times nine is twenty-seven." Roger was very interested in multiplication and enjoyed solving problems with multiplication whenever possible.

"Roger," Patrick said, "there are really ten squares in the first row and in the others, too. You figured it out like there were nine squares, I think."

Roger looked perplexed by Patrick's comment. "Can I come up and look under the squares to see what number is under the nine?" Roger asked. I nodded. Roger came up and looked, noticed the 10 underneath the 9 and began to count the rows quietly by tens. "Maybe thirty?" he said, uncertain of his guess.

"I think it's maybe twenty-nine," Brian said. "I notice that the other two numbers above it end in nine, so I think this new one should too. My brain also remembered about the zero. It takes up a square and it can't be nothing because it is a number."

"My answer is like Brian's, only I sort of did it differently," Michael said. "I counted by tens. I started with the nine at the top, then added ten and it was nineteen, then ten more would be twenty-nine. I think it should be twenty-nine."

"I think it's twenty-nine, too," Jose said. "I just counted by ones from nineteen and it was twenty-nine."

No one had anything else to add. Together we counted by ones from nineteen to the square I had indicated and agreed it should be labeled *29*, so I labeled it. I also pointed out that Brian's observation about all the numbers in the last column ending in nine seemed to work. We also counted by tens beginning with nine to verify that twenty-nine also worked when we counted by tens. The students were tired, so I ended the lesson at this point.

After the lesson, I completed numbering the strips underneath the notes from 1 to 100. To complete the 0–99 chart by numbering the notes, I planned to come back to the chart over the next several weeks and slowly fill it in by adding numbers as we had just done.

EXTENSIONS

Besides making a strip of one hundred sticky notes, students can work independently, in pairs, or in small groups to make their own strip of one hundred items, using stickers, stamps, thumbprints, footprints, or whatever. When they have completed their strip of one hundred, students can count the objects by twos, fives, and tens. Then they can cut their hundred strip into ten strips of ten to make a 0–99 chart or a 1–100 chart.

Questions and Discussion

▲▲

▲ *In an earlier lesson the students also created a 0–99 chart. Why would it make sense to do it a second time?*

For some classes it may not make sense to do both activities. For this class it did. There were still several children who had not yet resolved how there could be one hundred squares on a chart that ended with 99. This second experience provided them with an additional opportunity to grapple with that idea. Also, the discussion about why it made sense to label the squares with a particular number became more complex and interesting, indicating students were deepening their mathematical understanding of patterns and how the base ten number system works. As we continued to label the notes, more children made use of counting by tens rather than counting each individual square by ones.

Using notes was particularly helpful for some students, as once the chart was finished, they could see a 0–99 chart on top of the notes, while underneath, by flipping up the notes, they could see a 1–100 chart.

▲ *It seems like you spent a lot of the lesson focusing on various arithmetic problems rather than staying focused on making the chart. Why does this make sense?*

I did take time to have the students solve a variety of arithmetic problems. I did this for several reasons: The activity gave a context for thinking about arithmetic. The practice the students were getting as they solved the problems was meaningful practice, as the numbers derived their meaning from the activity. Also, I like students to practice computation whenever the opportunity arises. There were many opportunities in this activity. When students solve problems as they were doing in this activity, they also have an opportunity to share strategies, which helps clarify thinking for the person sharing as well as providing the listeners with new ways to think about something. I record the students' ideas using numerical notation to help them understand that their ideas and the language they use to express them can be represented by numbers; that is, numbers have meaning that can be linked to activities, language, and ideas that are theirs.

CHAPTER FOUR
DOLLAR SIGNS

Overview

This lesson provides students with another opportunity to experience counting large numbers of objects in several ways. Students repeat the experiment of drawing stars in one minute, but this time, rather than drawing stars, they draw dollar signs. This lesson can be done as a whole-group lesson, as was *Stars in One Minute*, or students can work in pairs. Working in pairs, one student times one minute while the other draws dollar signs. In this way, students also gain experience measuring time. After drawing the dollar signs, each child figures out in two different ways how many he or she drew and writes about the methods used to count.

Materials

▲ a clock with a sweep second hand or other timekeepers that measure one minute, 1 per pair of students
▲ optional: 3-by-3-inch sticky notes, 1 per student

Time

▲ one class period

Teaching Directions

1. Remind the students of the experiment they did in *Stars in One Minute*. Explain that they will repeat the experiment, only this time they will try to find out how many dollar signs they can draw in one minute.

2. If students will work on this activity in pairs, explain how to use the timekeepers to measure one minute.

3. Explain the directions for the activity: one person times one minute while the other person draws dollar signs, and then the students switch jobs.

4. After both partners have drawn their dollar signs, they each count in two different ways the number of dollars signs they drew. Then students write about how they counted.

5. Circulate and observe as children work.

Teaching Notes

This lesson is appropriate after children have had several experiences counting large quantities, including the lesson *Stars in One Minute*. Because of their prior experience, I was looking to see if this group of students would continue to count using the same numbers as they had before, or if they would try counting with new numbers. I was interested to see how many children still needed to count by ones to verify the total and who was still making errors when counting by twos and fives. Also, I was interested to know if any of the children would choose counting by tens as one of his or her ways. If ten wasn't one of a student's ways, which is typical, was figuring the number of tens and extras in his or her number of dollar signs trivial, did the student have to think about it, or was the student without a way into the problem? As I observed and talked with the children, I pushed a bit harder to have them figure out the number of tens and extras in their number and explain their thinking to help me better understand where they were with their learning and understanding about place value.

The Lesson

▲▲

"This is just like *Stars in One Minute*," I said, "but you draw dollar signs instead."

In the two previous years when I taught this unit, the classroom clock had had a sweep second hand. This year, however, there wasn't one, so I had borrowed stopwatches.

A few days earlier, I had taught Nick how to use the stopwatches—how to clear them and get them into stopwatch mode. I chose Nick because he was very good with machines of any kind. He was able to help others with the class computers, change the bag in the handheld vacuum cleaner, fix the stapler, and make the pencil sharpener work. However, Nick also had difficulty staying

focused during whole-class lessons. He often got excited, then a bit wild, and then lost his concentration. I felt that having some responsibility would be good for him and help him keep on track and stay engaged with the class. Nick was thrilled with the job and took the responsibility very seriously.

I showed the stopwatches to the students and showed them the button for starting and stopping the timer and the button for resetting the time. Several of the children were eager to investigate the timers.

I then asked Sarah to read the directions aloud: "One person times one minute, and the other person draws dollar signs. Then switch jobs. After you've each drawn dollar signs, count how many you drew in two different ways. Write about how you counted."

"How do you know when a minute is up?" Timmy asked.

"You use one of the stopwatches," I answered.

"I know," Timmy persisted. "But how does it tell you?"

"Ah," I said, "we should talk about this. The stopwatch works like a counter. It counts by seconds, like some of you did when I had you close your eyes and estimate one minute. It takes sixty seconds to make a minute."

"I don't know how to do it," Timmy said. Timmy wasn't very confident about his abilities and worried about not knowing.

"I can teach him," Nick said.

"Can I do it with Nick?" Timmy said.

"No," I answered. "You have to work with your regular partner. But you can both get help from Nick if you can't figure out how to use the stopwatch."

This task required little supervision from me. Children understood the directions and were eager to do the activity. As I observed, I noticed that most students grouped by twos and fives. Nick for example, wrote: *I counted by 2s and I had 30 then I counted by 5s and I still got 30.*

Some children counted by ones. Leslie, for example, wrote: *I couted by 2's and I came up with 44. I counted by 1's and i came up with 44.* (See Figure 4–1.)

Very few children grouped by tens. In my experience, I've noticed that grouping by tens isn't typically seen by children as useful for counting large numbers of objects. (If you were going to count a pile of objects, such as raisins in a small snack box or pennies in a jar, how would you group them?) Although grouping by tens is useful when adding numbers, it isn't always useful in the context of working with concrete objects.

I used to insist on this task that children group by tens. I've stopped doing so. I've come to realize that when I impose a sys-

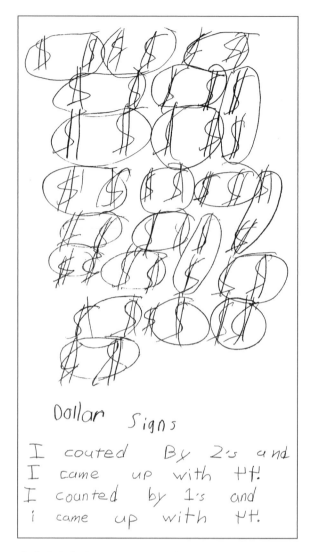

▲▲▲▲▲▲Figure 4–1 *Leslie grouped her dollar signs by 2s and 1s.*

tem on children, they get invested in following my rules rather than understanding the sense in the procedure. I've seen many children who can circle groups of ten objects and tell the total, but still not understand the tens and ones structure of our number system.

LINKING ASSESSMENT TO INSTRUCTION

As the children worked, I asked students who had counted their dollar signs to tell me how many groups they would have if they made groups with ten in each. For

Tomo, this was a simple question and he answered immediately.

"Three tens," he said.

"Any extra dollar signs?" I asked.

He thought for a moment. "No," he said, with a tone of voice that implied that I had asked a stupid question.

"How do you know?" I asked.

"You just go ten, twenty, thirty," he said.

Jason, however, didn't have a clue about the number of tens in his number. He had drawn thirty-six dollar signs. He counted them by ones and by fives. First he had gotten two different results, but after some recounting, he decided on thirty-six.

"If you circled groups of ten," I asked Jason, "how many groups of ten would you have?"

He thought for a moment. "Well," he said tentatively, "maybe one or two."

"Which do you think—one or two?" I asked.

"Hmmm, maybe two," he answered.

"Convince me," I said.

"I just guessed," he confessed.

"But what if you wanted to figure it out?" I replied. "What could you do?"

"I don't know," he said. "Oh yeah—I could count and draw circles."

Maria had drawn twenty-seven dollar signs. "If you circled groups of ten, how many groups of ten would you have?" Maria didn't have a clue.

"Can I draw on my paper to figure it out?" she asked.

"Yes, but I wonder if you could try to figure out the answer first," I said. "How many circles would you have to draw if you counted by tens?"

Maria sat quietly for a moment. Then she shrugged.

"Then try it on paper," I said gently.

MEETING A SPECIAL NEED

When I assess students informally, I'm interested in gathering information that will help me form a picture of their mathematical interests and abilities.

Sometimes, however, a student needs some extra attention.

Colleen called me over after she had counted her dollar signs. She had drawn circles to make groups of two. "I got twenty-eight," she said, "but then I counted them by ones and I got thirty-four."

"Show me how you counted by twos," I said.

Colleen began, but got confused in the teens, saying "fifteen" after "fourteen" and not sure what to say next. She started over, this time getting confused before she even reached ten. Colleen's number sense was very weak, and I sat down to talk with her. She didn't seem to have any understanding of even numbers. It seemed they were a string of words to be remembered, not a pattern of numbers to be understood.

"Show me how you would count the dollar signs by ones," I said.

Colleen didn't have a system for keeping track of the dollar signs as she counted them. She missed one and counted two of them twice.

"How about counting once more," I said. "This time, put a tiny check mark next to each dollar sign that you count. That way, you won't miss any or count them more than once."

Colleen did this and got to thirty-two. (See Figure 4–2.) "But that's not the answer I got when I did it before," she said. She was confused and getting frustrated.

"That's why it's important to count several ways," I said, "just to check."

"Which is right?" she asked.

Getting the right answer to the number of her dollar signs seemed like the least of Colleen's problems, but it was important to her to know.

"Watch as I count by twos," I said, "and we'll see what I get. I'll put a little X on each circle as I count that group." I counted by twos and got thirty-two.

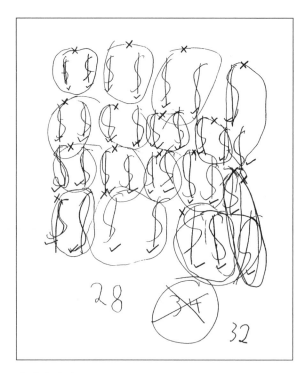

▲▲▲▲▲▲Figure 4–2   *On my suggestion, Colleen used check marks to keep track of the dollar signs as she counted them by 1s. I used Xs to mark each group of 2.*

"So it's thirty-two?" she asked.

"Let's count again by twos," I said. "This time, try to count along with me." Colleen was able to count with me up to ten, and then her voice faded.

"Would you like to know the secret of counting by twos?" I asked her. She nodded "yes."

"Would you be willing to do a special activity?" I asked her. She nodded "yes" again.

I had Colleen get the interlocking cubes. "Make a bunch of little trains with two in each," I said, "and then come and get me again."

"Does it matter what color I use?" she asked.

"No," I answered, "use any colors you'd like."

Colleen presented a special problem to me. Although she could count and used that as a way to add small quantities, she had little understanding of the relationships

among numbers. I felt I needed to intervene. I was interested, however, in giving Colleen help without making her feel deficient. Responding to different needs of children presents one of the big challenges of teaching.

Colleen called me over after she had made about a dozen trains of two. I moved the trains aside and put a piece of 9-by-12-inch construction paper in front of her.

"This is a game of count and record," I said. "You'll need a blank sheet of paper. How many cubes are on the construction paper now?"

"None," Colleen said, grinning.

"What number says none?" I asked.

"It's zero," she said. "Do you want me to write it?"

"Not just now," I said, "we'll get to that in a minute."

"Now I'll show you where the numbers come from when you count by twos," I said. "Just start by putting a train of two on the paper and then tell me how many cubes there are." Colleen did this easily.

"Put another train on and then tell me how many cubes there are altogether," I then said. Again, Colleen did this easily.

"So you started with zero," I reviewed, "then you had two, and then four." I removed the two trains from the paper, said "zero," and put each train back, counting "two, four" as I did so.

"Now add another train," I said, "and see how many cubes there are."

Colleen added a train and then counted the cubes by ones, touching each cube as she counted. I cleared the paper again and counted by twos from zero to six, putting the trains back on the paper. Then I had Colleen clear the paper and count by twos as I had done, adding each train as she did so.

"How many do you think you'll have when you add another train?" I asked.

Colleen shrugged. "Oh, wait," she said, "it would be seven, eight. Eight."

"Try it and see," I said. Colleen added a train and again resorted to counting all the cubes by ones. She was pleased to get to eight as she had predicted. I had her clear the paper and count by twos to eight, adding trains each time. I was trying to help Colleen link the sequence of even numbers to a concrete reference. I continued in the same way up until twelve, and then told Colleen that I'd leave her to continue, but that I wanted her to keep track of the numbers so I could check later.

I cleared the paper again. "That's zero," Colleen said.

"Write the number for zero on your paper," I said.

"Anywhere?" she asked.

"Near the top," I answered, "so you have room to write others underneath."

Then I had Colleen add a train. "I've got two," she said. "Should I write that, too?"

"Yes," I replied, "write it under the zero." I showed Colleen how to continue listing the numbers and left her to work. She was interested and engaged. When she got to twenty, she began to wonder about the numbers she had skipped and wrote them in a separate list. (See Figure 4–3.)

"Look," she said to me, "there's one in between all of them." She was surprised by this.

"Yes," I said, "those are the odd numbers." This information didn't seem to be of any interest to Colleen, another reminder that children learn on their own timetables. Later, I would have her color in the numbers on her list on a 0–99 chart and see the patterns that emerged. Children often benefit from several different ways to think about an idea.

I wasn't interested primarily in "fixing" Colleen's lack of understanding of even numbers. This lack was merely a symptom of the holes and confusions in her mathematical understanding. Although the activity focused specifically on the pattern of even numbers, I was interested in having Colleen

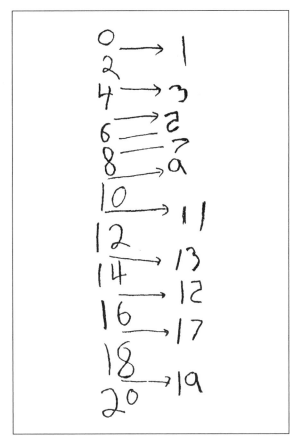

▲▲▲▲▲Figure 4–3 *Working with Snap Cubes, Colleen generated a list of even numbers and then wrote a second list of the numbers she skipped.*

see that number patterns come from logical, orderly relationships and in giving her an experience that could help reveal the logic and order to her. For many children, mathematical ideas are a jumble of random and isolated notions. They don't expect to see order or logic and therefore don't even look for it. I was trying to influence Colleen's basic understanding of mathematics while at the same time giving her access to the rationale for the pattern of even numbers.

Although I never have a surefire way to effect a student's learning, I know that it helps enormously to give children personalized attention, have them link abstractions to some concrete reference, and help them see the connection between standard numerical symbolism and a concrete experience.

EXTENSION

As with *Stars in One Minute*, this activity can provide an experience with data and statistics. Have students write the number of dollar signs they drew in one minute on a sticky note. Discuss how to organize the data into a graph focusing on the numerical data. Ask students to talk together about the information they notice in the graph. Lead a discussion and record the students' observations about the graph.

Lead a class discussion to find the total number of dollar signs the class drew. Encourage the students to count by twos and fives and then predict and check the number of tens.

Have students compare the differences in the numerical data shown on the graph. For example, what is the difference between the greatest and least number of dollars signs drawn?

Have students work in pairs and repeat the experiment, only this time drawing check marks or happy faces or something else that is of interest yet quick and simple to draw.

Questions and Discussion

▲▲▲

▲ *How did you find the time to focus on Colleen and help her while there were other children in the room?*

This was possible because the other children were engaged in an activity that was of interest to them. In addition, this activity was similar to *Stars in a Minute*, so the children knew what to do and did not need much direction from me to complete the task. When children did come to me with a question, I stopped and gave whatever help was needed. Also, Colleen did some of her special activity independently while I circulated around the room, checking on the other students' progress.

▲ *Did most children count by tens during this experience since they had had previous similar experiences?*

No, most children did not make use of tens as a way to count their dollar signs. This really did not concern me too much, as many adults don't typically count large numbers of objects by tens, but rather count by twos or perhaps fives. What was of interest to me, however, was who could easily tell me the number of tens and the extras in his or her number of dollar signs and who could effectively explain how he or she knew. This kind of information was useful in helping me know who was grasping with understanding how our number system relates to numbers in a real-world context.

CHAPTER FIVE
COUNTING FISH

Overview

In *Counting Fish*, children group and count objects in several ways. The lesson uses $\frac{3}{4}$-inch interlocking cubes to help children connect the tens and ones structure of our number system to a concrete material. The lesson is similar in intent to *Stars in One Minute*, but the new context and the use of the cubes make it different enough to be fresh and interesting for the students. Also, interlocking cubes can be easily organized into different-size groups and counted in several ways. Although the description provides details for a specific lesson, the overall structure of the lesson can be applied to other contexts. In the "Extensions" section there are suggested variations on this lesson that offer additional ways children can count.

Materials

▲ interlocking cubes, either Multilink, Snap, or Unifix cubes, 2 per child
▲ a bucket, bowl, or other container large enough to hold the cubes

Time

▲ two class periods

Teaching Directions

1. Have each child put two cubes into the bucket. (I used a plastic fishbowl and, on a suggestion from one of the children, my students decided to call the cubes "fish." This is not an essential part of the lesson, as the lesson worked just as well when I called it *Cubes in a Bucket*. But the imaginary context captured my students' interest and I've used it in other situations even when I didn't have a container that looked like a fishbowl.)

2. Write on the board the number of students in class. Then ask the children to figure out the number of cubes in the bucket and explain their reasoning. Put a prompt on the board to help them start their writing:

There are ___ fish in the bowl. I think this because

_____ .

3. After all the children have completed their papers (and perhaps the next day), gather the class for a discussion. Have several students show their papers and share their solutions. Discuss the variety of methods and recording systems they used.

4. Remove the cubes from the bucket, snapping them into trains of two cubes each, and stand the trains in a row so the class can see them and count with you. You may want to review first with the children how to count by twos.

5. Ask the children to predict how many trains there would be if you rearranged the cubes into trains with five in each. Ask if they think there would be extra cubes. Rearrange the cubes and count the number of trains and extras. Then count by fives to verify the number of cubes. (Not all children may be convinced that the total number of cubes stays the same when they're rearranged!)

6. Ask students to predict how many trains and extra cubes there would be if you rearranged the cubes into trains of ten. Give all children who have ideas the chance to express them. Then rearrange the cubes into trains of ten, count the number of trains and extras, and finally count the cubes by tens to verify the total.

7. From time to time, engage the children in other counting experiences, varying the contexts and materials. Each time, have the children put the objects into groups of two or five and then count. Ask children to predict how many groups of ten and extras there would be. Verify with the materials. See the "Extensions" section for additional counting ideas.

Teaching Notes

A wide range of understanding and abilities is typical in a class. The activities in this lesson are accessible and engaging to children who are just starting to think about the tens and ones structure of our number system as well as those students who fully grasp place value. Students who are ready are given many opportunities to explore, develop, and apply the understanding that a digit can represent an individual object in one instance and a group of objects in another, while those children needing additional opportunities to count by twos and fives have this need met.

The Lesson

▲▲▲

DAY 1

I brought out a plastic bowl and asked each child to put in two Snap Cubes. "Who remembers how many children are here today?" I asked.

Several children raised their hands and I called on Jonathan. "Twenty-five," he responded correctly.

I planned to have the children figure out how many cubes were in the bowl. Because I wanted to have them deal with a problem that was more unwieldy than doubling twenty-five, I put in additional cubes, two for me and two for each of three other adults—the student teacher, the music teacher, and the regular class-room teacher.

I wrote on the board:

25 children

4 adults

"How many people is that altogether?" I asked them. I gave the children a few minutes to think about the problem and waited until about half the students had raised their hands before asking for responses. I called on Molly first.

"It's twenty-nine," she said. "I did it by counting twenty-five, then twenty-six, twenty-seven, twenty-eight, twenty-nine."

I recorded on the board:

Molly   25 . . . 26, 27, 28, 29

I was pleased that Molly offered her reasoning without being prompted. She had learned that explaining her thinking is part of the process of giving an answer.

"Did anyone figure differently?" I asked.

I called on Leslie. "I knew I had to do twenty-five plus four," she began, "and I knew that five plus four is nine, so I knew that twenty + nine is twenty-nine." I

recorded Leslie's explanation numerically under Molly's.

Molly   25 . . . 26, 27, 28, 29
Leslie   25 + 4
*   5 + 4 = 9 so*
*   20 + 9 = 29*

Next I called on Teddy. He told me how to record his idea. "Write *twenty-five* and then a *four* underneath," he said. I did so. "Then you move the four up to the five with an arrow and then you write *twenty-nine* underneath."

Molly   25 . . . 26, 27, 28, 29
Leslie   25 + 4
*   5 + 4 = 9 so*
*   20 + 9 = 29*
Teddy   25 ◀━━┓
*   4   ┃*
*   29*

"Did anyone do it a different way?" I asked.

I called on Jason. "I did it like Leslie did," he said.

"OK," I said. "Does anyone have a new method, one that isn't the same as Molly's, Leslie's, or Teddy's?"

Seth raised his hand. "Mine is like Molly's."

Then Katy called out. "I did it like Molly, too." Several others called out as well.

I called them back to attention and restated my directions. "I'm interested in knowing if there are any different methods I could record on the board," I said. "Raise your hand only if you have a different idea."

Jonathan raised his hand. "Mine's kind of like Leslie's, but it's a little different," he said.

"Tell us about it," I said.

"Well," he said, "I know that five plus

two plus two is nine, so I did twenty-five plus two plus two is twenty-nine."

I added Jonathan's method to the others on the board.

Molly	25 . . . 26, 27, 28, 29
Leslie	25 + 4
	5 + 4 = 9 so
	20 + 9 = 29
Teddy	25 ◄─┐
	4 ──┘
	29
Jonathan	5 + 2 + 2 = 9
	25 + 2 + 2 = 29

No one else had a method to explain, so I told them that I would now present a problem for them to figure out. "How many fish are there in the bowl altogether?" I asked.

"What do you mean?" Timmy asked. Timmy was often anxious that he wouldn't be able to do the work.

I restated the problem. "There are two fish in the bowl for each child in the class," I said, "and for four grown-ups also. The problem is to figure out how many fish there are altogether." I wasn't sure that Timmy understood, but for the moment he seemed reassured.

"Is this a partner or individual problem?" Andrew asked.

Before I could answer, several children gave their opinions.

"Make it partners," Nick said.

"I want to do it alone," Molly said.

"I think we should work together," Jonathan said.

Several others had opinions as well. It was clearly an issue about which many of them had strong feelings. I called them back to attention and told them I was interested in their ideas. I had planned to have them work individually, but I was willing to hear their thoughts, and I was interested in their ideas.

"But you can't call out," I said. "Raise your hand if you want to tell your idea." More than half the class wanted to talk, and I gave all who wanted a turn the chance to speak.

"I think we should work together," Grace said, "because you don't waste time that way."

"It's funner if you have a partner," Rudy said.

"It's better if you do it together," Timmy said, "because you can talk and get help if you need it."

"I like to work alone," Andrew said, "because when I work with someone, I just tell the answer, and they don't always believe me." Andrew's math ability surpassed his communication skills.

"I don't have a partner," Molly said. Amelia was absent. "But Seth doesn't have one either, because Abby isn't here. Can I go sit with Seth?"

"Does that mean you'd rather work with Seth than alone?" I asked.

She nodded "yes."

"I think we should do it in partners," Leslie said, but she had no reason to offer.

"It's better to work in partners," Nick said, "because you don't have to do all the writing yourself."

As they were talking, I was thinking about what to do. Teaching often requires making decisions on the spot, and it's hard to give an idea careful consideration in the midst of a situation. Generally, I have children work individually when I'm particularly interested in getting a check on their individual abilities. However, I also know that when they're working in pairs I have a chance to assess as I observe and listen to them talk among themselves. I decided that in this case it really didn't matter. I was interested in information about each child's understanding of the tens and ones structure of our number system, and I planned to use this activity to assess their understanding, but this part of the lesson was just the introduction to the assessment

I'd planned. I collected my thoughts quickly and made a decision.

"Let me tell you how we'll work," I said, and waited for them to quiet down and give me their attention. "There actually are two parts to this problem. I know for sure that I want you to do the second part individually, because it will give me information that will help me know more about your thinking. But, for the first question, it's OK with me if you work alone or with a partner. So it's your choice."

I wrote the problem on the board:

How many fish are there in the bowl altogether?

Explain your thinking with numbers and words.

You can also use pictures.

I also wrote a suggestion for them to use to begin their explanation:

There are ___ fish in the bowl. I think this because _____.

"If you need help beginning your writing," I said, "you can start by copying this."

I continued with further directions. "I'll distribute the paper," I said. "When I come to your table, you tell me whether you're going to work alone or with your partner. If you're working alone, I'll give you your own piece of paper. If you're working together, I'll give you and your partner one piece to use. Decide now."

I walked around the room. Of the twenty-five students, only four decided to work alone. There were nine pairs and one group of three. I felt good about how this evolved. I want to support children in taking charge of their learning as much as possible. I was interested in their ideas about working alone or with partners and was interested to see the mode each student chose. It turned out that the two students who had expressed a desire to work alone, Grace and Andrew, wound up working with partners; Maria, who had

wanted to work with a partner, chose to work alone. This was the first time I had given the children a choice about how they were to work, and it seemed sensible to me.

Their papers reflected the usual range of responses. Some showed complete understanding of the problem and command over the numbers. Gwyn and Sarah, for example, wrote: $25 + 25 = 50 + 4 + 4 = 8 + 50 = 58$. *There are 58 fish in the bowl. I think this becaus if you add 25 & 25 it is 50 and then add 8 on it is 58.* (See Figure 5–1.) "That's the longest problem I've ever written," Gwyn told me when she gave me the paper. Three other pairs of children and one child who worked alone used this same reasoning.

Rudy and Nick's paper presented a different way of explaining the answer. They wrote: *There are 58 fish in the bowl. We think this because $25 \times 2 = 50$ and $4 \times 2 = 8$ and $50 + 8 = 58$.* In my experience, using multiplication is unusual for second graders, especially near the beginning of the school year, but Rudy knew a great deal about mathematics. His partners often benefited from his understanding.

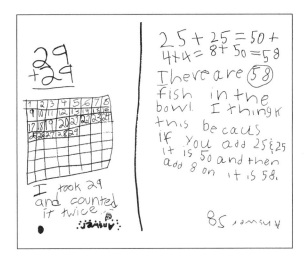

▲▲▲▲▲▲Figure 5–1 *Although Sarah and Gwyn worked together, they each used half of the paper for their own solutions. Sarah wrote the numbers from 1 to 29 on a grid and counted them twice. Gwyn added in her head.*

Some children relied on a pictorial representation. Teddy and Katy, for example, drew twenty-nine sets of two tallies. They wrote: *We think the ansar is 58 bkas [because] we catan [counted] by toos* (see Figure 5–2). Two other pairs of children also made drawings. Tomo and Colleen drew fish; Jonathan and Grace drew twenty-nine trains with two cubes in each.

▲▲▲▲▲▲Figure 5–2 *Teddy and Katy drew tallies in groups of 2 and counted them.*

Five children handed in work that showed their lack of understanding. Since they were free to talk with others, three of these children recorded the correct answer but were not able to offer any explanation, either on their papers or to me orally.

For example, Timmy and Jason weren't able to make sense of the problem, but they discussed it at length and worked hard on their paper. They wrote: *There are 32 fish in the bosl. I think this becuse we counted by 2 we came up 32.* Figures 5–3 and 5–4 show how three other students worked on this problem.

DAY 2

I gathered the children on the rug to talk about their work from the day before and then to count the cubes. Seeing one another's papers sparked their interest, and

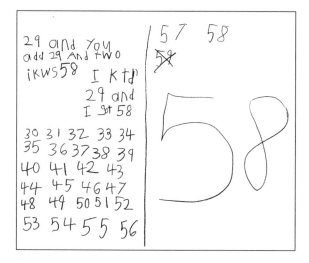

▲▲▲▲▲▲Figure 5–3 *Eli worked alone. He counted on by writing numbers beginning with 30. He went to 59 but realized he had written one number too many.*

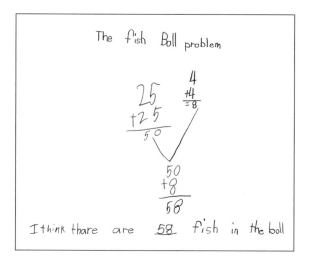

▲▲▲▲▲▲Figure 5–4 *Seth and Andrew worked together and solved the problem symbolically.*

a lively discussion resulted about different ways to solve problems and think about numbers. After showing a paper, I asked the children for comments or questions. Also, I asked other questions that occurred to me.

For example, Tomo and Colleen had drawn fish on their paper and also had written a numerical solution: $25 + 25 + 4 + 4$. I asked how they kept track of the fish to know when they had drawn enough. They both looked surprised.

"How many fish did you draw?" I asked.

"I don't know," Tomo said.

"We just decided to draw them," Colleen added.

"Suppose you wanted to draw the actual number of fish," I said, "how could you keep track?"

Tomo shrugged.

"Does anyone have an idea?" I asked.

Timmy raised his hand. "One of you could count while the other draws," he suggested.

"But we both wanted to draw," Colleen said.

"You could each draw some and then write down how many you drew," Molly said.

Sarah had a different suggestion. "One of you could draw for the adults and one for the children," she said.

After we discussed some of their papers, I focused the children once again on the bowl of cubes. "How could we be sure how many fish are in the bowl?" I asked.

"Count them!" they responded in a chorus.

"Since you each put in two cubes, we'll count them by twos," I said. "But first, let's practice counting by twos, and I'll record the numbers." As they counted aloud, I listed the numbers on a piece of chart paper. I did this for two reasons. One was that I wanted to have the children examine the patterns of the digits in the sequence of numbers—the repeating pattern of 0, 2, 4, 6, 8 in the ones digits and the pattern of five 1s, five 2s, five 3s, and so on, in the tens digits. Also, I wanted to have the numbers accessible to children who weren't yet sure how to count by twos. I stopped writing when I reached 58. "Why did I stop here?" I asked.

More than half the hands went up. "I know," Seth said. "Because there are fifty-eight fish."

"How many numbers did I write on this list?" I then asked.

Only a few children raised their hands, and they were eager to respond.

"I think there are about twenty, or maybe a few more," Nick said.

"That can't be," Andrew blurted out. "There has to be twenty-nine because there were twenty-nine people."

"I don't get it," Maria said.

Sarah raised her hand to explain. "She wrote one number down for each person," she said, "and there are twenty-nine numbers, so we got to fifty-eight." Sarah was the student who had characterized the problem as 29 + 29.

Maria was still confused. "I still don't get it," she said. Some of the others also seemed confused.

I tried to explain. "I agree with Andrew and Sarah," I said. "I wrote one number for each child and each adult. So the first number could be for your fish, Maria, and the next for Sarah's fish, and the next for Gwyn's, and so on. I put a check mark next to each number as I talked. "I wrote just enough numbers to account for everyone's fish," I concluded.

I wasn't sure my explanation helped. I've become more and more convinced that teaching by telling has a dismal return in terms of helping children learn. I decided to refocus the class on the cubes.

"Let's count the cubes," I said. "I'll set them on the bookcase in twos and we'll see how many there are."

I had the children count out loud as I put each pair of cubes on the bookcase. I noticed that some of the children were referring to the chart to help them count. We found out that there were fifty-eight cubes.

"Raise your hand if you know how many pairs of cubes I put on the bookcase," I said. I wondered if more children would be able to answer this question because of the concrete context. More than half of the children raised their hands. I called on Amelia.

"There have to be twenty-nine because there was one for each child and each adult," she explained. We counted the pairs to make sure, and I continued with another question.

"If I rearrange the cubes into fives, then how many trains would there be?" I asked. As I asked the question, I connected two pairs of cubes and added one cube from another pair to make a train with five cubes. I stood it on the bookcase.

No one knew the answer to my question, but I could tell that several were interested and thinking about it. The rest of the class focused on my making trains of five cubes and standing them on the bookcase. The children counted by fives as I did this.

In the middle of the activity, Teddy called out his discovery. "There will be three extras," he said. "No, maybe four. No, three." Several other children got interested in Teddy's idea and began to chat about it. Although I was curious about Teddy's thinking, I didn't stop to have him explain. I felt it was better to continue with the lesson, as I knew the children would get restless after a while.

Finally, I got to fifty-five and showed the three remaining cubes. "You were right, Teddy," I said. "There are three extras." He smiled his pleasure.

Grouping by Tens

"I have another question that I'd like you to answer," I then said. "What if we rearranged the cubes again and put them into trains of ten each? Before we do it, I'm interested in how many trains you think we would have and if you think there would be any extras. If you know, don't call out, but think about a way to explain your idea to others."

For some children, the answer was obvious. Others, however, thought they knew but weren't sure, and some children didn't seem to have any way to think about the problem. My goal was to have those who understood present their ideas so that those who didn't understand would hear a variety of ways to think about the problem. Also, I was curious about how many different ideas the children would generate.

Andrew was eager to report, as always. He was waving his hand with eagerness and insistence. I decided not to call on him. The other children were so ready to accept Andrew's thinking that I wanted to give others the chance to offer their ideas first. Having a class discussion like this was hard on Andrew when the problem seemed trivial to him.

"I know you're eager to report, Andrew," I said, "but you'll need to wait just a bit. I will call on you, but I'm going to give some other children a chance first." I had learned that this sort of acknowledgment helped with Andrew.

I called on Grace. "Before Grace starts," I said, "I want to remind you to listen carefully to her idea and see if it's different from yours."

"You just count by tens," Grace said. "You go ten, twenty, thirty, forty, fifty, and then you go fifty-one, fifty-two, fifty-three, fifty-four, fifty-five, fifty-six, fifty-seven, fifty-eight." She showed with her fingers as she counted.

"So how many tens and extras are there?" I asked.

Grace needed to count again, and did so quietly to herself, but still using her fingers. Some other children were counting to themselves along with her. "Five tens and eight more," she finally said.

"I can see that some of you agree," I said. "Does anyone have a different way to think about it?" I called on Sarah.

"I think mine is sort of like Grace's, but a little different," she said.

"Let's hear," I responded.

"Well, I just know that five tens are fifty," she said, "and then it takes eight to go from fifty to fifty-eight. So it's five and eight."

"So you agree with Grace," I said. Sarah nodded. I called on Nick next.

"Do you have a different idea?" I asked him.

"It's a little different," he said. "I did ten plus ten plus ten plus ten plus ten, and that's fifty, and then I did five plus three and that's eight." Nick was pointing to the cubes.

"What do you mean?" Catherine asked.

"Can I show?" Leslie asked. I nodded. She stood up and went over to the bookcase where the cubes were organized into trains of five. "See, you can push them together and get tens," she said, but then she got confused. "Then you wouldn't have as many, but I'm not sure how many you'd have. I forgot my idea."

"I can help," Jason said. "Can I?" He looked at me. I nodded and Jason went up to help her.

"It's easy," he said, "you get, like, two for one. Can I move them?" He looked at me for permission. I nodded again. (Jason was a nervous boy who needed approval or reassurance in situations where other children just barreled ahead. I tried to always be gentle and encouraging with him.) Jason pushed the trains together to make groups with two trains in each.

"Oh, I get it now," Leslie said.

"Why don't you count and see if you get the same answer that Grace and Sarah and Nick did?" I said. Together, Leslie and Jason counted and proved to themselves, and to the class, that there were five tens and eight extras.

Finally, I called on Andrew. "You just look at the number," he said.

"What do you mean?" I probed.

"You look at the front of fifty-eight and it's a five," he said. "Then you look at the end and it's 8. So that tells you."

I was pleased with the variety of ideas, but I knew that the children were at different stages of constructing understanding of the relationship of tens and ones to our number system. I knew many needed more time and more experience, and I planned to involve the class in similar counting activities on other days.

EXTENSIONS

1. Repeat *Counting Fish*, having students each put three, four, or five cubes into the bucket. As before, have students count by twos, fives, and tens.

2. Have the children put one cube in each of their pockets and then make a train to show how many they have. Ask them to predict the number of pockets in the entire class, then organize the cubes into trains with two in each and count to find the total. Have them predict the number of groups of five and ten cubes they can make and explain their reasoning. Verify with the cubes. Repeat for several days and compare the different numbers of pockets. This same lesson structure can be used to count buttons on students' clothing, pockets on their backpacks, books in the class library, and so on. (A complete description of this lesson is in Chapter 6 of *A Collection of Math Lessons from Grades 1 Through 3*, by Bonnie Tank and Marilyn Burns, Sausalito, CA: Math Solutions, 1988.)

3. Ask the children to bring pennies from home for a class penny jar and count how many there are, again by twos, fives, and tens. Continue over several days and then have the children decide what they can buy with their money. You may want to read *A Chair for My Mother* (New York: Greenwillow Books, 1982), by Vera B. Williams, to stimulate interest in collecting pennies.

4. An additional activity that provides children with opportunities to count large numbers is *Fill the Cube*. Besides counting, students are also involved in measuring and estimating. When students make comparisons during this activity, they're challenged to reason proportionally.

Before beginning this activity, cover the hole in the top of a Unifix cube with a piece of tape. Explain to the students that they will be estimating the number of popcorn kernels it will take to fill a Unifix cube. Model for them how to record their estimates by writing the following on the board:

I think there are _____ kernels in the cube.

Next, explain that they are to spill the kernels onto their desks and then count the kernels in two ways and record. Write on the board:

I counted by _____ and by _____.

Distribute lentils so students can compare the sizes of the lentils and the popcorn kernels. Pose the following question to the students: *Suppose there were 50 kernels of popcorn in the cube. How many lentils do you think there might be?* Have students estimate the number of lentils to fill a cube, record their estimate as with the popcorn kernels, count the lentils in two ways, and record the results on their papers.

Questions and Discussion

▲▲

▲ *What is the purpose of recording students' explanations on the board as you did early in the lesson?*

Recording students' explanations numerically helps children to see the link between their language and mathematics. It provides models for using numerical symbols to express their thinking. Also, recording students' ideas gives the message that their thinking is important and valued. Varying the ways you record is important so children can see that there are different ways to represent mathematical ideas symbolically.

CHAPTER SIX
OUT FOR THE COUNT

Overview

Kathryn Cave's *Out for the Count* provides an engaging context for children to count by tens. The book is also a vehicle for helping children see how the place value structure of our number system determines how we write numerals, a concept with which students need a great deal of experience. For each illustration in the book, the children verify that the actual number of ghosts, animals, pirates, and so on shown matches the number in the story. They also create and illustrate their own endings for the story, organizing their illustrations into tens and ones.

Materials

▲ *Out for the Count*, by Kathryn Cave (New York: Simon and Schuster, 1991)

Time

▲ one class period

Teaching Directions

1. Read the first page of the story. Have children figure the number of drinks, hugs, and good-nights Tom got before his dad suggested he count sheep.

2. Continue reading the next two pages. After reading about counting the twelve wolves by twos, ask students if there would still be the same number if the wolves were counted by tens. Verify by counting. Record on the board:

12 = 1 group of ten plus 2 ones
12 = 10 + 2

3. Read the page about the twenty-three pythons. Ask children to think about how the pythons are arranged, have them share their ideas, and then show them the illustration to verify their thinking. Record on the board:

23 = 2 groups of ten plus 3 ones

23 = 20 + 3

4. Continue sharing the book as described through the page about the eighty-eight ghosts.

5. Stop reading and explain to the students they're going to make up their own endings to the story following these directions:

Decide what Tom sees next and how many.

The number of things Tom sees must be in the nineties.

Draw what Tom sees, grouping them into tens and ones.

Write about what Tom sees and how many.

6. After students have completed their stories, finish reading *Out for the Count*.

7. Share the endings the students created.

Teaching Notes

Tom has difficulty getting to sleep, even after three drinks of water, six hugs, and four good-nights. Finally, he tries his dad's suggestion of counting sheep. The seventh sheep coaxes Tom out of his room and on a wild adventure involving twelve wolves, twenty-three pythons, thirty-six goats, forty-five pirates, fifty-four penguins, sixty-one bears, seventy vampire bats, eighty-eight ghosts, and one hundred shadows. The illustrations show each collection Tom encounters arranged in groups of ten.

The story provides a natural context for students to explore quantities using tens and ones. The students in the vignette that follows had many previous experiences counting large numbers of objects by ones, twos, fives, and tens. This story focuses them on groupings by tens and ones.

Students are asked to create their own ending to the story and draw a collection of ninety-something objects arranged in groups of ten and ones. It's helpful to remind the students to keep their illustrations simple so the assignment does not become frustrating or tedious. Choices made by students in the vignette that worked well included stars, Cheerios, doors, houses, fish, rotten eggs, surfboards, happy faces, and balls, to name a few.

Providing the students with the opportunity to create their own ending is a way to assess how easily and efficiently students are able to use the structure of the base ten number system.

The Lesson

▲▲

"I have a book to share with you today," I began. "It's called *Out for the Count.*"

"Does it have math in it?" DeAndre asked.

"What makes you think it has to do with math?" I responded.

"The title has the word *count* in it," DeAndre explained. "I hope it does have math because then we're doing two things at once, math and literature."

"I'll read the story and let you decide," I said. "The book is written by Kathryn Cave."

"My middle name is Kathryn," Angie said proudly.

"Do you have a middle name?" Andy asked me.

"I do have a middle name and it's not Kathryn," I said. The students giggled.

I shared the first page of the story, stopping to ask the students how many drinks of water, hugs, and good-nights Tom had before Tom's dad went off to bed.

"He had nine," Amy said.

"Tell me more," I responded.

"Three drinks and six hugs. That's nine," Amy explained.

"I think you forgot something," Samuel said. Amy looked at Samuel with surprise.

"Like what?" Amy responded with a bit of annoyance.

"Like the good-nights," Samuel said. I reread the first page to verify that what Samuel had noticed was correct.

"In that case," Amy began rather dramatically, then paused and used her fingers to help her figure the answer, "in that case it's thirteen. Three plus six is nine and four more is thirteen."

I recorded Amy's thinking on the board:

$$
\begin{array}{cc}
3 & 9 \\
+6 & +4 \\
\hline
9 & 13
\end{array}
$$

"Who has another idea to share?" I asked.

"I took one off the four to make three," explained Rachel. "Then I added three plus three, and that was six. I did six and six to make twelve, then added one more from the four and that was thirteen."

I recorded Rachel's idea:

$4 - 1 = 3$

$3 + 3 = 6$

$6 + 6 = 12$

$12 + 1 = 13$

"I knew four and six was ten," Shawn explained. "So I started with that and then added the three, so that was thirteen."

I recorded Shawn's idea:

$$
\begin{array}{cc}
4 & 10 \\
+6 & +3 \\
\hline
10 & 13
\end{array}
$$

No one had any additional ideas. I continued reading the second and third pages, stopping at the bottom of the third page.

"Tom counted the wolves by twos and found out there were twelve wolves. Do you think there would still be twelve wolves if we counted by tens?" I asked. "Put your thumb up if you think there would still be twelve, put your thumb down if you think there won't still be twelve, and put your thumb sideways if you aren't sure." Most students put their thumbs up, although a few had their thumbs down or sideways. Even with all the work we'd done with counting objects, I wasn't too surprised.

"Let's try it and see," I said. I showed them the illustration, which has the wolves grouped into one group of ten and one group of two. Pointing to the group of ten, I counted ten and then added the two to make twelve. "How many tens in twelve?" I asked.

"One," chorused the class.

"How many extras, or ones?" I asked.

"Two," they responded.

I recorded on the board:

12 = 1 group of ten plus 2 ones

12 = 10 + 2

I pointed to the 12 I had written on the board. "Which number tells how many groups of ten?" I asked.

"The one means there's one group of ten and the two means there are two extras," Shawn responded. Although Shawn was correct, and my goal was for all children to come to this understanding, I knew that not all of them understood this yet. I also knew that children need many experiences to make sense of the place value structure of our numbers. I moved on knowing that the lesson would provide more opportunities for others to make this important mathematical connection. I continued by reading the next page, about the twenty-three pythons.

"If the illustrator uses the same pattern of arranging the things Tom sees into tens and ones, think in your brain how the pythons are arranged," I said. After a moment I asked who would like to share.

"Maybe they're in two groups with ten and three extras," Amy suggested.

"I think what Amy thinks," Andy said.

"Me too," Antonio added.

"Put your thumb up if you agree with Amy's idea that there'll be two groups of ten and three extras or ones, put your thumb down if you disagree, and put your thumb sideways if you aren't sure," I said. Most students were quick to put their thumbs up.

"Let's see," I continued as I showed them the illustration to verify that their thinking had been correct.

I recorded on the board:

23 = 2 groups of ten plus 3 ones

23 = 20 + 3

"If I count the pythons by twos, will there still be twenty-three?" I asked.

"There has to be," Tony said. "The pythons in the picture can't change, so there still has to be twenty-three."

"Can I count to be sure?" Angie asked. I nodded and Angie came to the front and carefully counted the pythons in the illustration by twos as her classmates watched. "There's twenty-three!" she concluded.

"What if we count them by fives?" I asked.

"I think there will be still be twenty-three," Samuel said, "but can I count to see?" Samuel counted by fives and there were twenty-three pythons, just as he thought.

"I don't think it matters how you count," Rachel said. "Unless you make a mistake or change the number of what you are counting, nothing should change."

I read the page about the thirty-six goats. "How many tens will there be?" I asked.

"Three tens," the class responded.

"How many ones?" I asked.

"Six," they said.

I recorded on the board:

36 = 3 tens plus 6 ones

"You could write that another way," Ellie said. "Three tens is the same as thirty, and six ones is the same as six, so you could write thirty plus six.

I added Ellie's suggestion to what I'd written before. If Ellie hadn't suggested this, I would have done so, as I did for twenty-three.

36 = 3 tens plus 6 ones

36 = 30 + 6

I continued sharing the story in this way until we got to the page with the Bengal tigers. Rather than read this page to the students, I stopped. I recorded on the board the different numbers of things Tom had seen:

12

23

36

45

54

61

70

88

"What number of things do you suppose Tom will see next?" I asked.

"I think it has to be ninety-something," Maya said.

"Convince me," I said.

"Because the numbers are going up, one, two, three, four, five, six, seven, eight," Maya explained, pointing to the tens column, "so the next one has to be nine."

"I think the next number will be odd," Shawn said. "The pattern goes even, odd, even, odd."

"I disagree," Karly said. "It does that mostly, but not at the end. The end goes even, even."

"If the next number is in the nineties and it's odd, as Shawn thinks, what could the number be?" I asked.

"Ninety-one," "ninety-seven," and "ninety-five," were some of the responses. I listed these on the board.

"If the number is in the nineties and even, what could it be?" I asked.

"Ninety-four," "ninety-eight," and "ninety," the students replied. I made another list with these.

"That's not all of the odd or the even numbers," Samuel noticed. "Ninety-three is odd and ninety-two is even." I added Samuel's suggestions to the lists.

"Do we have all the possibilities?" I wondered aloud.

"I think ninety-six is even," Rachel said.

"I think ninety-nine is missing," DeAndre said.

"Is ninety-nine even or odd?" I asked.

"Odd," DeAndre replied. I added Rachel's and DeAndre's suggestions to the lists.

"We really don't know about the next page, do we?" I asked. "Your job is going to be to finish this story in your own way. You may choose where Tom goes next and you may also choose how many of something he sees as long as the number is in the nineties. If the number has to be in the nineties, what does that mean?"

"It could be ninety or ninety-one or ninety-two, up to ninety-nine," Samuel said.

"Samuel's correct," I said. "You need to put what Tom sees into groups of tens and ones just like the book's illustrator did. The last thing you need to do is write about what Tom sees next and how many he sees."

To remind the students about what to do, I wrote the following directions on the board:

Decide what Tom sees next and how many.

The number of things Tom sees must be in the nineties.

Draw what Tom sees, grouping them into tens and ones.

Write about what Tom sees and how many.

I read the directions I'd written on the board one last time to reinforce what the students were to do. I also suggested to them that they draw something simple such as happy faces or question marks since drawing ninety or more things could take a long time and get tiring. There were no questions. I handed each student a sheet of unlined paper and they got to work immediately. They worked quietly, carefully drawing and counting. Angie drew ninety-five stars, grouping them into tens and extras easily. She wrote: *I think that there are ninety five stars. and they are going to be thrown out Tom's window and go up in the sky and create the univers.* (See Figure 6–1.)

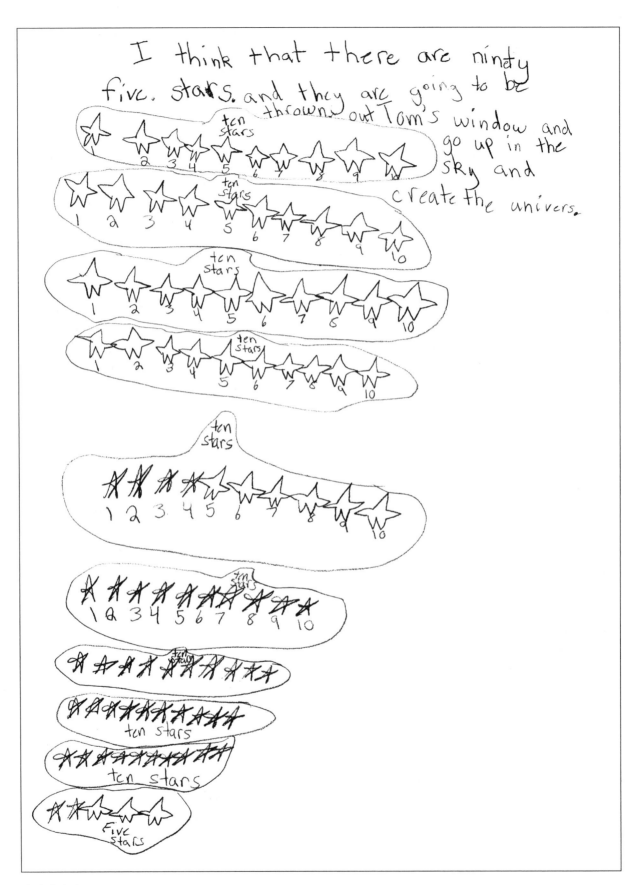

I think that there are ninety five stars. and they are going to be thrown out Tom's window and go up in the sky and create the univers.

▲▲▲▲▲▲Figure 6–1 *Angie easily grouped 95 stars into 10s and 1s.*

Andy drew the faces of ninety-nine proboscis monkeys. He wrote: *He was climbing a tree and met 99 proboscis monkeys then he swung down and landed on a branch.* (See Figure 6–2.)

Karly wrote: *In the juggal ther whus 97 lios [lions]. The boy whus friten so much. In the drek [dark] thay sleep. The boy tipetowe over the lios. Then he with bake to sleep.* (See Figure 6–3.)

Bonnie drew ninety-three surfboards. She wrote: *Next Tom runs into 93 surfbords!!! After that he rides on all 93!!! He rides at Hawaii! Then he runs into the soft sand!! Now he wishes he is back in bed. But he's not!!!!!!* (See Figure 6–4.)

Samuel, a child easily frustrated, became completely involved with this activity. He drew an underwater scene on one side of his page and on the back he drew nine groups of ten sharks plus eight extras. He wrote: *I think he well meat 98 sharks he ned it to run to land.* (See Figure 6–5.)

All the students were able to group the objects in their drawings by tens and ones accurately. A few students had difficulty finishing because they drew objects that took some time, such as ponies. When most students had finished, I gathered them on the rug to finish sharing the story with them.

"I noticed as I watched you work that some of you had some wonderful ideas about how this story should end," I said. "I'll go through the pile of work you have done and ask you if you'd like me to share your story ending." I went through the pile, asking each child if I could share his or her story. A few said no but most were pleased to have me share their work.

▲▲▲▲▲▲Figure 6–2 *Andy drew 9 groups of 10 on the left and the remaining 9 tucked in with his explanation.*

In the jugol
ther whus 97 lios.
The boy whues friten so
much. In the drck
thay sleep. The boy
tipetowe over the
lios. Then he with
bake to sleep.

The end

Next Tom runs into 93 surfboards!!!. After that he rides on all 93!!! Then he rides at Hawaii!!. Now He runs into the soft sand!! He wishes he is back in bed. But he's Not!!!!!!!

▲▲▲▲▲Figure 6–4   *Bonnie drew 93 surfboards.*

EXTENSIONS

1. There is a board game inside both the front and back cover of *Out for the Count.* Students may be interested in playing the game as an independent activity.

2. Create a class book. Students can choose, draw, or illustrate a number that you assign. They can write about Tom's adventure with that number, drawing the illustration in groups of tens and ones as done previously. Collect their work and assemble it into a book.

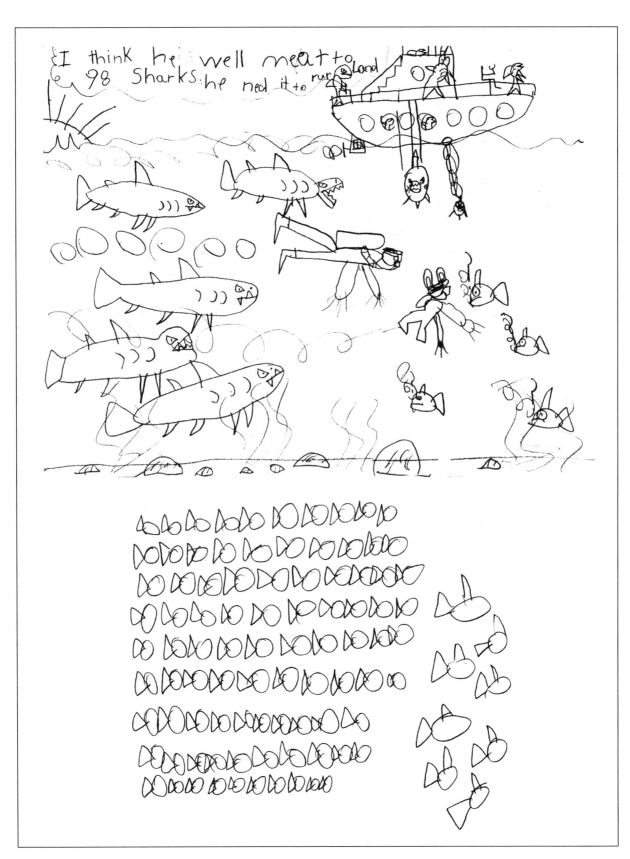

▲▲▲▲▲▲Figure 6–5 *Samuel drew 98 sharks on the back of his paper.*

Questions and Discussion

▲▲▲

▲ Isn't ninety or more objects a lot for children to draw?

This can become tedious quickly if children draw things that are too complicated. Remind them to keep it simple. A few children ignored this advice initially. After working for a short while and noticing their progress was slow, they asked if they could change their idea. I gave them another sheet of paper and they worked happily and successfully to complete the task.

▲ Why did you choose such a large number?

I chose a number in the nineties for several reasons. Children enjoy working with large numbers. These students had had many previous experiences counting large numbers of objects, and I was interested in learning how they could apply what they knew about counting and about tens and ones to this situation. Also, asking them to draw ninety-something objects fit with the story.

▲ In many of the previous activities, students were asked to count objects in several ways. Why didn't you ask them to do so in their independent activity?

Because these students had had many previous experiences doing this, I felt it was not necessary. During the discussion as I shared the book, most children had no problem with the idea that counting the same number of objects in different groupings still produced the same total. Had a child needed to work on this idea, I would have modified the assignment for that child, asking that he or she count the objects in at least two ways.

▲ What if a child is unable to get started with the writing?

This is a very real problem, especially for young children. The class in the vignette was a very creative group of children, so this problem did not present itself. However, it has with other classes. In those cases I ask the children to tell me what they imagine could be on the next page of the book. Usually this gets a response that provides a place for the child to start. If that doesn't work, ask the child to pretend he or she is Tom and ask, "What would you like to find ninety-something of?" Once children have an idea, they can start drawing and usually complete the task easily.

▲ Why did you sometimes record a problem vertically and sometimes horizontally? For example:

$$3$$
$$\underline{+6}$$
$$9$$

$$4 - 1 = 3$$

When number sentences are written using only one format, children come to believe that only that way is correct. Writing their ideas using both the horizontal and vertical formats increases students' flexibility and comfort with multiple methods of writing number sentences.

CHAPTER SEVEN
THE KING'S COMMISSIONERS

Overview

The King's Commissioners, by Aileen Friedman, provides an imaginary context for the same sort of problem as the *Counting Fish* lesson does (see Chapter 5). In the story, forty-seven king's commissioners are counted by twos, fives, and tens. The lesson asks students to make sense of different ways of counting, offering them another opportunity to see the relationship between groups of ten and the numbers that represent them. This lesson is appropriate after children have had a variety of grouping and counting experiences.

Materials

▲ *The King's Commissioners*, by Aileen Friedman (New York: Scholastic, 1994)

Time

▲ two class periods

Teaching Directions

1. Read the book to the class.

2. Stop reading before the Princess steps in and after the Royal Advisors have reported. Ask the students how many commissioners they think there are and have volunteers explain their reasoning. Then finish the story.

3. Begin a class discussion of the story. On the board, write the numbers that show how the Royal Advisors and the Princess counted:

23 2s and 1 extra

9 5s and 2 extra

10 4s and 7 extra

Ask: "Why was the King confused? What did he mean when he kept saying, 'That doesn't tell me anything'? How can you explain why the First Royal Advisor was correct? Why was the Second Royal Advisor also correct? Why was the Princess's method easy for the King to understand?"

On the board, you may want to draw the tally marks as the Royal Advisors did.

4. To prepare children for the writing assignment, again ask them to explain why the First Royal Advisor's answer of twenty-three twos and one extra made sense. As students explain, record their thinking numerically on the board to model ways to represent children's ideas with mathematical symbolism.

5. Give the writing assignment of explaining why each counting method in the story made sense. Write the following prompts on the board:

> The First Royal Advisor made sense because _____.
> The Second Royal Advisor made sense because _____.
> The Princess made sense because _____.

6. As children finish their work, have them bring it to you and read it aloud. If you have time, use this opportunity to conduct informal assessments. Ask: "Suppose there were fifty-four commissioners instead of forty-seven. If the Princess lined them up in tens, how many rows and extras would there be?" Note which children see the question as trivial, which need to think before answering, and which aren't able to figure it out.

7. On the next day, return to the story by reminding the children about the King's comment at the end of the book about the number of commissioners: "'That's not so many,' he said. 'We can still have more.'" Ask children to think of other commissioners the King might appoint and how many he might need. You may want to list the children's estimates on the board or even graph them. Pick several of the numbers suggested and have students discuss how many rows and extras there would be if those numbers represented commissioners that the Princess lined up in tens.

Teaching Notes

In *The King's Commissioners*, by Aileen Friedman, the King wants to know how many commissioners he has. His two Royal Advisors count the commissioners in different ways. One counts by twos and reports that there are twenty-three twos and one extra; the other counts by fives and reports nine fives and two extras. Their methods confuse the King, who wants only to know the total number of commissioners. The Princess steps in to help. She has the commissioners line up in rows of ten, counts four rows of ten with seven left over, and convinces the King that there are forty-seven in all. She proceeds to explain why the Royal Advisors' methods were also correct.

This lesson builds on the counting experiences students have had in prior lessons. The lesson, as presented, is more abstract than the previous experiences children may have had, as children are relying on a book and its illustrations rather than on concrete objects. If this is a problem for your students, providing them with cubes or other counters, or having them draw the forty-seven commissioners, can help make the experience more concrete and accessible.

The Lesson

▲▲▲

DAY 1

I told the students the title of the book and asked if they knew what commissioners did. Several had ideas.

"They work for the police," Jason said, "doing investigations and things."

"They take care of stuff in offices," Leslie said.

"They're like the king's men," Nick said.

"I think they're something royal," Andrew said.

"Let's see what you think after you hear the story," I said.

After I read how the two Royal Advisors kept track of the commissioners and reported their counts to the King, Tomo's and Andrew's hands shot up. Several children began talking to one another. I stopped reading and called on Tomo.

"I know it," he said, excitedly. "It's forty-seven."

"How did you figure that out?" I asked.

"I did five, ten, fifteen, twenty, twenty-five, thirty, thirty-five, forty, forty-five, and then two more is forty-seven," he said. He had used his fingers to be sure he counted nine fives.

"I got the same thing," Andrew said. "I did it the same way."

"What about the First Royal Advisor?" I asked. "He had reported twenty-three twos. Is that forty-seven also?" Neither of the boys or any of the other children knew. Somehow, twenty-three seemed like too many twos to work with.

I continued reading the story. The Princess decided to arrange the commissioners into rows of ten and organized them into four rows with seven commissioners left over. Before the Princess counted by tens, about half of the children figured out that there were forty-seven commissioners in all.

I asked the children if they had any comments about the story.

"I liked the things the commissioners did," Seth said.

"I think that there should be a commissioner for messy rooms," Sarah said.

"I don't think the King was a very good king," Nick commented.

"Why not?" I asked.

"He didn't know very much," Nick responded.

Teddy jumped in. "You can't really tell if he's a good king from the story. Maybe he just wasn't good in math."

"But he's a grown-up," Amelia said.

"Why do you think the King was confused?" I then asked, trying to turn the conversation toward some mathematical thinking. This question didn't help, however.

"He didn't know how many commissioners he had," Colleen said.

"He had too many people working for him, and he didn't know what they all did," Teddy offered.

"He didn't remember what he learned in school," Katy added.

I then asked a different question to elicit responses about the counting. "The

Princess said that the two Royal Advisors were correct," I said. The children nodded their agreement.

"How could you prove that the First Royal Advisor was right when he reported twenty-three twos and one extra?" I asked. I gave them a few moments to think about this, taking the time to draw tally marks on the board to show twenty-three groups of two and one extra. By then, about eight of the children had raised their hands. I called on Teddy.

"You count by twos to twenty," he began, "and that uses up ten of them. Then another ten is twenty, and twenty plus twenty is forty. Then you go two plus two plus two plus one equals seven. So it's forty-seven."

"Let me see if I can write down what you explained," I said. I often record the children's explanations numerically to model for them how mathematical symbolism can be used to describe their thinking. I wrote on the board, verifying with Teddy as I did so:

Count by 2s to 20 (10 2s)

20 + 20 = 40 (20 2s)

2 + 2 + 2 + 1 = 7

40 + 7 = 47

"Does anyone have a different way to prove that twenty-three twos and one extra equals forty-seven?" I asked. I called on Molly.

"I figured that twenty-three plus twenty-three is forty-six," she reported, "and one more makes forty-seven." I recorded on the board:

23 + 23 = 46

46 + 1 = 47

"How come you decided to add twenty-three and twenty-three?" I probed.

"Because you have twenty-three two times," she said, referring to the twenty-three groups of tally marks on the board.

"Does anyone have a different way?" I asked. I called on Grace.

"First I did five twos," she said. "I made a bundle and it has ten." Grace showed a piece of paper on which she had drawn tally marks and a loop around groups of five twos.

"Then I made more bundles the same size," she continued, "so I had four bundles, and that's ten, twenty, thirty, forty. Then I did the three twos and the one more, and it's forty-seven altogether." I made loops around the tally marks on the board to show the class what Grace had done on her paper.

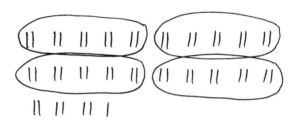

I also wrote:

5 2s = 10

10, 20, 30, 40, and 3 2s and 1 more = 47

"Does anyone have another idea?" I asked again. Nick raised his hand.

"Mine is kind of like Grace's," he said.

"Tell us," I responded. I then told the class, "Be sure to listen carefully to see if Nick's idea is the same as Grace's idea."

"I did five twos," he began, "and then I did five more, and that was ten twos, and that was twenty. Then I did twenty and twenty is forty, and that used up twenty twos. Then I counted the seven and got forty-seven." I wrote:

5 2s = 10

10 2s = 20

20 + 20 = 40 + 7 = 47

The King's Commissioners   73

"Any other ideas?" I asked. I called on Rudy.

"I have a trick," he said. "I know two and two is four, so I know that twenty and twenty is forty, and then you go forty-two, forty-four, forty-six, forty-seven." I wrote:

2 + 2 = 4, 20 + 20 = 40

42, 44, 46, 47

"Any more ideas?" I asked. There were none.

A Writing Assignment

"You'll each do some writing now about the story and the math thinking," I said. "There are three parts."

"First, you explain one of the ways to prove that the First Royal Advisor was correct," I said. "You can use one of the ways on the board, or any other way you want. Here is how you can start your writing." I wrote on the board:

1. The First Royal Advisor made sense because _____.

I explained the other two parts. "Then you'll do the same for the Second Royal Advisor and the Princess. Watch as I write how you can start writing for each." I wrote on the board:

2. The Second Royal Advisor made sense because _____.

3. The Princess made sense because _____.

"What do we use for a title?" Seth asked, always concerned about being correct. I usually give the children a title for their papers, but I decided to listen to their ideas. I was curious to know how the story had stimulated their imaginations.

"What do you think would be a good title?" I asked the class.

"How about 'Counting for the King'?" Sarah said.

"I think 'How Many Commissioners?'" Abby suggested.

"Maybe 'It Made Sense,'" Hassan said.

"I'll let you each decide," I told the class. "It will be OK if you have different titles."

I gave one last direction. "Remember," I said, "you must use words and numbers on your paper and, if you'd like, pictures." Several of the children said "pictures" with me. They'd heard me give this direction many times for writing assignments.

The children got to work with the typical confusion that erupts when I give a writing assignment. Writing is difficult for some children, and I need to do a great deal of encouraging and prodding to get them all started and to keep them going. Sometimes it feels like trying to keep a dozen or more balloons in the air. I persist, however, not only because writing helps children clarify their mathematical reasoning but also because their written work provides me with evidence of their thinking and reasoning. Figures 7–1 through 7–3 show how three students responded to this assignment.

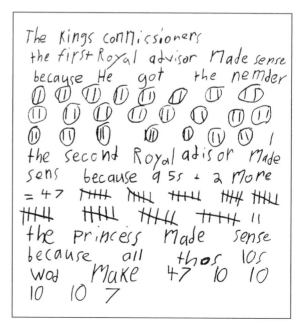

The Kings commissioners the first Royal advisor made sense because He got the nemder ① the second Royal adisor made sens because 9 5s + 2 more = 47 ⊞⊞ ⊞⊞ ⊞⊞ ⊞⊞ ⊞⊞ ⊞⊞ ⊞⊞ ⊞⊞ ⊞⊞ 11 the princess made sense because all thos 10s wod Make 47 10 10 10 10 7

▲▲▲▲▲▲Figure 7–1 *Katy tried to explain each of the three methods.*

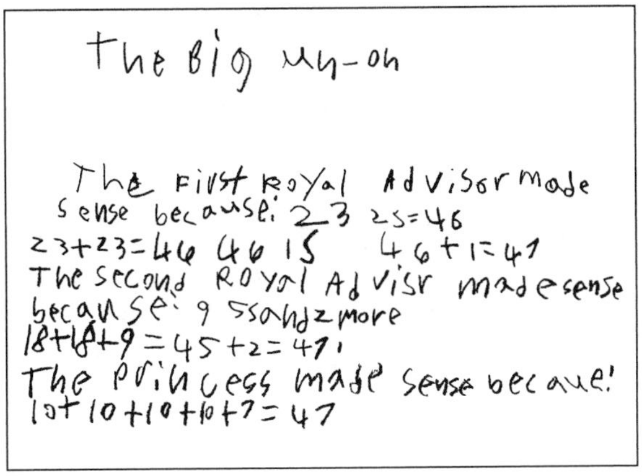

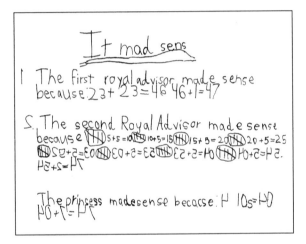

The Big My-oh

The First Royal Advisor made
sense because: 23 25=46
23+23=46 46 1S 46+1=47
The Second Royal Advisr made sense
because: 9 5s and 2 more
18+18+9=45+2=47.
The Princess made sense because!
10+10+10+10+7=47

▲▲▲▲▲▲**Figure 7–2** *Hassan's math ability surpassed his writing ability. He turned 9 fives to 5 nines and added 18 + 18 + 9 to get 45.*

It mad sens

1 The first royal advisor made sense
because: 23+ 23=46 46+1=47

S. The second Royal Advisor made sense
because 5+5=10 10+5=15 15+5=20 20+5=25
25+5=30 30+5=35 35+5=40 40+5=42
42+5=47

The princess madesense because: 4 10s=40
40+1=41

▲▲▲▲▲▲**Figure 7–3** *Molly was still having difficulty with reversals when she wrote numerals.*

Informal Assessment

As each child brought his or her paper to me, I posed another problem. For example, I said to Tomo, "Suppose there were fifty-four commissioners instead of forty-seven. If the Princess lined them up in tens, how many rows and extras would there be?"

The problem was trivial for Tomo. Without hesitation, he answered, "Five rows and four extras." Amelia, Molly, Rudy, Leslie, and Nick answered similarly.

Andrew gave an extra explanation. "The number tells you," he said. "The five

means five rows and the four means four extras." Andrew's understanding of place value was solid.

About half the class gave correct responses but took time to figure it out. Katy, for example, counted by tens on her fingers before reporting that there would be five rows and four extras.

Five of the children didn't have any idea or any way to think about the number of tens and extras in fifty-four. When I asked Colleen, for example, she just shrugged. On her paper, she had ignored the prompts I had put on the board and had written *47 ones: 1 + 1 + 1 +. . . .* Actually, I doubted that there were exactly forty-seven ones, as Colleen frequently miscounted.

I took Colleen's paper and asked her a question. "Suppose there were only fifteen commissioners," I said, "and the Princess lined them up in tens. How many rows do you think there would be?"

Colleen thought for a minute and shrugged again.

"Do you think there are enough com-missioners to make a row of 10?" I asked. Colleen immediately nodded.

"Do you think there are enough to make two rows of ten?" I continued.

Colleen thought for a minute. "Maybe," she said, "I'm not sure."

"I have an idea," I said. "Would you go over and count out fifteen Snap Cubes and take them to your desk?" Colleen nodded eagerly. "Then come and get me, and we'll see if there are enough for one row of ten or more."

At this time, I didn't demand more from Colleen's writing. She needed to work with smaller quantities first.

Timmy was another child who didn't know how many rows and extras there would be with forty-seven commissioners. Timmy had a difficult time focusing on activities and writing. When he brought his paper to me, it had only his name, the date, and a title: "The King Count."

"I don't know what to write," he said. I'd learned that referring Timmy to the prompts on the board didn't help him. And I didn't want to focus him on the writing before we had a chance to talk about the mathematics.

I gave Timmy the same problem I gave to Colleen. "Suppose there were only fifteen commissioners," I said, "and the Princess lined them up in tens. How many rows do you think there would be?"

"That's easy," Timmy said. "She could make one row and there would be five more."

"Why is fifteen so easy for you?" I asked.

Timmy thought for a minute. "It just is," he said.

"What about if there were twenty-three commissioners?" I asked.

"Ooh, that's harder," he responded. "Oh, I know, ten and ten are twenty, with three left over. Oh, I get it." Timmy got excited and continued.

"I know how to do forty-seven," he said. "You go ten, twenty, thirty, forty." He didn't complete the thought but took his paper and went back to work. Timmy still didn't follow the directions for the complete assignment, but he wrote about what he understood. (See Figure 7–4.)

After talking with a few more children, I went to check on Colleen. She was putting fifteen cubes together in trains, sorting them by color. "Let's pretend these

are commissioners," I said to her. Colleen nodded.

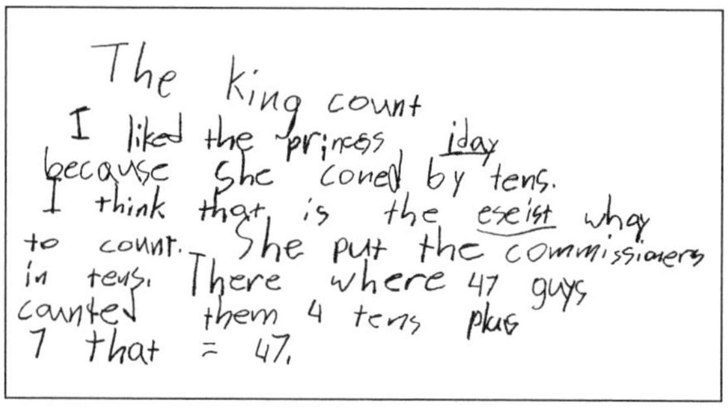

"Can you make a row of ten?" I asked. She nodded again and picked up a train of four red cubes and a train of three yellow cubes. She snapped them together and counted them. Then she added a train of four green cubes and counted again. When she got to eleven, she removed one cube and looked at me.

"How many in that train?" I asked.

"Ten?" she said tentatively, and then counted them again.

"So if the Princess lined up the commissioners in tens, these ten would be in one row," I said. Colleen nodded.

"Do you have enough for another row?" I asked.

Colleen counted the extras and said, "No, there are only five more."

"So with fifteen commissioners," I said, "there's one row of ten and five extras. Could you do the same with forty-seven cubes?"

"Maybe," Colleen responded.

By now, however, it was time for lunch. I told Colleen to put away the cubes for now, and I asked the class to get ready for lunch dismissal.

DAY 2

I began class the next day by reminding the children about the King's comment at the end of the story after he was convinced there were forty-seven commissioners. "'That's not so many,' he said. 'We can still have more.'"

"What other commissioners do you think he could have?" I asked the class. The children had a wide range of ideas. Some seemed to think of their personal or classroom needs and suggested commissioners for cleaning out pet tanks, sharpening pencils, picking up dirty socks, brushing hair, making breakfast, bandag-

The king count
I liked the princes iday
becauce She coned by tens.
I think that, is the eseist why
to count. She put the commissioners
in tens. There where 47 guys,
counted them 4 tens plus
7 that = 47.

▲▲▲▲▲▲Figure 7–4 *Timmy wrote only about the Princess, explaining the benefit of grouping by 10s.*

ing bad cuts, and more. Some ideas seemed to be related to how the children perceived the King's needs, such as commissioners for crown cleaning, putting the Princess to bed, and cutting beards. Nick, who was more savvy than most of the children about the world at large, suggested that there be a commissioner for Elvis sightings.

The children were eager to continue talking about the different jobs for commissioners, but I wanted to direct the class discussion toward some mathematical thinking. "You have lots of ideas," I said, "and I'm interested in giving you more time to think about them. But right now I want to ask another question."

Eli raised his hand. "I think one should be for kicking out the cook if the food isn't good," he said. The children laughed, and others began to raise their hands.

"Please put your hands down and listen," I said, quieting the class. "I will give you more time to think about commissioners and to write about your ideas and draw some pictures, if you like. But now I'd like you to think about a different question."

When I had the children's attention, I asked, "How many commissioners do you think the King should have? Think about this for a moment, and when you have an idea, raise your hand."

The children's estimates ranged from Colleen's suggestion of 10 commissioners to Andrew's 347. Most of their numbers ranged from the 20s through the 60s.

Molly reported her answer in a different way. "I think the King needs eight more commissioners," she said, "one for taking pictures, two for cleaning, and a couple more."

To avoid letting the discussion shift to what the commissioners might do, I asked the class, "If the King appointed eight more commissioners, and he had forty-seven already, how many would he have altogether? Talk to your partner about this."

The room buzzed with conversation. Many children used their fingers to count. Two children went to the 0–99 chart to figure. After a few minutes, I called the class to attention.

"Since it was Molly's suggestion, I'll let her report," I said.

"It's fifty-five," she said, and explained using her fingers. "I went forty-eight, forty-nine, fifty, fifty-one, fifty-two, fifty-three, fifty-four, fifty-five." Other children nodded.

I wrote 55 on the board. "Now my question is this," I said. "If the Princess lined up the fifty-five commissioners, how many rows would there be and how many extras?"

A few children immediately raised their hands. I waited a minute and a few more children raised their hands. Children reported the same sorts of methods they used when I'd asked them the question individually the day before. I took the time to allow as many different students to report as wanted to. I find that when students explain their thinking, they not only cement their own ideas but also offer their classmates different ideas.

EXTENSIONS

Present another writing assignment. Have children list other commissioners the King might appoint, then explain how many he would have altogether and how many rows and extras he would have if they all lined up in tens. (See Figures 7–5 through 7–7.)

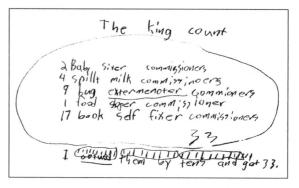

The king count

2 Baby Siter commissioners
4 spillt milk commissinoers
9 bug exterminater Gommioners
1 toad paper commissioner
17 book sdf fixer commissioners

33

I counted them by tens and got 33.

▲▲▲▲▲▲Figure 7–6   On this paper, Timmy was able to explain how he grouped 33 into 10s and extras.

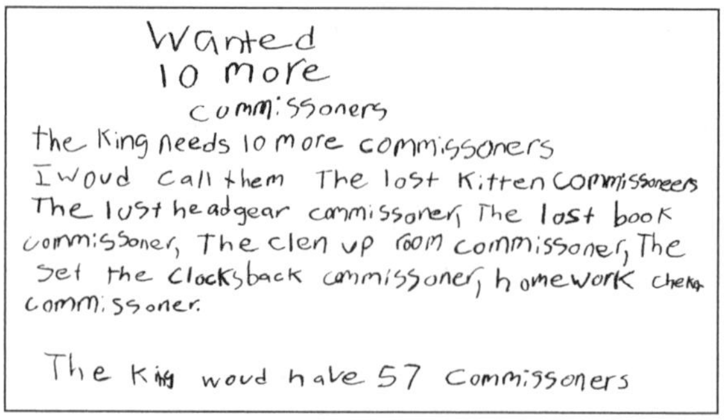

comissinors math

1. The king needs 20 more comissinors

2. I would call them: fixing electronics comissinors

3. make sure you brush your teeth comissinors

4. Sharpening pencils comissinors

5. keep track of the calender comissinors

6. there would be: 67 comissinors all together.

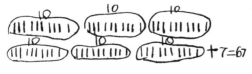

▲▲▲▲▲▲Figure 7–5   Annie added 20 more commissioners.

Wanted
10 more
commissoners

the King needs 10 more commissoners
I woud call them The lost Kitten Commissoners
The lost headgear commissoner, The lost book
commissoner, The clen up room commissoner, The
Set the clocks back commissoner, homework checker
commissoner.

The King woud have 57 Commissoners

▲▲▲▲▲▲Figure 7–7   Sarah thought the King would need 10 more commissioners, but she didn't explain how many 10s and 1s there would be.

Questions and Discussion

▲▲

▲ *Why do you often ask the class if anyone has another idea?*

Continuing to ask the class for other ways to explain reinforces the idea that there is more than one way to think about a problem. Also, it encourages children to keep thinking when someone else offers a correct solution or explanation and to search for new and different approaches. When the ideas that students share are recorded and left posted during the math period, children are more likely to try ideas they might not have tried otherwise, strengthening their own understanding.

▲ *When children have difficulty writing, how do you encourage them?*

Sometimes when students are having difficulty writing it is because they don't know where to start. To help them I ask such questions as

▲ What do you know about the problem?
▲ What are you trying to figure out?

▲ Can you draw a picture of what you know about the problem that might help you solve it?

▲ Tell me the problem using your own words.

Often these will trigger ideas and students will be able to explain their thinking and solutions orally. When they have done this, I tell them to take what they said to me, make it go from their brain, to their arm, to their hand, then out their hand, to their pencil, and onto their paper. This usually brings about giggles, but it also lets the students know what is expected and what should go on their paper.

If these ideas are not helpful to the child, then I have found it useful to present the child with a related, simpler problem, as I did with both Colleen and Timmy during this lesson.

As the children work, I circulate throughout the room, constantly looking over their shoulders, monitoring their thinking by reading what they have written and asking questions, and answering questions as they come up.

▲ *What are your goals for children when you give them an assignment in math that requires them to write?*

It is important to remember that the primary goal of a lesson is not to have children write but to have them think and reason. Writing can serve as a tool for children to explore their thinking or as a record of the ideas they've already formulated. But the emphasis must be kept first and foremost on children's thinking. The written product provides a record of their ideas. Teachers need to make the decision about when to push for written evidence, when to accept oral evidence, and when to push for both.

CHAPTER EIGHT
FIVE-TOWER GAME

Overview

The *Five Tower Game* provides another way for children to generate a large number of objects to count. In this game, they use interlocking cubes. They take turns rolling the dice and making towers. After five turns each, they snap their towers into long trains and count the cubes in two ways. Finally, they compare their trains and figure out how many more cubes are in the larger train.

Materials

▲ interlocking cubes, such as Multilink, Snap, or Unifix cubes, 100 per pair of students
▲ dice, 2 per pair of children
▲ optional: rules for *Five-Tower Game*, 1 per student (see Blackline Masters)

Time

▲ one class period to introduce the game, then additional time for playing

Teaching Directions

1. Show the children the cubes and the dice, and tell them they'll use the materials to build towers, then count their cubes two ways.

2. Model the game for the class by playing with a child or by having two children play with each other.

3. Reinforce that they are to pay attention to what their partners are doing so they are sure they agree.

Teaching Notes

Rolling two dice ensures that each of the five towers a child builds has at least two cubes and at most twelve cubes. Combining the five towers creates a train from ten to sixty cubes long. This activity, therefore, involves the children with two-digit numbers. Counting the cubes in their trains in two different ways reinforces the experiences children had in other activities, for example, *Stars in One Minute* and *Counting Fish.* To compare their trains to figure out who has more cubes, most students this age place the cube trains side by side and count the extras in the longer train to find the difference between them. By doing this, children are building their understanding of the comparison model of subtraction.

Consider the following problems:

Jazmin has nine marbles. Maya has six marbles. How many more marbles does Jazmin have?

Jazmin has nine marbles. She gave six to Maya. How many marbles does Jazmin have now?

Both use the same numbers, nine and six. The first problem requires a comparison of two amounts to figure who has more marbles, while in the second problem, marbles are taken away and students must figure how many are left.

The Lesson

▲▲

To teach the *Five-Tower Game,* I assembled a bucket of $\frac{3}{4}$-inch interlocking cubes, two dice, and copies of the directions for students who might want them. "I'm going to teach you a new game today," I began. "Please watch and listen so you can learn the rules." I asked Annie if she would help me teach the class the game by being my partner. I read the beginning of the first direction: "Take turns. On your turn, roll the dice. The sum tells the number of cubes to take. Snap them into a tower."

I asked Annie to roll first and report the numbers to the class. "I rolled a six and a five," she said.

I said to the class, "Raise your hand when you've figured out how many cubes Annie should take."

I called on Gwyn. "It's eleven," she said.

"How do you know that?" I asked.

"I know it because I know that five plus five is ten and you just need one more, so it's eleven," she answered.

Usually, when children present their ideas for computing, I record their methods on the board to model for them how to use mathematical symbols to describe their thinking. But today I was more interested in getting on with my explanation of the game, so I merely accepted their verbal explanations.

"Did anyone figure it out a different way?" I asked. I called on Jason.

"I started with five," he explained, "and I counted up like this: six, seven, eight, nine, ten, eleven." Jason demonstrated with his fingers.

"Is there another way?" I continued. I called on Amelia.

"I knew six plus four is ten," she said, "and then you plus one more and you get eleven."

I'm always interested in hearing the variety of children's methods. We'd had class discussions like this enough times previously so that the children knew that I would listen to all their different ideas.

I called on Andrew next. "I did it kind of like Gwyn," he began. "I took one from the six and made it five and then did five plus five and then added the one back on."

I called on Leslie next. "Mine is like Jason's, but different," she said. "I started with six and five more. I did seven, eight, nine, ten, eleven."

Hassan reported next. "I just knew it," he said.

Nick had a new method. "I did six plus six," he said, "and then you take away one."

Grace reported last. Her method was a bit more involved. "I took one from the five and put it on the six, and that made seven," she said. "Then I had four more, so I added two more, that made eight, nine, and then I added two more, and that made ten, eleven."

No other children had suggestions, so I returned to teaching the game. During this time, Annie had snapped her eleven cubes together. I asked her to stand the tower up carefully. I then read the next rule, "When you're done, pass the dice to your partner. Then your partner follows Steps One and Two." When Annie handed me the dice, I took a turn. When I reported that I had rolled a 4 and a 2, I heard a chorus of "six." I built my tower.

"Let me read some more of the directions before Annie and I continue," I said, and read, "Do this until you each have five towers."

"Remember," I said to the class, "you must wait until your partner hands you the dice to take your turn." I handed the dice back to Annie to indicate it was again her turn. Annie and I continued rolling dice and making towers. I didn't stop to discuss the sums of the two dice each time we rolled, as I wanted to move the game along. As Annie and I built our towers, some children commented on who they thought was winning. Finally, we each had built five towers.

I read the rest of the directions: "Each player makes a long train with his or her five towers. Count your cubes in two different ways. Then compare your trains to see who has more and who has less. Figure out how many more cubes are in the longer train. Record."

"I'll start by counting my cubes by twos," I said. "Count along with me quietly." I pointed to the cubes as we counted. There were thirty-six cubes.

"I'm going to count them by tens next," I said. "Raise your hand if you know how many tens I'll have." More than half the students raised their hands. I called on Molly.

"You'll have three," she said.

"How do you know?" I asked.

"Because three tens make thirty," she answered.

"And you'll have six extras," Rudy called out.

"How do you know?" I asked.

"Because it's thirty-six," he said, "and you need six more to make thirty into thirty-six."

I carefully placed Annie's train next to mine.

"You win," Eli said.

"Annie doesn't have as many," Leslie said.

"How many more do I have?" I asked.

Several children who were close counted. "You have seven more," Eli said.

"How many cubes do you think there are in Annie's train?" I asked.

About two-thirds of the class seemed totally perplexed about how to figure this out. After a few moments, only six children had raised their hands. I called on Hassan.

"I think it's thirty-one," he said.

"Explain how you figured," I said.

Hassan shrugged. "I just guessed," he said.

"Listen to someone else's idea," I said, "and that may give you a way to think about how to solve the problem."

"It's twenty-nine," Andrew said. I could always count on Andrew to give a correct answer and be able to explain his reasoning. "Because if you take away six," he continued, "you have thirty, and you have to take away one more, and that makes twenty-nine."

"He's right," Annie said. She had counted the cubes.

"How many tens can Annie make with her train?" I asked. Several children called out that there would be two tens. Andrew disagreed.

"There would be almost three," he said. "Just one would be missing."

The students were eager to get to work and play the game themselves. As they played, I circulated and observed, giving assistance as needed. I hadn't provided specific directions about the recording children were to do, and as they worked, several children asked me about what they should write. I gave them my stock answer: "Use words, numbers, and, if you'd like, pictures." Children interpreted this in different ways.

Jason and Leslie were partners. After playing a game, Jason wrote: *We got a ti. I had 38. She had 38.* For the same game, Leslie wrote: *I counted by 5's and I got 38. and Jason got 38. I counted by 10's and I got 38.* (See Figure 8–1.)

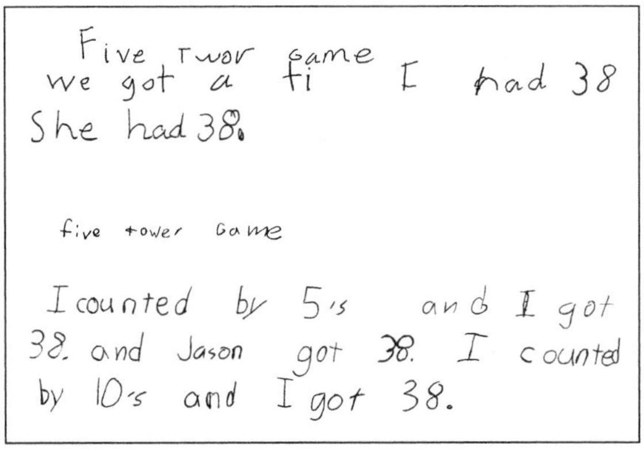
Five Twor game
we got a ti I had 38
She had 38.

five tower Game

I counted by 5's and I got 38. and Jason got 38. I counted by 10's and I got 38.

▲▲▲▲▲Figure 8–1 ***Leslie and Jason described the same game differently.***

Sarah and Rudy were partners, and their papers revealed a collaboration that wasn't evident in Jason's and Leslie's work. Sarah wrote: *I got 46 cubes and Rudy onley got 38. We played for about 2 minits it seemed liked. And . . . . . . best of all I won!* Rudy wrote: *Sarah got 46 cubs and I got 38 cubs. I canted by 2's and 5's. I think it took abut 3 min. it seems like.* (See Figure 8–2.) Both of them drew pictures of their towers of cubes.

Some children included different kinds of information. For example, Amelia wrote: *Molly had 37 and I had 33. All together there was 70.* Hassan wrote: *I count by 2. I count by 5. Catherine got 41. She wun by 3.* He wrote *38* for his answer. (See Figure 8–3.)

Reading the children's work gives me insights into their different responses to the activity and into their writing ability.

▲▲▲▲▲▲Figure 8–2   *Rudy included a drawing of the game he played with Sarah.*

LINKING ASSESSMENT TO INSTRUCTION

I intervene when I perceive that children need encouragement to stay involved or are confused about directions. I also interrupt children when I see an opportunity to probe their thinking and informally assess their understanding.

▲▲▲▲▲▲Figure 8–3   *Hassan explained how he counted and how many more cubes Catherine had.*

Assessing Jonathan and Jason

Jonathan and Jason were partway through the *Five-Tower Game* when I interrupted them. Each boy had made three towers.

"Who has more cubes right now?" I asked.

Each boy started to count his cubes. Jonathan counted forty and Jason counted twenty-seven.

"He does," Jason said.

"Can you figure out how many more cubes Jonathan has?" I asked. This question was too difficult for them. Jonathan typically solved numerical problems either by counting concrete objects or by making tally marks on paper. He was not able to think about quantities merely from written numbers. Also, he didn't use counting on as a strategy. Jason was at a similar level.

The boys connected each of their three towers into a long train, stretched them out side by side, and counted the extra cubes in

Jonathan's train. Even though they worked carefully, they miscounted.

Once they had connected their cubes into long trains, the boys were confused about how to continue with their game. Also, a piece of one of the trains had broken off and the boys began to argue about whose cubes they were. Jason grabbed them, Jonathan grabbed them back, and I could see we were headed for trouble. I think my questioning raised their level of stress.

"I'm sorry I messed up your game," I told the boys. "How about starting over so you both have a fresh start?" That suggestion seemed OK to them, and they began the game once again.

Deciding when to interrupt children and when to let them continue working on their own is a professional decision that isn't always easy to make. I'm not sure it was a good choice to interrupt the boys as I did. Although the interaction confirmed my understanding about their limited ability with numbers, it also made them uncomfortable. In a few minutes, however, they were back to work, fully engaged with the game.

Assessing Grace and Andrew

A little later, after playing the *Five-Tower Game*, Grace and Andrew dismantled their towers and returned the cubes to the bucket. Grace became upset because she realized that they hadn't counted the cubes in their trains and therefore didn't have the information to write about their results. Andrew, however, wasn't at all concerned. He avoided writing whenever possible. But Grace was persistent and called me over to help them solve the problem.

"Tell me about your game," I said.

"I won by two," Andrew said. Grace nodded in agreement.

"Can either of you remember the numbers you rolled?" I asked.

"I can," Grace said. "First I rolled two twelves, then two fours, and then a five."

"Then I think you have enough information to solve the problem," I said. Now I had Andrew's interest. He loved problems like this one. Grace wasn't so confident. She liked working with numbers, and her mother gave her a good deal of practice at home, but she didn't always transfer her skills to problem situations.

"Do I have to build my towers again?" she asked.

"You can if you want to," I answered.

"I don't think we need to," Andrew said, and he got up to get some paper.

"Can you help?" Grace asked me.

"What sort of help would you like?" I asked.

"Maybe you could just sit here," she said.

I sat down at their table. Andrew returned with a piece of paper for each of them and they started to talk. Neither asked me for help. (I think perhaps the reassurance of my presence was helpful to Grace.)

While Grace and Andrew talked, I answered questions that other children brought to me. I then noticed that Grace and Andrew were working separately, each writing on a separate paper.

Finally, Grace interrupted me. "Is thirty-three right?" she asked.

"What's the question?" I asked.

Grace showed me her paper. On her paper she had written *12 + 12*, then *4 + 4 + 5.* "I know that twelve and twelve is twenty-four," she explained, "and then I counted the fours and got thirty-three."

"That's not right," I said. She recounted and got thirty-two, which I confirmed. She then added on five, again by counting, and returned to work by herself.

Meanwhile, Andrew had completed his

paper without any additional help from me. He figured out that Grace had had thirty-seven cubes in all and he, therefore, had had thirty-nine. He wrote: *I know 12 + 12 = 24 then I added up the other numbers by counting. I knew that I had two more so we added up Grace's numbers and it was 37 so I have 39.*

Shortly afterward, Grace was finished. She had written: *I had double 12 and double 4. I had 15. all together is 37. My answer is 37. Andrew had 2 more then me so I think he has 39.* (See Figure 8–4.)

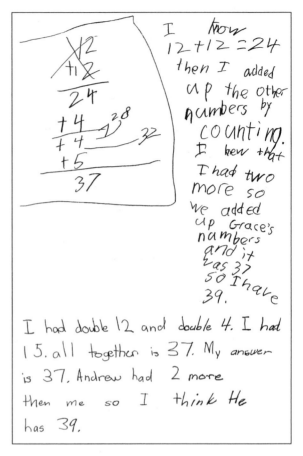

▲▲▲▲▲▲Figure 8–4 *Andrew and Grace separately figured out how many cubes they each had in their trains.*

Questions and Discussion

▲▲

▲ How could this game be adapted?

For less experienced or less able students, the game can be adapted by having students use only one die. For students who are ready for a greater challenge, have the students build eight, nine, or ten towers instead of five.

▲ You insisted that the person who had rolled the dice hand them to the other player before continuing the game. Why?

This process has several benefits. First, it prevents students from grabbing the dice from each other and the problems that occur with this behavior. Also, having one player hand the dice to the other slows the game down so that both players can consider and discuss all moves and reach agreement. Additionally, this process sets the tone for students to treat each other respectfully.

CHAPTER NINE
MAKE A SHAPE

Overview

In this activity, children each draw a shape that they think can hold thirty-five color tiles. They test their shape by placing color tiles inside their shape, using ten tiles of one color, then switching to another color, and so on. *Make a Shape* not only encourages children to count by tens but also provides experience with geometry and area measurement.

Materials

▲ color tiles, 10 each of four colors per student
▲ *Make a Shape* sample (see Blackline Masters)
▲ optional: directions for *Make a Shape*, 1 per student (see Blackline Masters)

Time

▲ one class period

Teaching Directions

1. Show the class the *Make a Shape* sample and explain to the students that you think thirty-five tiles will cover the inside of the shape. (**Note:** If you have overhead color tiles, you can use an overhead transparency of the *Make a Shape* sample and the overhead tiles.)

2. Model for the class how you'll test the shape. Place ten tiles of one color inside your shape, then switch to another color and place ten more, and continue this way until the shape is full. **Note:** The sample shape holds fewer than thirty-five tiles.

3. Count the tiles by tens. Have the children figure how many more tiles would make exactly thirty-five. Ask for suggestions about how to adjust the shape to fit thirty-five tiles.

4. Take another sheet of paper and draw a shape that you think would be more likely to hold thirty-five tiles. Test it as you did with the first, reading the rules to the children. If you'd like, distribute a copy of the rules to each student.

5. Model how to record.

6. Have the children get to work. Circulate and observe.

Teaching Notes

This activity gives students the opportunity to work specifically with tens and ones to fill the inside of a geometric shape. The activity is open enough that those students who aren't ready to utilize the tens and ones structure of our number system will still be engaged and thinking about groupings as well as developing their spatial skills.

In this activity, students compare the number of tiles required to cover the inside of their shape with the number thirty-five. Comparing groups can be difficult for students of this age. Through this activity, students gain concrete experience that supports the development of this understanding.

It's important to be correct when using language to describe mathematical ideas. In this case, a choice had to be made between "cover the shape" and "cover the inside of the shape." A square, as an example of the kind of shape this task calls for, is made up of four line segments that enclose a region. The region enclosed isn't the square; technically, it's the inside of the square. So it isn't correct to ask children to cover the shape. This may seem picky, and it is. But the language we use is important in that it influences the language children use.

The Lesson

▲▲▲

I gathered the students on the floor so they could see the *Make a Shape* sample. "How many tiles do you think it will take to cover the inside of my shape?" I asked the students. Hands shot into the air; students were eager to share their thinking. As students shared, I asked them to explain their reasons for their guesses, and then I listed their ideas on the board, using a tally mark to indicate when more than one student had the same estimate.

After all who wanted had shared I said, "I think it will take thirty-five tiles to cover the inside of my shape."

"That's two more than I thought," Rudy said.

Grace added, "That's way less than I thought."

"I'm going to use the tiles to find out how many it will take," I explained. "First I am going to use blue tiles." I began counting and filling in the shape and many of the students were quick to join in as I counted to ten.

I then said, "I used ten blue tiles so far. Now I am going to change and use red tiles." I continued covering the inside of the shape and counting, stopping when I had used ten red tiles.

"How many more tiles do you think it will take to cover the inside of the shape?" I asked.

"About five," Katy volunteered.

"I think exactly five," Andrew said.

"Maybe four or maybe six," Teddy suggested.

"Let's see," I said as I continued to cover the inside of the shape with yellow tiles.

"One, two, three, four, five," the children counted.

"It took twenty-five tiles to fill in the shape!" Rudy said.

"Who can explain how you know the number of tiles it took to cover the inside of my shape?" I asked.

Molly explained, "There is one group of blue tiles, that's ten, and there is one group of red tiles, that's ten more. Ten plus ten is twenty. Then there are five yellow tiles. Twenty plus five is twenty-five." I recorded on the board:

10 + 10 = 20

20 + 5 = 25

"That's what I think, too," Amelia added.

"Who has a different way?" I asked.

Jason explained, "I knew there were five yellow tiles, and I added those to the ten blues, that's fifteen, then there were still ten red, and that makes twenty-five." On the board I wrote:

5 + 10 = 15

15 + 10 = 25

No one had another idea and I wanted to keep the lesson moving so the students would have time to work on the activity.

"My prediction was that it would take thirty-five tiles to fill in my shape. It only took twenty-five tiles. If I wanted to draw a new shape that could have the inside covered by thirty-five tiles, what should I do?" I asked.

"Make it bigger," Tomo said.

"Why should I make it bigger?" I asked.

"The one you have only holds twenty-five tiles," Tomo said, "so if you want to have a shape big enough to hold thirty-five, it has to be bigger because thirty-five is bigger than twenty-five." The students nodded their agreement as Tomo explained his reasoning.

"How much bigger is thirty-five than twenty-five?" I asked the class.

This seemed difficult, and I encouraged the students to talk it over with their partners. After a few moments, I asked for the students' attention. Several had their hands in the air. I called on Leslie.

"We think it's ten more," Leslie said. "We counted by fives. Twenty-five to thirty is five and then thirty to thirty-five is five more, so five and five makes ten." I recorded on the board:

25, 30, 35

25 to 30 is 5

30 to 35 is 5

5 + 5 = 10

Teddy explained, "I counted: twenty-six, twenty-seven, twenty-eight, twenty-nine, thirty, thirty-one, thirty-two, thirty-three, thirty-four, thirty-five. Every time I said a number, I put a finger up. When I was done, I had ten fingers up." I wrote on the board:

26, 27, 28, 29, 30, 31, 32, 33, 34, 35

No one else had a different idea. "You are each going to have the chance to draw your own shape in just a few minutes," I said. I distributed to each child a copy of the Make a Shape directions. I asked students to identify the materials required and explained to them that they would be working on this activity individually.

"The directions give you all the information you need about what to do," I said and then read the first direction, "Draw a shape. You want to be able to cover the inside with thirty-five tiles." I began to draw a shape on a piece of unlined paper, commenting aloud as I did so. "It helps me to think about the different shapes I cut for the zero to ninety-nine puzzle," I said. "Those shapes give me ideas for the kind of shape I'd like to make."

I held up my shape to show it to the class and then read the next direction, "Test by covering the inside of the shape with color tiles. Use ten tiles of one color, then ten of another, and so on, until it's covered."

As I had done before, I put my paper on the desk and began placing tiles inside my shape. I started with green tiles first, then switched to blue, and finally to red. I used ten green, ten blue, and four red tiles.

I continued reading the directions, "Count the color tiles." Several children called out that there were twenty-four.

"Raise your hand if you can explain how you know there are twenty-four tiles on my shape," I said.

I called on Molly. "Because ten and ten makes twenty and four more makes twenty-four," she said, using a strategy similar to the one she had used earlier.

"Does anyone have a different way of explaining?" I asked. There were no other responses.

I returned to the directions. "Record the number of tiles inside your shape." I removed the color tiles and wrote the number 24 inside the shape.

"So what do you think I learned about the shape I made?" I asked the class.

"It's still not big enough. The first one held twenty-five and this one held twenty-four. I think it's smaller than the other one," Sarah said.

"You need one that uses more tiles," Jason added.

"How many more tiles do I need to use thirty-five?" I wrote on the board as I asked the question:

I used 24.

I want to use 35.

How many more do I need?

The idea of "how many more?" is difficult for children this age. I take every opportunity that comes up to have a class discussion about the idea to help children develop strategies for dealing with problems of this type.

I called on Rudy first.

"I think it's eleven," he said, "because if you add one more ten to twenty-four, you get thirty-four, and then you need to add one." I recorded on the board:

24 + 10 = 34

34 + 1 = 35

Next I called on Hassan. "I think it's nine," he said.

"Explain how you figured," I responded.

"Well," he said, "four plus five is nine, so you need nine more."

"I agree with you that four plus five is nine," I said, and wrote on the board:

4 + 5 = 9

"If I started with twenty-four tiles and add nine, how many tiles would I have?" I asked, and wrote on the board:

24 + 9 =

Hassan and several other children began to count on their fingers. Several responded, and there were a variety of answers, including thirty-two, thirty-three, thirty-five, and thirty-six.

"I'm not convinced," I said. "I hear different answers."

I called on Katy. She didn't respond to Hassan's idea, but had a different thought. This was fine with me, as it gave Hassan some time to think more about his solution.

"What I did," she said, "was count. I went twenty-five, twenty-six, twenty-seven, twenty-eight, twenty-nine, thirty, thirty-one, thirty-two, thirty-three, thirty-four, thirty-five. I ran out of fingers at thirty-four and had to go one more. So I know it's eleven." I wrote on the board:

25, 26, 27, 28, 29, 30, 31, 32, 33, 34, 35

Then I counted the numerals to verify that there were eleven. I then called on Seth.

"I kind of did it like Katy," he said, "but a little different."

"What did you do?" I asked.

"I know that if you have twenty-four," he said, "you need six more to get to thirty because I counted twenty-five, twenty-six, twenty-seven, twenty-eight, twenty-nine, thirty. Then you need five more to get to thirty-five. And six and five makes eleven." I recorded on the board:

25, 26, 27, 28, 29, 30

30 + 5 = 35

6 + 5 = 11

I called on Teddy next. "I think that twenty-four plus nine is thirty-three," he said, returning to Hassan's idea. "So you need two more to get to thirty-five, and nine plus two equals up to eleven."

"What do you think, Hassan?" I asked.

"Yeah, that's right," he said. "You need two more." I wasn't sure that Hassan understood, but he seemed relieved and satisfied, so I didn't probe further.

"Any other ideas?" I said. Sarah raised her hand and came to the board.

"My mother taught me how to do this," she said, and wrote on the board:

24 + ___ = 35

"Then you put the eleven on the line," she said.

"How do you know you're supposed to write eleven on the line?" I asked.

"I don't know, but I think it's right," she replied.

Several more hands were raised, but I told the children that I was going to stop the discussion. "I want to be sure that you understand the entire task," I said, "and then you can get to work. Remember that it doesn't matter if exactly thirty-five tiles cover the inside of your shape. It didn't for me. In this activity, you have the chance to draw a second shape and see if you can get closer to thirty-five. And, if you'd like, you can try more shapes as well."

With that, the children quickly got to work.

OBSERVING THE CHILDREN AT WORK

I noticed differences among the students as I observed them at work on this task. For example, some children placed tiles carefully inside the shape, nesting them close together with their edges touching. Other children, however, placed tiles with no regard to their position in relation to one another and were content even when some overlapped to the outside of the shape. Some students were bothered when some portion of the inside of the shape was left uncovered. Others were unconcerned and merely ignored the gaps.

As I circulated, I talked with children. I tried to help some see the importance of placing tiles together so that more of them would fit inside the shape. I talked with others about how they might deal with the spaces yet uncovered, tentatively encouraging them to think about halves of spaces, yet not pushing the idea if it didn't seem to make sense to the individual. I took note of different children's responses.

Some children were disturbed when exactly thirty-five didn't cover the inside of their shape. Some chose to adjust their shape so that thirty-five tiles covered the inside, either by redrawing lines and then rechecking, or by arranging thirty-five tiles and tracing around them. Other children seemed totally unconcerned when they didn't use thirty-five tiles and were happy to leave their papers as they were. I noted these differences as well.

Also, while some of the children followed the directions of the activity and used ten of one color and then switched to another color, others either arranged tiles in a color pattern that pleased them or merely chose tiles at random. I talked with students who weren't following the system of using ten of one color and then switching colors and pointed out its advantage. (After all, seeing the usefulness of grouping by tens in a problem-solving situation was an underlying goal of this activity in the context of the unit.) I observed what the children did when I left them to get back to work by themselves and tried to judge their readiness and understanding. See Figures 9–1 through 9–3 for three students' work on this activity.

▲▲▲▲▲▲Figure 9–2 *Molly claimed that both times she tried the activity she drew shapes that called for exactly 35 tiles.*

▲▲▲▲▲▲Figure 9–1 *Corrine's shape wasn't large enough for 35 tiles, but she did not attempt to figure out how many more she needed.*

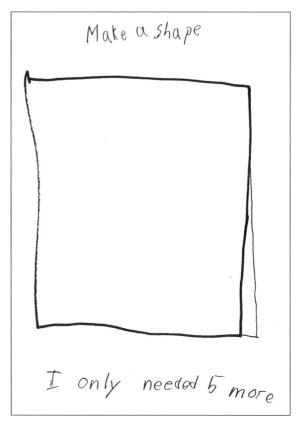

▲▲▲▲▲▲Figure 9–3 *Andrew indicated that his shape needed 5 more to hold 35 tiles.*

Questions and Discussion

▲▲

▲ *How can I adapt this activity for more or less experienced children?*

The numbers you choose can make the activity easier or more challenging. For less experienced learners, give the students half a sheet of paper and ask them to draw a shape that would take fifteen, twenty, or twenty-five tiles to cover the inside. Using half a sheet of paper keeps the shapes and the number of tiles to cover the inside of the shape smaller and more manageable.

For learners who need more of a challenge, ask them to draw a shape that would need thirty-seven or forty-three tiles to cover the inside. Thirty-seven and forty-three are not as friendly and easy for most students to think about as thirty-five. Another suggestion is to give more able students a larger sheet of paper and ask them to draw a shape that would require fifty tiles to cover the inside. As in the vignette, have students compare the number of tiles it actually took to cover the inside with fifty or whatever number you have chosen.

▲ *You spend a lot of time on class discussion. What is your purpose?*

One of the key purposes I see for class discussions is the opportunity to emphasize children's thinking. By asking children to explain their reasoning, teachers give the message that an answer alone is not sufficient and that the thinking that leads to the answer is also important. Also, when one child gives an explanation, always ask for other ideas. This effort supports the notion that there are different ways to think about a problem. Also, the sharing that goes on during discussions enhances students' understanding about and confidence in mathematics.

▲ *Weren't you bothered by the different ways children approached this activity and their different levels of understanding? It seemed at times you were assessing students and then at other times you weren't. What was your intent?*

I am not particularly bothered by the differences in children's approaches to this task. Their approaches provide me valuable insights into their learning and understanding. As they worked, I was able to suggest new ideas to them. It was interesting to see if the child tried out a new idea I had suggested or returned to doing the task as before. These observations provide me with important information about my students and their understanding.

Something important to consider is the purpose of the task. Is it an assessment task, a learning task, or both? As the students worked, I observed. I was assessing what they were doing during this observation time. When I thought it appropriate, I offered suggestions or posed questions to probe or push their thinking. Posing suggestions or questions can lead students to a new learning or insight or can help you assess students' knowledge and understanding. In this lesson, I was doing both. I was assessing the students' understanding and, when it seemed appropriate, I was pushing them toward new learning and insights. My choices about what to do with each student were based on my observations. In this way, assessment and learning are very closely linked and difficult to separate.

CHAPTER TEN
HIPPETY HOP

Overview

Students use hops of one, ten, and one hundred to move to a target number on a 1–100 chart. The goal is to reach the target number with the fewest hops possible. Students explore this activity first as a whole group, next as table groups, then in pairs, and finally the activity becomes a game.

Materials

▲ 1–100 charts, 1 per pair of students (see Blackline Masters)
▲ overhead transparency of the 1–100 chart
▲ game markers, 1 per pair of students
▲ 3-by-5-inch index cards cut in half and numbered as follows: 37, 68, 54, 97, 13, 44, 53, 75, 22, 68 (or any ten numbers from 1 to 100), 1 set per pair of students (**Note:** When making the cards, use a different color marking pen for each set. This will allow for quick sorting if the sets should get mixed up.)
▲ optional: rules for the game of *Hippety Hop,* 1 per pair of students (see Blackline Masters)

Time

▲ one class period to introduce the activity, additional class periods to play and discuss the game

Teaching Directions

1. Project the overhead transparency of the 1–100 chart on the wall. Tell the students that they will investigate moving a marker to move to a target number in as few hops as possible. Place a marker above the chart and explain: "There are three ways to hop to the target number—hops of one, hops of ten, and hops of one hundred."

2. Discuss with the class ways to hop to the target number of 11. Record students' ideas, for example:

$$1 + 10 = 11$$

$$10 + 1 = 11$$

$$1 + 1 + 1 + 1 + 1 + 1 + 1 + 1 + 1 + 1 + 1 = 11$$

With the students, determine which ways use the fewest hops.

3. Repeat Step 2 for other numbers until the students are comfortable finding different ways to hop to the target numbers. Be sure to include numbers such as 67, for which using hops of one hundred are needed for the fewest moves.

4. Have students work as table groups and then as pairs hopping to target numbers you give them. Give them 1–100 charts and game markers. Have children share their moves and strategies. Record their solutions.

5. The next day, present the game of *Hippety Hop* for students to play in pairs. The object of the game is to move to the target number using the fewest number of hops possible. Model the game with a student using the following rules.

The Game of Hippety Hop

You need:
  a partner
  a 1–100 chart
  1 game marker
  1 set of number cards

Rules
1. Draw a score chart and write your names at the top of the columns.

2. Place the marker above the top row of the 1–100 chart.

3. Player 1 draws a card and hops by ones, tens, and/or hundreds to reach the target number in as few hops as possible. Both players must agree on the number of hops. Player 1 records the number of hops in his or her column on the score sheet.

4. Player 2 follows Steps 2 and 3.

5. Continue until each player has drawn five numbers.

6. Both players figure their total hops. The player with the fewest number of hops for all five numbers wins the game.

---

6. After the children have had a chance to play, lead a discussion about the strategies they discovered as they played.

Teaching Notes

This activity is appropriate after students have had many experiences counting by twos, fives, and tens. Also, familiarity with the hundred chart is important. Students need to know that the numbers on the chart increase or decrease by one when a marker is moved one square horizontally and increase or decrease by ten when a marker is moved vertically.

Most activities in this book suggest the use of the 0–99 chart. For this activity, it is suggested that the hundred chart be used, as students have the option of making a hop of one hundred. While this is possible on the 0–99 chart, it is more obvious on the hundred chart.

As students gain confidence and familiarity with this activity, they are building their number sense and laying a foundation for understanding how numbers are rounded. It becomes evident why numbers below five are rounded down and why numbers above five are rounded up. That leaves five in the middle. Students cannot discover why five is rounded up, as it is a decision made by and agreed upon by mathematicians. This is information that you need to provide.

The Lesson

▲▲

DAY 1

"Today we are going to play a game using the hundred chart," I began as I placed a transparency of the hundred chart on the overhead projector. "In this game, you will need to think little instead of thinking big, as in many games. The object of the game is to get to a number in as few hops as you can."

"Where do we start?" Shamera asked.

"You begin by placing your marker above the numbers on the chart," I explained as I set a cube on the overhead to show the class. "Here is some very important information. You can move three ways. You can hop by ones; that is, you can move one space," I said as I modeled on the overhead.

"If you hop onto the board and land on one, then that's one hop?" Sonny asked. I nodded.

"A second way you can move," I continued, "is to hop by ten. If I were to hop by ten for my first hop, where would I land?" Most hands were in the air immediately. Maritza came to the overhead and moved

the marker to 10 to show us. I asked the students to indicate their agreement with Maritza's move by putting their thumbs up if they agreed, thumbs down if they disagreed, or thumbs sideways if they weren't sure. Thumbs went up quickly, indicating their agreement.

"Tell me in a whisper voice how I can move," I said, to reinforce what we had discussed so far.

"By tens and by ones," the class whispered back.

"Hopping by ones and tens, how could I get to eleven?" I asked. "Talk with your table group." The room was immediately engulfed in animated discussion. After a minute or so, I asked for the students' attention once again.

"Who would like to share one way your group discussed to get to eleven?" I asked. I called on James.

"You could hop ten once and land on ten and then hop one more time by one and land on eleven," James explained.

"How many hops did James's way take?" I asked.

"Two," Dane said. "One for ten and one for one, so that's two hops."

I recorded James's explanation on the board:

10 + 1 = 11   2 hops

"Who has another way?" I asked.

"My way is sort of the same and sort of turned around from James's," Kasey said. "We hopped one space and then we hopped one ten. It still comes out to be two hops."

I recorded Kasey's idea:

1 + 10 = 11   2 hops

"I have a different way," Derrick said. "You could hop by ones eleven times."

"That's too many; you're supposed to think small," BJ said.

"The object is to get to the number in as few hops as possible," I replied. "Let's see if Derrick's way works because we are interested in knowing many different ways so we can find the shortest." Together we tried Derrick's suggestion of counting to eleven by ones and found that it took eleven hops. I recorded Derrick's idea:

1 + 1 + 1 + 1 + 1 + 1 +
1 + 1 + 1 + 1 + 1 = 11   11 hops

"Does anyone have a way of getting to eleven in fewer than two hops?" I asked. No one did.

"I told you there were three ways to move," I said. "You can hop by ones, and you can hop by tens. The third way is to hop by one hundred."

"Wow! That's clear to the end of the chart!" BJ said.

"Why would you do that?" Jazmine asked. I paused for a moment to give the students time to consider Jazmine's question.

"Why would you want to hop to one hundred?" I asked. "Talk with your partner. First one of you talks for thirty seconds, then the other. No interruptions," I said as I started timing thirty seconds. After thirty seconds, I reminded the students to switch roles. At the end of one minute, I asked for the students' attention. I called on Sean.

"If you have a number like ninety-nine, it would take less hops to go to one hundred and then go back one to ninety-nine," Sean explained. As Sean shared his idea, I modeled it for the other students using the overhead.

"That's what we thought, too," Kasey said with a giggle.

"How many had Sean's idea?" I asked. Many raised their hands. "Does anyone have a different idea?" No one did.

"I would like you to work with your table group to find the way that uses the fewest number of hops to get to the number I am going to give you," I said. "You and your table group will have one minute to figure this out. What are the ways you can hop?"

"By ones, tens, and hundreds," the class responded, eager to move on.

"Can we use the hundred chart?" Maritza asked.

"Yes," I said. "I put several on each table before class and you may use those if they help you to solve the problem." There were no further questions.

"The number is sixty-seven," I said. The room broke into excited conversation. While keeping track of the time, I listened and observed as the students worked together to solve this problem. I gave the students a five-second warning and then asked for their attention.

"Which group would like to share?" I asked as hands flew into the air. I called on Shamera's table.

"Can we come up to show you?" Shamera asked. I nodded. "First, hop one hundred—that's one hop—then go up the chart to ninety, then eighty, then seventy. Next, go across from seventy to sixty-nine, sixty-eight, sixty-seven."

"That's seven hops," said James, who had been keeping track with his fingers as Shamera explained their table's solution.

I recorded their way on the board:

100 – 10 – 10 –10 – 1 – 1 – 1 = 67   7 hops

"Did anyone else think of it like Shamera's group?" I asked. Students at a couple of tables raised their hands, indicating they had. "Who has a different way?"

"Ours was seven hops, too," Corrine shared. "We hopped to one hundred, then we hopped across by ones to ninety-seven, then we hopped up the chart by tens to sixty-seven. That's seven hops!"

I recorded the solution for Corrine's group on the board:

$100 - 1 - 1 - 1 - 10 - 10 - 10 = 67$ *7 hops*

"I know another way," Dane offered. "You could hop by tens to sixty and then hop by ones until you get to sixty-seven."

"How many hops would that be?" I asked Dane. Dane used his marker and the hundred chart to count and discover that it took thirteen hops to get to sixty-seven in this way. I recorded Dane's idea:

$10 + 10 + 10 + 10 + 10 + 10 +$
$1 + 1 + 1 + 1 + 1 + 1 + 1 = 67$ *13 hops*

"Dane's way certainly works," I commented, "but it's not the way with the fewest hops."

"This time I'm going to ask you to work in pairs," I said. "Work with the person sitting beside you. Together you'll try to find the way to get to the number I choose with the fewest hops. You may use the hundred charts to help you." I checked to be sure each student knew who his or her partner would be and that each pair had a hundred chart with which to work.

"Here's your first number," I said as the students waited with anticipation. "It's fifty-six."

"Easy!" "I know!" were some of the responses as the partners began their task. It took about a minute for most pairs to come to an answer. As I watched, I saw many children trying multiple solutions rather than just accepting the first way that came to mind. If a pair didn't attempt to find more than one way, I intervened with comments such as "Your way works, but I think there's a shorter way. Can you find it?" or "Your way works. Could you get to fifty-six if you hopped to one hundred first?" or "Your way works. Why does it make sense to go to sixty and hop down to fifty-six rather than going to fifty and hopping up to fifty-six?" After the pairs had the chance to finish, I asked for the students' attention.

"Who has an idea to share about how to get to fifty-six in the fewest hops?" I asked. Almost all students had their hands raised. I called on Juan.

"You hop to one, then two, then three, then four, then five, then six, then to sixteen, twenty-six, thirty-six, forty-six, and fifty-six," Juan said. "That's fourteen hops."

"Let's check the number of hops Juan made by counting them together," I suggested. As Juan explained, I moved the marker and the students counted each hop aloud. We discovered that Juan had hopped eleven times.

I recorded Juan's way on the board:

$1 + 1 + 1 + 1 + 1 + 1 +$
$10 + 10 + 10 + 10 + 10 = 56$ *11 hops*

"We did it a different way," Shamera shared. "We hopped to one hundred, then went to ninety, eighty, seventy, sixty, fifty-nine, fifty-eight, fifty-seven, fifty-six."

"That's nine hops," added BJ, her partner. "I'll show you."

BJ came to the front of the room and moved the marker on the overhead as the students counted each hop.

"Yep, it comes out to nine!" Corrine said.

I recorded Shamera and BJ's thinking on the board:

$100 - 10 - 10 - 10 - 10 - 1 - 1 - 1 - 1 = 56$
9 hops

"Did anyone else do it like BJ and Shamera?" I asked. A few hands went up.

"We did it sort of the same, only we did a different order," Jazmine said. "We hopped to one hundred, then hopped one to ninety-nine, ninety-eight, ninety-seven, ninety-six, then hopped a ten to eighty-six, seventy-six, sixty-six, fifty-six. That's nine, isn't it, Derrick?" Derrick was Jazmine's partner. Derrick repeated what Jazmine had said quietly to himself as he used his fingers to keep track of the number of hops.

"Uh-huh," Derrick confirmed with an uncertain nod.

"Let's check together," I said as I moved the marker across the overhead chart while Jazmine repeated her suggestion. The children counted the hops quietly as I moved the marker.

"It is nine!" Derrick said with excitement. "I knew it!"

I recorded Derrick and Jazmine's idea as follows:

$$100 - 1 - 1 - 1 - 1 - 10 - 10 - 10 - 10 = 56$$
$$9 \text{ hops}$$

"We have a different way," Maritza said. "We did six ten-hops, ten, twenty, thirty, forty, fifty, sixty, and four one-hops, fifty-nine, fifty-eight, fifty-seven, fifty-six. Six hops and four hops is ten hops. Besides, I counted with my fingers, too." Maritza held up ten fingers to show she had kept track of the hops as she counted aloud. I recorded Maritza's suggestion:

$$10 + 10 + 10 + 10 + 10 +$$
$$10 - 1 - 1 - 1 - 1 = 56 \qquad 10 \text{ hops}$$

No one had any additional ideas. "I have one last number for you to try today," I said as I noticed it was almost time to go to lunch. "This time, find out the fewest number of hops to reach twenty-three." Again the students were immediately engaged. After a minute or so, all pairs had finished. I called on Corrine and Dane to share.

"Easy," Dane began.

"Yep," Corrine interjected.

"You hop two ten-hops and three one-hops," Dane continued.

"Two hops and three hops is five hops altogether," Corrine said, completing their explanation.

"Did anyone else think of it like Dane and Corrine?" I asked. Most hands went up.

"We got five hops, but we did the three one-hops first and then the two ten-hops," Shamera said. No one else had any other ideas.

"Can we play tomorrow?" Luz asked.

"We're going to play again tomorrow, but I'm going to teach you a little different way," I said. The students were pleased with this. I was pleased with their enthusiasm.

DAY 2

"Are we going to play a game today?" Janelle asked.

"That's exactly what we are going to do," I responded. There were cheers from the rest of the class.

"Do we get partners?" Maritza asked.

"I'll tell you all about the game and the rules," I said as I settled the class. "Yesterday Greg and Diego were absent, so I'm going to ask you to explain to them what we did so they can understand the game we're going to play today."

"Well, we were moving our markers on the hundred chart," Kaitlyn began.

"There were three ways you could move your marker," James said. "You could hop by ones, or you could hop ten, or you could even hop one hundred. All those ways of hopping counted as one hop."

"You had to hop to a target number in the fewest hops," Dane added.

"Does anyone else have anything to add about yesterday?" I asked.

"Maybe you should show Greg and Diego," Shamera suggested.

"That's a good idea, Shamera. Would you like to help me?" I asked. Shamera nodded and came to the overhead projector. "Would you like to think of a number and I'll try to move the marker to the target number, or would you rather I think of a number and you move the marker?"

"You think of the number," Shamera said.

"How about sixty-six?" I said.

Shamera grinned and started to move her marker while the rest of the class counted the hops she made.

"Explain to us what you did," I said.

"I hopped to one hundred, then I did three ten-hops up to seventy," Shamera explained. "Then I did four one-hops to get to sixty-six. I think that's. . . . eight hops."

"I think I get it," Greg said.

"I need a partner. We'll model a game as the rest of you watch and that should help make it clear to everyone how to play," I said. Students put their hands up immediately to volunteer to be my partner. I chose Kaitlyn.

"We'll need to keep track of our scores," I said as I drew a score chart on the board.

Mrs. Wickett	Kaitlyn

"We'll each take a turn," I began. "The first player will draw a card from this pile of number cards, and that number will become the target number." I showed the students the pile of number cards. "Then the object is to get to the target number with the fewest hops. Would you like to go first, Kaitlyn, or would you like me to go first?"

"You!" Kaitlyn said, pointing her finger at me and grinning.

"OK," I said. "What do I do first?" I asked the class.

"Draw a card," came the response. I did as they said and drew 37. "Now what?"

"Hop!" the class chorused.

"I need some advice," I said. To keep the students involved and focused, I asked them to work with their table groups to come up with advice on how I could move. After a minute or so, hands were in the air. I called on Greg.

"You could do four ten-hops and then go back three one-hops," Greg suggested.

"How many hops is that?" I asked.

"Seven," Greg responded.

"I know another way," BJ said. "You could do three ten-hops and seven one-hops."

"How many hops is that?" I asked. BJ shrugged. "How could we figure it out?" I probed.

"Do it on the chart," BJ suggested.

"Use your chart and see if you can figure it out," I said. BJ used the chart and found that he needed to make ten hops to reach thirty-seven his way.

"The other way uses less hops," Kasey said.

"Both ways do work, but the first way does use fewer hops," I responded. "Does anyone have a way that uses fewer than seven hops?" No one did. "I guess seven is the least number of hops, so that is my score for this round." I wrote my score on the score sheet. "It's Kaitlyn's turn."

Mrs. Wickett	Kaitlyn
7	

Kaitlyn drew a card and got 97. She grinned and looked at the class. "I don't need any help with this one. I go one hundred-hop and three one-hops, and I'm there. Four hops is all I need." Kaitlyn recorded her score on her side of the score sheet.

I drew again and this time got 13. "I got a thirteen and I need your help," I told the class.

"That's easy," James said. "You do a one-hop and land on one, then you do a ten-hop and that puts you on eleven, and then do two more one-hops and you're on thirteen. It only takes four hops."

"You could just hop to ten," Kasey said, "and then one hop to eleven, another to twelve, and then one more to thirteen. That's four hops, too, but in a different order."

"I guess four is the fewest hops," I said. "I'll write the four under the seven for the first round and then add them together to see how many hops I've taken altogether."

Mrs. Wickett	Kaitlyn
7	4
+4	
11	

Kaitlyn took her turn. The students were starting to get restless and were eager to begin playing. I thanked Kaitlyn for being my partner and she returned to her seat. "You'll be playing the game with the person sitting beside you," I said. "You already have hundred charts and markers on your tables. I'll bring you paper to keep score and the number cards. You'll each need to keep your own score sheet, but you'll keep track of both scores on your own sheet, just as Kaitlyn and I were doing." I passed out the paper and number cards as I answered the usual questions about who should go first.

As I circulated I noticed most students were able to move about the board with ease and efficiency. I reminded partners to watch each other's moves and to be sure they agreed. Maritza and BJ called me over. "BJ thinks he can do a six-hop," Maritza complained.

"What are the three hops you can make?" I asked, directing my question to both students.

"One-hops, ten-hops, and hundred-hops," Maritza said.

"Do you agree?" I asked BJ.

"Yeah," BJ responded.

"If you can't do a six-hop, what other way could you use to get to six?" I asked.

"Six one-hops," BJ replied.

"Do you agree?" I asked Maritza. She nodded. I left the two to resume their game. I then watched Sonny and Shamera for a moment.

"Sonny has eleven and he just had to hop seven," Shamera explained.

"How many does Sonny have now?" I asked.

"Ten and seven is easy, that's seventeen, and then one more because it was eleven, not ten, so that's eighteen," Sonny explained.

"Do you agree?" I asked Shamera.

"It's eighteen," Shamera agreed. "I counted on my fingers: eleven, twelve, thirteen, fourteen, fifteen, sixteen, seventeen, eighteen."

"Shamera has fifteen and Sonny has eighteen," I said. "Who is winning?"

"Shamera," both children replied at once.

"She has the least," Sonny said.

"How many fewer does Shamera have?" I asked. Both students thought for a moment. Shamera used her fingers to keep track as she counted from fifteen to eighteen.

"I know," Sonny said suddenly. "I have three more than Shamera, so Shamera has three less than me!" Sonny was quite surprised and pleased by this discovery. I left the children to continue playing their game.

Kasey and Kaitlyn then called me over. "We think we have an idea about this," Kasey said with considerable confidence. "We think if you get a number in the middle of the row, it will take more hops to get to it then if you get a number at the end or the beginning."

"Give me an example to help me better understand your thinking," I said.

"If you get ninety-seven, you can get there in four hops," Kasey explained as she also demonstrated using the hundred chart.

"And a number like ninety-six, which is more in the middle, would take five hops," Kaitlyn added.

"Why do you think that is?" I asked.

The girls looked at each other and then started talking between themselves. "Would you like to think about it and I'll come back in a few minutes?" I asked. I made the decision to let them choose if they wanted further assistance from me because they seemed to be making sense of the situation on their own.

"Yeah, come back!" Kasey said. As I walked off, the girls put their heads together and were involved in an animated discussion.

"Look," Dane said, "Jacob and I are tied. We only have one more turn each."

Each boy had a score of 23. "How many hops have the two of you made together?" I asked. I paused to give them a moment to think about this. Dane looked at the hundred chart and decided to use it as a way to figure out the sum. Jacob seemed oblivious to what Dane was doing, totally absorbed in his own thinking. Dane looked up, ready to tell me his answer. I asked him to whisper it in my ear to give Jacob a chance to finish his thinking.

"I know now," Jacob said.

"What did you come up with?" I asked.

"It's forty-six," Jacob said.

"Do you agree?" I asked Dane. Dane nodded.

"How did you figure it out?" I asked Jacob.

"I did two tens and two tens from the twenty-threes. That's four tens, or forty. Then I did three and three and that's six, so it's forty-six," Jacob explained.

"Dane, show us how you used the hundred chart," I said.

"I went to twenty-three, then went down two squares, ten and twenty, so I had to go over three to make twenty-three, and I landed on forty-six," Dane said.

"We both agree!" Jacob said.

I checked back with Kasey and Kaitlyn next. "What have you found?" I asked.

"I think the ones on the end get less hops because the only way you can get to the middle is with one-hops and the more in the middle it is, the more one-hops you have to do," Kaitlyn explained. Kasey listened, quietly nodding that she agreed with Kaitlyn's explanation.

"Do you have anything to add?" I asked Kasey. She shook her head "no."

After most of the students had finished their first game, I called them back to order. "What did you notice as you played the game?" I asked.

"It's sometimes better to get either real small numbers or real big numbers instead of in-the-middle numbers," Janelle shared.

"Tell me more," I encouraged her.

"Like, it works better to get ten than fifty," Janelle said. "You only need one one-hop to get to ten and five to get to fifty. Or ninety is good, too. You could do a hundred-hop and a ten-hop, and that's still less than it takes to get to fifty."

"Kasey and me think it's better to get numbers at the beginning or the end of the rows than in the middle of the rows," Kaitlyn explained.

"Yeah, it's because you can only get to the middle of the rows with one-hops, so you don't want to have to do too many one-hops," Kasey added.

"Do you mean it would be better to get twenty-one than twenty-five?" Greg asked thoughtfully. Kasey and Kaitlyn nodded as Greg thought about this. "Oh," Greg continued, "I think I get it; you have to do one one-hop for twenty-one and five one-hops for twenty-five!"

No one had anything else to add.

"Can we play again?" Derrick asked.

"You'll have a chance to play again if you make that choice during menu time," I replied.

EXTENSIONS

1. Have less confident students play in partner pairs. The partner pairs decide on four target numbers. Both partner pairs use the same four target numbers. Working together, each pair tries to move to each of the four target numbers in the fewest hops. The pair who has the lowest total hops wins. As students gain skill with the game, tie scores will result.

2. Once students are familiar with the activity, use it as a warm-up. Post a target number on the board and have the students work to find the fewest hops needed to reach the target number.

3. Increase the difficulty by playing on a two hundred or three hundred chart.

Questions and Discussion

▲▲

▲ *Why did you teach the activity using the sequence described in the vignette?*

I chose to introduce the activity as a whole-group activity, followed by small groups, then pairs, and finally as a game. The activity can be confusing and the game requires additional instructions for scorekeeping. When I introduced it as a game rather than going through the sequence described, some children were overwhelmed and frustrated. A learning opportunity was lost for these students. The sequence in the vignette keeps all students involved, excited, and successful, thus increasing the likelihood of learning and deepening mathematical understanding.

▲ *Can this game be used as a menu or choice-time activity?*

This game, along with several others described in this book, makes an excellent menu or choice-time activity once it has been introduced and students are comfortable with how to play the game. As students gain additional experience with the game, leading class discussions to share what the children have discovered can deepen mathematical understanding.

▲ *What do you mean by a menu activity?*

A menu is a list of activities available for students to explore. During menu time, students make choices about how they use their time and what they learn about and explore. Because students work independently or in pairs, menu activities should be familiar to students or have directions simple enough that students can read and follow them themselves. Menus can provide children with additional meaningful practice of concepts and skills that have already been introduced.

An added benefit of menu time is that the teacher has time to talk with students to probe and assess understanding or to give those who need it additional help or added challenges.

CHAPTER ELEVEN
THE GAME OF TENS AND ONES

Overview

The game of *Tens and Ones* provides students with an opportunity to use the 0–99 chart to play a game involving the addition and subtraction of tens and ones. Students roll specially labeled dice to determine how they will move on the 0–99 chart. The goal is to be the first to reach 99. After students have had experience playing the game, they are shown two ways to record their game. One is to visually represent how they moved on the 0–99 chart, while the other uses number sentences to tell the story of the game. Writing the number sentences provides a way for students to link the structure of our base ten number system to the way it is represented numerically. Students also gain practice with addition and subtraction as they play the game.

Materials

▲ dice, 1 per pair of students, with faces labeled as follows: +10, +10, +10, –10, +1, –1
▲ 0–99 charts, 3 or 4 per student (see Blackline Masters)
▲ markers, 1 per student
▲ *The Game of Tens and Ones* record sheet, 2 or 3 per student (see Blackline Masters)
▲ optional: rules for the game of *Tens and Ones* to distribute to students (see Blackline Masters)

Time

▲ one class period to introduce the game, then additional time for playing and discussion

Teaching Directions

1. Model the game by playing with a student. Follow the rules below.

The Game of Tens and Ones

You need:
- a partner
- 2 0–99 charts
- 2 markers
- 1 die with faces labeled +10, +10, +10, –10, +1, –1

Rules
1. Each player places a marker on the zero on his or her own 0–99 chart. Players take turns rolling the die.

2. Player 1 rolls the die and moves a marker according to the roll on his or her own 0–99 chart.

3. Player 1 checks that Player 2 agrees and then hands the die to Player 2.

4. Player 2 follows the same steps as Player 1, using his or her own chart.

5. The winner is the first player to move his or her marker to 99. To win, a player must land on 99 exactly. For example, if a player lands on 90 and rolls a +10 on the next turn, the player must pass, as there are only nine boxes from 90 to 99. Players may not move their markers past 99 and off the chart.

---

2. Have students play the game in pairs. As students play, ask them questions such as:

How far ahead of one player is another?

How many tens have you moved your marker?

How many more tens do you need to move your marker to reach ninety-nine? How many more ones?

How many spaces have you and your partner moved altogether?

3. On another day explain to the students how to record their games on the 0–99 chart. Players put an X on zero to show where they started the game. For each move, players color in the boxes where their markers land.

4. After students have had practice recording on 0–99 charts, explain how to record the game using number sentences to represent moves made. For example, a player is on 23 and rolls a 10. The player moves forward ten spaces, landing on 33. The number sentence would be 23 + 10 = 33. Make the *Game of Tens and Ones* record sheet available for students.

Teaching Notes

This game provides a context for adding and subtracting ones and tens. During the course of a game, students typically calculate between twenty and thirty addition and subtraction problems before reaching 99 on the 0–99 chart. This is meaningful practice, and the students' work in the following vignette was virtually error-free.

Students looked for patterns that resulted when one or ten was added or subtracted. While this was difficult for most students, it provided a foundation on which students could build their understanding.

This game also provides students with a context for recording number sentences. The moves in the game give meaning to the numbers in the number sentences used to record the game.

The Lesson

▲▲

DAY 1

I gathered the students around a large table so all could see what I was going to do. "Today we're going to use a zero to ninety-nine chart to play a game," I began. "You'll need a partner, a special die, two zero to ninety-nine charts, and two markers." As always when I mention that students will need partners, there was an initial move by the students to find a partner. In this case I asked for their attention, explaining to them I would assign partners later.

"To begin," I said, "each of you will use your own chart and place your marker on zero." I demonstrated as I talked. I asked DeAndre to be my partner and instructed him to place his marker on zero on his chart as I'd done on mine.

"The dice are special dice because the numbers on them are different from the numbers on regular dice," I explained as I held up a die.

"A die is a cube," Maya interrupted.

"That's correct," I responded, "but please remember to raise your hand if you have something you wish to say."

"How many faces are on a cube?" I then asked, taking Maya's lead.

"Six, I think, because a die is a cube and the numbers go to six on a die," Bonnie explained. The students nodded their agreement.

"Let's count the faces and see," I suggested. We quickly counted.

"A die has six faces and is a cube," I continued. "The faces of these dice aren't labeled one through six as they usually are. Three of the faces are labeled 'plus ten,' one face is labeled 'plus one,' one face is labeled 'minus one,' and the last face is labeled 'minus ten.' The plus and minus signs tell you something about how you move your marker on your zero to ninety-nine chart. What do you suppose they could tell you?" Most hands were up quickly.

Ellie explained, "The plus means you go forward and the minus means you go backward. The number probably means how many you have to go forward or backward."

"That's it," I said. "Here's a tricky part. If you can't move the way the die tells you, then you must pass and give the die to your partner. If I rolled a minus one for my first turn, could I move my marker?"

"You could but it would go off the chart," Dalton said.

"That's right, I'd have to move off the chart, so I can't use the minus one. If I rolled a minus one, I'd have to stay where I was, on zero, and pass the die to my partner, DeAndre."

"It would work if you added some more boxes," Samuel said.

"Where would I add them?" I asked.

"On the side," Abby suggested.

"On the bottom of the chart maybe," Karly suggested, then immediately changed her mind, adding, "Oh, that wouldn't make sense because that's where one hundred and numbers like that would go. Maybe on the top of the chart."

"Yeah," responded several other children quietly.

I redirected the lesson toward the game. "DeAndre and I are going to play so you can see what to do when you play," I said. DeAndre chose to have me go first.

"I rolled a minus one," I said sadly. "What now?"

"You lose your turn because you'd have to move off the chart and you can't do that," Abby said with a giggle.

"That means l have to pass the die to DeAndre," I said.

DeAndre rolled a +10. The students cheered for DeAndre as he carefully moved his marker ten squares on his chart, landing on 10.

"What's a number sentence that I could write that would show what DeAndre did?" I asked. The students thought for a few moments and hands started to go up slowly. I waited until about half were up. I called on Angie.

"You could write zero plus ten equals ten," Angie said.

I recorded Angie's suggestion on the board:

$0 + 10 = 10$

"Explain why your number sentence tells about DeAndre's turn," I said.

"Well, the zero tells where DeAndre started," Angie explained. "His marker was on zero when he rolled the die. Then he rolled plus ten and that's the 'plus ten' part, and when he counted up ten boxes, his marker was on ten and that's the 'equals ten' part."

DeAndre handed me the die and I rolled +1. "I'm starting on zero," I said. "The die is telling me to move forward one on my chart, so now I'm on one. What number sentence would tell the story of my turn?"

"Zero plus one equals one," Samuel said. "The zero is where you started, the 'plus one' is how many boxes you moved, and the 'equals one' is where you landed."

"Here's how we can write what Samuel said using numbers," I said as I wrote on the board:

$0 + 1 = 1$

"To show I'm all finished with my turn, I'm handing the die to DeAndre," I said to reinforce this rule for the students.

DeAndre rolled a –1. "That means I have to go back one. I guess I'll be on nine now," he said with a sigh as he moved his marker back one on his chart.

"What number sentence should I write?" I asked.

Maya said, "Ten minus one equals nine." I recorded:

$10 – 1 = 9$

"DeAndre's at nine and I'm at one. How many boxes would I have to move to catch up to DeAndre?" I asked.

I paused, watching the students carefully as they thought about this question. Some seemed to have an answer almost immediately while others used their fingers to point to the boxes as they counted the difference. A few counted the boxes more than once. "Who would like to share?" I asked. Most hands were up immediately, as the students had had a few moments to solve the problem before I asked for volunteers to share. "Show me with your fingers what you think the answer is," I said to the class. Almost all were showing eight fingers. "It looks to me like you think the answer is eight. Who would like to share your thinking?"

"I just counted the squares beginning with two and went to nine, and there were eight," Allie explained.

I recorded on the board:

start with 2: 3, 4, 5, 6, 7, 8, 9   eight squares

"How many of you solved it like Allie?" I asked. About half the students raised their hands. "Who has a different way?"

"I just did nine minus one because DeAndre is on nine and Mrs. Wickett is on one, so nine minus one," Dalton shared.

I recorded Dalton's idea:

9 – 1 = 8

"My idea is sort of like Allie's but different," Angie said. "I thought in my brain, 'One plus something is nine. Hmm, what's the something? Well, one plus eight is nine,' so I knew it must be eight boxes."

I recorded Angie's idea on the board:

1 + □ = 9   □ = 8

"I just counted on my fingers is all," Katya said. "I started on one and then said 'two' and put up one finger, 'three,' put up another finger, so that's two fingers altogether, and kept doing that until I got to nine, and I had eight fingers up." Katya demonstrated her method as she talked. "It's really sort of like the first way except instead of counting the boxes, I was using my fingers."

"Mine is sort of like Katya's and Allie's except backwards," Abby said. "I started at nine and counted the boxes until I got to one."

I recorded Abby's strategy on the board:

start at 9, then count backward:
8, 7, 6, 5, 4, 3, 2, 1   eight boxes

"I have a way that is sort of different," Ramon volunteered. "I knew that to go

from zero to ten it was ten spaces. So Mrs. Wickett moved one space, so that was only nine, and then DeAndre had to move one back, so that was eight."

I recorded Ramon's idea on the board:

0 + 10 = 10
10 – 1 = 9
9 – 1 = 8

There were no further suggestions. The students seemed to have the idea of the game and were eager to get started. "There's one last rule you need to know. When it gets close to the end of the game, remember that you can't go off the board. That means you must use all of the number you roll and land on ninety-nine, or pass the die to your partner." I didn't dwell on this point because I knew most students would not remember it and it would make more sense to them if I explained it as it came up during the game.

I asked the students to return to their seats. They were seated in groups of four. Once they were settled, I explained that their partner would be the person sitting next to them. I reviewed the rules with them quickly and showed them where they could get the 0–99 charts, dice, and markers.

Observing the Students

As the students got to work there were the usual questions such as who goes first, who should get the materials, where they should put their markers, and so on. I answered the various questions, then looked around the room and noticed that most students were involved in playing the game. The noise level was high, but the students were engaged and cooperating by checking each other's moves and passing the die rather than grabbing it. I noticed that a few students knew that if they rolled a +10 or a –10, they could just move their marker down or up one space; however, most of the students had to count out ten spaces. As the games progressed, a few more students figured this out and started using this strategy.

Rachel and Dalton were especially focused on their game, discussing each move that was made. Dalton's marker was on 52 and Rachel's was on 70. "How many spaces would I have to move from fifty-two to get to seventy?" I asked. Both students thought quietly for a moment. Rachel started to move down her chart, counting by tens, while Dalton counted each individual box. I asked Rachel to wait just a moment before telling me her answer to give Dalton a chance to finish figuring. Both students figured eighteen as their answer.

"Rachel's marker is on seventy. How many more does she need to win the game?" I asked.

Rachel immediately responded with "Thirty," while Dalton counted the boxes one by one from 70 to 99.

"Twenty-nine," he said.

"Huh?" Rachel responded with a confused look on her face.

I paused, giving Rachel a chance to sort out her confusion before intervening. Then I said, "Explain how you got thirty."

"I started with seventy and counted by tens to one hundred. Eighty, ninety, one hundred," Rachel explained, holding up three fingers for each of the three tens she had counted. "Ten, twenty, thirty," she said as she counted by tens for each of the three fingers she had held up.

"Dalton," I began, "explain how you got twenty-nine."

"I started with seventy and counted the boxes to ninety-nine," Dalton explained. "It was twenty-nine boxes."

"*Ooohhh*, man!" Rachel said with a giggle, "I know what happened. The chart only goes to ninety-nine, but when I counted I figured it out like it went clear to one hundred! Now I get it. Dalton's right. It is twenty-nine."

"Thanks for letting me interrupt your game to talk with you," I said before I moved on.

I then watched quietly for a few moments as Ellie and Antonio played. I noticed that Antonio easily and accurately moved up and down the chart when he rolled a +10 or −10, while Ellie needed to count each box. I moved on to observe Conner and Bonnie. Conner could move down the chart easily when he rolled a +10, but when he rolled a −10, he had to carefully count back one by one. After observing this, I decided to interrupt their game. "Conner, I notice that you seem to know what to do when you roll a plus ten," I said.

"That's easy," he explained. "You just go down a row. It works because when you add ten, you don't do anything to the ones; you just add another ten. Like, in this column, all the numbers end with eight, so I just knew they were ten apart."

"I also noticed that minus ten did not seem so easy. Why is that?" I probed.

"Um, maybe because I have to count back by ones and it takes longer and take away is much harder for me because it goes backwards or something," Conner explained.

I took another marker and laid it on Conner's chart. "I put a marker on twenty-five," I said. "Where will my marker be if I add ten?"

"Easy! Thirty-five!" Conner replied proudly.

"OK, now I want to move back ten. Where will my marker be?" I asked.

"That's the hard part," Conner said. "Can I use the chart to count?"

"See if you can figure it out without counting on the chart first," I said, hoping he might make the connection that minus ten was the opposite of the plus ten he'd just done. After a few moments I could see his frustration building. "Go ahead and use the chart to help you," I said. He counted back ten boxes and landed on 25. "Did you notice what happened?" I asked.

"I came back to where I started," Conner said. "I went forward ten and then when I went back ten, I was in the same spot again." Conner seemed to be thinking about this, so I left him to think and continue playing the game.

As I continued to ask partners about the difference between their markers or how many more boxes were needed for one player to finish the game, I was surprised at how many students had to count by ones to figure the answers to these questions. A few students did count down the chart by tens to figure the tens and then across to figure the ones, but most had to count by ones. These students had had previous experience counting by tens beginning with any number and I had expected them to apply this prior information to this new situation. This reminded me that I must be careful about assumptions I make about students' understanding and when and how they might apply it.

DAY 2

To give the students additional experience and opportunity to apply their understanding of ones and tens, I decided to have them spend another day playing the game. I began by showing the students an overhead transparency of the 0–99 chart.

"Today we are going to play the same game we played yesterday, only I am going to have you record what happens each time it's your turn," I explained.

"Like a game story?" Angie wondered aloud.

"Yes, that's one way of thinking about it," I replied.

"You'll record right on your zero to ninety-nine chart," I explained as I placed a transparency of a 0–99 chart on the overhead projector. "To begin your story, place an X on zero because that's where your marker will be," I continued. "Next, roll the die and move your marker according to what the die tells you. If I roll a plus ten, then I could move ten spaces."

"Or you could just move your marker one space down, right below where it is now," Karly suggested.

"Would Karly's idea work?" I asked the class. The students started talking and sharing ideas among themselves. In order to give them all a chance to have their ideas heard, I asked them to talk with their partners. After a few moments, I asked for their attention. Many hands were up and students were eager to share their thinking.

"I think it'd be better to start with zero and count to ten. That way each box will get counted and there won't be any that get skipped," Allie said.

"Maybe for another number besides ten that would be good," Bonnie said. "But with ten, all I have to do is move down one space because I already know it takes ten to get there. I know because I have counted it about a hundred million times or so!"

"Does anyone have any different ideas?" I asked. I had not expected the students to have any other ideas, as I had listened when they shared with their partners and their thinking seemed to fit one of the two ways shared, but I asked to be sure. No one had anything further to add.

"You may choose either way of moving your marker as long as what you are doing makes sense to you and you can explain it," I said. I returned to explaining the game.

"I have marked an X to show where I put my marker at the beginning," I reviewed. "Now I'll roll the die and see how I can move. I rolled a minus one. I can't do that, so I have to pass the die to my partner."

Because the students had already played the game and my goal was to show them a method of recording, I did not actually model the game this time by playing with a partner. I told the students that since they knew how to play the game, they could pretend I had a partner. This would save time and show them how to record their games. This was not a problem for them.

"Pretend my partner took her turn, recorded her move on her chart, and handed the die back to me. Now it's my turn to roll," I said as I rolled the die and got a +1.

"I got a plus one, so I get to move one space, starting with zero and landing on one," I said as I moved my marker. "I can show this by coloring in the box with one since I landed on one." I quickly colored the box.

"My turn again," I continued as I rolled the die. "I rolled a plus ten. Where will I put my marker?" I asked the class.

"Eleven!" they replied.

I placed my marker on 11. "I began on one, rolled a plus ten, and moved to eleven. How should I show this?" I asked.

"Color in the eleven on the chart," came the reply. I did this.

"My turn again and I rolled a minus one. What should I do now?" I asked.

"Go back one space to number ten," Angie volunteered.

"I noticed something," Ramon said. "You were on eleven and that space is colored and then you had to go back one space because of the minus one you rolled and now you're on ten. You could put an arrow that goes from eleven to ten to show you had to go back one space."

"Cool idea, Ramon," DeAndre blurted out.

"If you'd like, you may use Ramon's idea of using arrows to show the directions if that makes sense to you," I said. "I think you have the idea of how to record your game. Are there any questions?" There were none. I reminded the students about the materials they needed and where they were. Almost all the students were instantly engaged in the game. As I observed the students, I noticed that a few more of them were able to move down one square rather

than counting by ones when they rolled a +10. A –10 still presented a challenge for most students.

Some students may become confused when they land on the same number more than once. One way to help avoid confusion is to have them use arrows, as suggested by Ramon. Another way is to have them color the number a different color each time they land on it. A third possibility is to have them use a checkmark to show each time they land on a number.

Dalton called me over with a giggle. "Look," he said, "I'm stuck. I rolled plus one and then plus ten and then minus ten and then plus ten. I keep going back and forth! I need some luck!"

Abby, Dalton's partner, seemed to be having better luck. While Dalton's marker was on 11, Abby's was on 41. "Tell me the story of your game so far," I said.

Using her chart, Abby explained, "I rolled a plus ten first. So I moved my marker from zero to ten. Then I rolled and got a plus ten again. That's how I got to twenty."

I interrupted Abby to ask, "How many tens are there in twenty?" She paused to think about this.

"Oh," Abby began, "I know, three, no wait . . . two. Yeah, two. I rolled two tens to get to twenty, so there must be two. Ten, twenty—that's two tens!"

Abby continued with her explanation. "I rolled another plus ten to get to thirty. My luck was swollen with plus tens! Then I rolled a plus one and went to thirty-one. Then my luck was swollen again and I got a plus ten and landed on forty-one."

"How many tens are in forty-one?" I asked Abbey.

"That's hard!" Abby replied. Dalton had been listening and was also thinking about the question. He picked up the die and examined it carefully as if it held the answer.

"I know," he said. "I used the die to figure it out. There would be four tens in forty-one. I thought to myself, 'How many plus tens would I have to roll?' There are three plus tens on the die, so I counted those up and that was thirty. Then I counted one more ten and that was forty. Anymore tens and then it would be too much."

Abby listened carefully to Dalton. To check his idea, she used her fingers to keep track of tens as she counted, putting up one finger for each ten. "He's right!" she said. I left the students to continue playing.

I watched Rachel and DeAndre for a moment as Rachel won the game.

DeAndre looked up at me and said, "I got stuck. I kept rolling plus ten, minus ten, plus ten, minus ten, like that, and I kept going up and down the chart from fifty-one to sixty-one to fifty-one to sixty-one. And Rachel just kept getting plus tens."

"Well, I did mostly get plus ten." Rachel said. "But I got a plus ten, then another plus ten, then a minus one. That's how I got to nineteen. Then I just got plus tens!" As I looked around the room, most students were close to finishing their games. I gave a two-minute warning signal, indicating their time to play the game was almost up. At the end of two minutes, I asked for the students' attention.

"What did you notice about the game?" I asked. I paused until most students had their hands raised. I called on Shawn.

"When you roll a ten, you can move fast. But in the last row, it's bad because you have to use up all of your number," Shawn said.

"I got stuck in the last row on ninety," Angie shared. "I thought I could win by rolling a plus ten, but there was no box under ninety, and when I counted there were only nine boxes left on the chart."

"Were you stuck for the rest of the game?" I asked.

"No, I rolled a minus one and moved to eighty-nine, and then I rolled a plus ten and landed on ninety-nine," Angie said.

"I noticed something about the dice," Conner said. "There are mostly plus tens, and it seems like I rolled mostly plus tens." Several other students indicated their agreement with Conner's observation.

"There's only one plus one," Antonio said, "and I think that's why it was so hard for me to win the game. I got to ninety and then I had to keep rolling ones if I wanted to move. It took a while!"

"Wow! That would take nine rolls if you only got plus ones!" Andy added. "That's a lot!"

"Can we play again?" Karly asked.

"Yes," I replied. "There's another way I would like to teach you to record your games. Would you like to learn it now or wait to learn it and play another game first?" Most students wanted to know my other way of recording. The purpose of the game was to give children experience adding and subtracting tens and ones and the opportunity to notice patterns when this occurs. Coloring in the squares provided a visual model for them to consider. My second way of recording was less concrete. I wanted them to use mathematical notation to represent their moves. The game provided a context for writing number sentences that connect to a real situation.

"In the last game, you told the story of your game by coloring in boxes to show your moves," I explained. "This time you'll tell the story of your game using numbers. For example, I begin on zero as always. Then if I roll a plus ten, I move to box ten by counting across by ones or by moving one square down. I could show this as a number sentence." I wrote the following on the board:

$$0 + 10 = 10$$

"Why do you suppose I wrote a zero first?" I asked.

"That's where you began," Shawn said.

"What about the 'plus ten'?" I asked.

"I think that's what you rolled," DeAndre said.

"I know what the 'equals ten' stands for," Katya said. "It's where you landed at the end of your turn." Since I had recorded in this way when I introduced the game the day before, the recording made sense to the children.

"That's what I was thinking," I said. "I'd like a volunteer to help me show you more clearly." I invited Katya to be my partner. I drew two large rectangles to represent paper on the board. To help students organize their work, I divided each of the rectangles into sixteen smaller rectangles.

Katya		Mrs. Wickett	

Katya and I each placed our marker on the zero on our own chart. I rolled first. "I rolled a minus one. I can't do that or I'll go off the chart and that's against the rules. I have to skip my turn and give the die to Katya." I recorded nothing for that turn, as I had to pass. Katya rolled a +10. She moved her marker to 10 on her chart. Then she looked to me for guidance.

"Your number sentence should tell a story about your turn. Where did you start?" I asked her.

"Zero," she replied.

"That's the beginning of your story—where you started," I said.

Katya recorded a zero in the first box on her recording sheet.

"What did the die tell you to do?" I asked.

"Go ten boxes," Katya said. "Should I write 'plus ten' next to tell I moved ten boxes?" I nodded my head "yes." "I get it, then I should write 'equals ten' because that's where my marker is now." Katya completed her number sentence and handed me the die.

Katya	
0+10=10	

"I rolled a plus one," I said. "My number sentence should begin with zero because that's where my marker was at the beginning of my turn. Then I'll write 'plus one,' because that's what I rolled on the die and how far I moved on my chart. The 'equals one' tells where my marker is at the end of my turn." I handed the die to Katya.

Mrs. Wickett	
0+1=1	

Katya rolled a +1. She smiled and moved her marker forward one space on her chart, to 11. In the second box on her recording sheet on the board she wrote: *10 + 11 = 1.* Several children snickered, and I reminded them about how they needed to treat others.

"Where did you start, Katya?" I asked.

"On ten," she replied.

"What did you roll on the die?" I continued.

"Plus one," she replied.

"Your number sentence tells me you rolled an eleven. How could you fix it to show what you really rolled?" I asked.

"Oh," Katya whispered after a moment's thought and then she erased the 11. "I rolled a one, not an eleven. I landed on the eleven, so my sentence should be 'ten plus one equals eleven.' I get it now."

Katya and I played a couple more rounds in front of the class. Then the other children got to work playing the game. As before, the children found the game engaging and were immediately involved. For most children, the recording was not a problem. Allie was confused in the same way as Katya had been. That is, in her number sentence, she tried to add the starting place and the ending place rather than adding the starting place and the number rolled on the die to give the ending place. I sat with her for a few turns, leading her through the same questions I had used with Katya, and soon she was able to record accurately.

As the students worked, I circulated, asking them questions such as: "Who is ahead? By how much? How many tens did it take to get to the space with your marker? How many ones? How many more times will you need to roll plus ten to get to the bottom row? Once you get to the bottom row, how many plus ones will you need to get to ninety-nine?" With some

students I would point to a number sentence they had written and ask them to show me using the chart what happened. Explaining the story behind the number sentence using their chart was something the students especially enjoyed doing. Also, I asked students to look over the number sentences they had written to find patterns. Ramon noticed that the ones place of the starting number was the same as the ones place of the ending number each time he added ten. Angie noticed that the ones place of the starting number increased by one when one was added, but it was the tens place of the ending number that increased by one when ten was added and the ones place stayed the same. Unlike Ramon and Angie, finding patterns for most children was difficult. They needed more time and experience.

EXTENSIONS

1. As students gain experience and confidence in this game, change the numbers on the dice. For example, replace one +10 with +20.

2. Another way to challenge students is to start at ninety-nine and move back to zero using a die labeled –10, –10, –10, +10, +1, and –1.

Questions and Discussion

▲▲▲

▲ *What is the role of discussion during this lesson?*

Discussion is key to student learning in this lesson. Through discussion, students are confronted with misconceptions and must explain their thinking. Explaining their thinking is a very effective way for them to clarify and solidify ideas. Also, through discussion, students hear new ideas and I gain insight into how they are thinking.

▲ *How do you know what questions to ask?*

I have two purposes for asking questions: to push children's thinking or to assess their understanding. Often these two purposes overlap. When I plan a lesson, I clarify the math goal for myself. Then I have a starting place for thinking about questions to ask. These questions provide a framework on which to "hang" the lesson. As the lesson progresses and the students raise questions and issues, I adjust my questioning so that I can better understand what they are thinking. Students' misconceptions provide another source of questions. One important aspect of questioning is to listen carefully to what students actually say, not what you'd like them or expect them to say.

CHAPTER TWELVE
TARGET NUMBERS

Overview

This activity provides students practice combining ones and tens to reach a target number. The activity and the resulting discussions help students relate tens and ones to the notation of the base ten number system. In addition, students gain flexibility with reasoning numerically and also have the opportunity to practice computing mentally.

Materials

▲ 3-by-5-inch index cards, 1–2 per student
▲ optional: dice, 1 per pair of students with faces labeled +10, +10, +10, –10, +1, and –1
▲ optional: 0–99 charts, 1 per student for reference (see Blackline Masters)

Time

▲ one class period

Teaching Directions

1. Begin by writing on the board: *Target* _____.

2. Explain that the students' task is to figure out ways to reach the target number using the options on the dice from the game of *Tens and Ones*, by adding or subtracting ten or one.

3. Fill in the blank: *Target 12.*

4. Lead a discussion about different ways to reach twelve using the dice from the game of *Tens and Ones*. For example, starting on zero, rolling a +10, a +1, and a +1 would make twelve. Record students' explanations on the board.

5. Give the students the target number of fourteen. This time have them write at least two ways to go from zero to fourteen using the options on the dice. Ask them to write a short way and any other way they like.

6. For students who finish early, offer them the "challenge" number seventeen.

7. Lead a discussion for children to share how they reached fourteen and seventeen. Record their ideas on the board. Most likely a student will share rolling a +10 once and a +1 four times as a way to reach fourteen. If not, offer it as another way. Use this idea to link the numbers rolled on the die to how the number is written.

```
     1      4
   +10    +1
          +1
          +1
          +1
```

8. If needed, do a few more numbers together. Otherwise, allow students to choose their own target number, write it on one side of an index card, and on the other side, record one way to get to their target number.

9. Have a student share how to get to his or her target number while the rest of the class guesses the target number.

Teaching Notes

It's useful for students to have prior experience playing the game of *Tens and Ones* (see Chapter 11). Because of this experience, throughout the lesson I reminded them to think about the dice used to play the game as a way to think about reaching, or rolling, a target number. Using the dice to think about how to reach the target number provided a connection between using tens and ones and the way we represent numbers. It may be helpful to have the dice used to play the game of *Tens and Ones* available for students to look at, or you can list the possible moves on the board: *+10, –10, +1, –1*.

During the discussions there are opportunities for students to think about several ways to make target numbers. This kind of discussion helps build flexibility in reasoning numerically. For example, twenty-four can be made with twenty-four ones, two tens and four ones, or one ten and fourteen ones. Being able to think about numbers in these ways supports future work with addition and subtraction when regrouping is involved.

Near the end of the lesson students choose their own target numbers. As students share how they reached a number, the rest of the class tries to guess what the target number is. This provides students with an excellent opportunity to practice mental math skills.

The Lesson

▲▲▲

By playing the game of *Tens and Ones*, the students had become adept at adding and subtracting ones and tens on the 0–99 chart. When they rolled a +10, most knew they did not have to count ten boxes individually but could move the equivalent of plus ten by vertically moving down one space. They were not as quick when moving their marker if a –10 was rolled; many still had to count back ten by counting individual squares. I wanted to build on what students seemed to understand and begin to link it to the place value notation we use to represent numbers.

I wrote on the board:

Target _____

"In a moment, I am going to fill in the blank with a number," I explained. "I want you to think silently, in your brain, about the ways you could get from zero to the target number using the dice we have been using to play the game of *Tens and Ones* the past few days." As the students watched I filled in the blank:

Target 12

"I don't think you can do that in one roll, right?" Conner asked.

"Tell me more about your thinking," I encouraged.

"Well, you can only roll a plus one, minus one, plus ten, or minus ten," Conner explained, referring to the numbers on the face of the die.

"That makes sense," I responded. "I guess you'll have to think about getting from zero to the target number using more than one roll." With this piece of information, hands began to go up. I waited until most were up and then called on Shawn.

"You could roll plus ten, then plus one, plus one, plus one, minus one," Shawn said with a smile, indicating he was pleased with his cleverness.

"Where do you start?" I asked Shawn.

"Oh," Shawn said, "you start at zero and then do plus ten, plus one, plus one, plus one, minus one."

I recorded Shawn's idea on the board:

Shawn   0
          +10
          +1
          +1
          +1
          −1
          12

"Let's check Shawn's idea," I said as I started to solve the problem aloud.

"Isn't the answer fourteen?" Dalton asked, with a very confused look on his face. "There is a ten and four ones on the board."

"You're right, Dalton," I explained. "There's one ten and there are four ones written in the problem. The minus sign tells us we need to subtract the last one, not add it." I pointed to the plus and minus signs as I explained to Dalton.

"Let's count it together," I said. Together Dalton and I counted, "Ten plus one is eleven, plus one is twelve, plus one is thirteen, minus one is twelve."

"Oh, I see what happened now," he said.

"Does someone have a different way?" I asked.

"You could roll plus one twelve times," Ellie suggested.

I recorded Ellie's way on the board:

Ellie   0 + 1 + 1 + 1 + 1 + 1 + 1 + 1 + 1
          + 1 + 1 + 1 + 1 = 12

"Who has a different way?" I asked.

"You could do plus ten, minus ten, and then roll twelve plus ones," Angie suggested. I recorded:

Angie $0 + 10 - 10 + 1 + 1 + 1 + 1 + 1$
$+ 1 + 1 + 1 + 1 + 1 + 1 + 1 = 12$

"I have another way," Bonnie volunteered. "It's short. Roll a plus ten and plus two."

"That is short," I agreed. "But how can you roll a plus two using our dice?"

"Oh, you have to roll two plus ones for the plus two," Bonnie clarified.

I recorded:

Bonnie $0 + 10 + 1 + 1 = 12$

"You could do plus ten and then another plus ten and then minus one eight times," Tony said.

I recorded on the board:

Tony $0 + 10 + 10 - 1 - 1 - 1 - 1 - 1$
$- 1 - 1 - 1 = 12$

Samuel shyly raised his hand. Because he was generally reluctant and did not feel good about math, I was delighted. I called on him immediately. "I'm not sure if this is different or the same. It's kind of both," he explained very tentatively. "Could you roll a plus one, a plus ten, and one more plus one?"

I recorded Samuel's idea on the board as follows:

Samuel $0 + 1 + 10 + 1 = 12$

"What makes you think this might be like one of the others already on the board?" I asked.

Samuel took his time responding. His classmates waited patiently for him. "I think it's kind of like Bonnie's. The numbers are the same."

"I agree so far with your thinking. What makes you think your idea is different?" I carefully probed.

"Well, they're in a different order," Samuel replied.

"You've just brought up an important idea in mathematics," I said. Samuel beamed. "In addition, the order in which you add the numbers doesn't matter. That means that whether we add the numbers

Bonnie's way or your way, the answer will still be twelve. Mathematicians call this idea the *commutative property*."

Now I wanted to change the direction of the conversation and move the students toward an informal discussion linking base ten notation with the rolls of the dice they'd been using. In an area of the board where I'd written both Bonnie's and Samuel's ideas, I wrote *12*. Pointing to the 2 in 12, I asked the students what that represented when rolling the dice. A few hands went up.

"Maybe it's the two plus ones," Antonio said. "Plus one two times would make two, and that's what I think." Several other students nodded, indicating Antonio's explanation made sense to them.

"Any other ideas?" I asked. There were none. "What about the one in twelve?" I asked, pointing to the 1.

"Oh, I know," Ramon said. "It's the plus ten. You had to roll a plus ten and two plus ones with Bonnie and Samuel's way."

I recorded on the board:

$$\begin{array}{ll} 1 & 2 \\ +10 & +1 \\ & +1 \end{array}$$

"I have a task for you to do." I said. "I'm interested to know what each of you is thinking, so I'm going to ask you to work by yourself. I'm going to give you a new target number, the number fourteen. First put your name on your paper. Then please write a short way, like Bonnie's and Samuel's ways, to get to the target number using our dice. Then figure out and write one other way to get to the target number of fourteen." As I explained, I briefly listed on the board the steps the students needed to follow.

Write your name on your paper.

Write a short way to get to 14.

Write one other way.

I handed each student a sheet of paper and most quickly went to work. A few students needed reassurance that they understood the task, then they also got to work.

As is typical of tasks such as this, some students finished before others. As students finished, I talked with them about their work, and offered a "challenge number." The challenge number was seventeen. Seventeen is interesting because the shortest way using rolls of the dice would be two +10s and three –1s rather than one +10 and seven +1s. A few finished the challenge number and wanted a harder number still. When asked what a harder number was, the students typically thought it was a larger number. I gave these few students thirty-nine. By this time, most students had finished with both the original number, fourteen, and the challenge number, seventeen. I asked for the students' attention.

We briefly discussed the shortest way to make fourteen and determined it was one +10 and four +1s. I wrote on the board:

$$1 \qquad 4$$
$$+10 \qquad +1$$
$$+1$$
$$+1$$
$$+1$$

"Who would like to share a short way you could get seventeen with our dice?" I asked. My reason for asking for a short way for both seventeen and fourteen was to use students' experience as the bridge to understanding the notation we use to represent numbers.

"You could roll a plus ten and seven—I mean, seven plus ones," Ellie shared.

I recorded Ellie's way on the board:

Ellie $0 + 10 + 1 + 1 + 1 + 1 + 1 + 1 + 1$
             $= 17$

Rachel shared next. "You could roll two plus tens—that's twenty—then roll three minus ones. That would be twenty, minus one is nineteen, minus one more is eighteen, then minus one more is seventeen." I recorded:

Rachel $0 + 10 + 10 - 1 - 1 - 1 = 17$

"These are two short ways to roll seventeen," I said. "Does anyone have another way?" No one did.

"Let's look at Ellie's way," I said, again wanting to take the opportunity to link place value notation to the context of the dice. "What does the one in seventeen tell us?" Many hands went up quickly. I called on Tony.

"It means there is one ten," Tony replied confidently.

"What about the seven in seventeen? What does that tell us?" I continued.

"It tells you someone had to roll plus one seven times," Angie explained.

I recorded the information on the board as I had done for twelve and fourteen:

$$1 \qquad 7$$
$$+10 \qquad +1$$
$$+1$$
$$+1$$
$$+1$$
$$+1$$
$$+1$$
$$+1$$

While Rachel's way of getting seventeen was shorter than Ellie's, it did not clearly connect to how we write numbers.

I then wrote 21 on the board. "How could I get this using our dice?" I asked.

"Easy!" Dalton announced. "You roll two plus tens for the twenty—ten plus ten equals twenty—and then a plus one for the one in twenty-one."

"I noticed that the numbers in the number, like the two and the one in twenty-one, tell you how many tens and ones!" Conner said.

"I don't think I get that," Samuel said.

The students started talking to Samuel at once. I quieted them and reminded them they should raise their hands if they had something to share. Several hands went up. I called on Antonio.

"OK, Conner said that the numbers tell you how many tens and ones you had to roll, or how many tens and ones," Antonio began. "To get to twenty-one you would have to roll two plus tens and that would be twenty. Ten plus ten makes twenty. Then to get twenty-one, the one in twenty-one tells you you need one more plus one." Conner nodded his agreement with Antonio's explanation. Samuel still looked a bit unsure, but I decided to go on and check back on his understanding after a bit more discussion. I recorded:

$$2 \qquad 1$$
$$+10 \qquad +1$$
$$+10$$

"I know another way of rolling the die to get twenty-one," Karly said. "You could roll just one plus ten and then roll eleven plus ones and that would make twenty-one."

I recorded on the board:

Karly
$$2 \qquad 1$$
$$+10 \qquad +1$$
$$+1$$
$$+1$$
$$+1$$
$$+1$$
$$+1$$
$$+1$$
$$+1$$
$$+1$$
$$+1$$
$$+1$$

"With Karly's way, are there still two groups of ten in twenty-one?" I asked. "Talk with your neighbor. To be sure each of you has the chance to speak, I'll tell you when to change speakers." Initially the room was quiet, but after a few seconds of studying what I had written on the board, the students began to discuss my question. After thirty seconds, I reminded the students to change speakers. Then after another thirty seconds, I asked for the students' attention.

Many students had their hands up, ready to share. I called on Tony.

"Maya and I think there's another group of ten." Tony explained. "It's just on the side with all the ones. There are eleven ones, so you could take a group of ten ones and that would leave one one." Maya nodded her agreement.

"How can the ones be ten?" Allie asked . "They're on the ones side."

"If you wanted, you could put ten of the ones into one group of ten and move it to the tens side," Angie explained. Angie came to the board and circled ten of the +1s. "See, there are ten ones in the circle. Ten ones is the same as one ten."

"It's like money," Ramon said. "Ten pennies and one dime are worth the same amount."

"Can we make up our own numbers and tell how many plus tens and plus ones we need?" DeAndre asked.

"I'll give you a choice. I have one last thing I would like you to do today. I'm going to give you an index card," I said as I held up a 3-by-5-inch card. "On one side put your own target number. On the other side, show how you could reach that number using the dice." Using an index card, I modeled by writing the number *15* on one side and on the other, I wrote: *0 + 10 + 1 + 1 + 1 + 1 + 1.* "If you're still a little confused, you may choose to stay here and we can work together some more." All but four children immediately got to work choosing their own number and explaining how many tens and ones were needed to make it. With the small group, we explored how to make sixteen and then twenty-four using tens and ones as we had with the dice. This little bit of reinforcement seemed to build their confidence and they were able to join their classmates. As the students worked, I circulated, looking over their shoulders and reading their work.

Tony had written on one side of his card: *0 + 10 + 10 + 10 + 10 + 10 + 10 + 10 +*

1. "Let me see if I can figure out the number you have written on the back side based on what I can see," I said. "Is the number on the other side seventy-one?" I asked.

Tony grinned and turned his card over to show me that 71 was on the other side. (See Figure 12–1.) "What does the seven in seventy-one tell us?" I asked.

"You need seven," Tony said with a questioning voice.

"I'm not sure what you mean. There's no seven on the die," I replied as I handed him a die to look at.

"Ahhm, you need to . . ." Tony paused. He looked at the list of +10s and +1 he had written on his card, then quietly began to count the +10s. "Oh, the seven means I have to roll seven plus tens! And the one means I have to roll one plus one."

"What if my number were seventeen?" I probed.

"Oh, that's easy. That would be one ten and seven ones," Tony responded.

When most students had finished, I gathered them on the rug. I asked for a few volunteers to read the series of numbers on their cards so we could try to guess their target number. I called on Katya.

"I wrote ten plus one, plus one, plus one, plus one, plus ten, plus ten," Katya said. (See Figure 12–2.) Most students raised their hands to guess her target number. Katya called on Bonnie.

"Thirty-four," Bonnie replied.

"Yep! That's my number," Katya said.

I called on Samuel next. "I did one hundred minus ten, minus ten, minus ten, minus ten, minus ten," Samuel said with a sly grin.

"It's sixty," Allie said.

"Nope, I don't think so," Samuel replied. He paused to double-check his work.

"It's fifty. You started at one hundred and you subtracted five tens, so it has to be fifty," Angie said.

"That's right," Samuel said, slightly disappointed he hadn't stumped the class a bit longer.

"Hey, I did fifty a different way," Conner said. "I did four tens and then ten ones and that's forty plus ten, which is fifty." (See Figure 12–3.)

"I have a tricky one," Rachel said. "Start with one hundred, then minus one, minus one, minus ten, minus ten, minus one, minus ten, minus ten, plus one, plus one, plus one, plus one." (See Figure 12–4.)

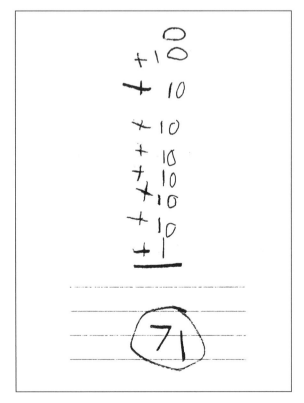

▲▲▲▲▲Figure 12–1 *Tony showed how to make 71 using 10s and 1s.*

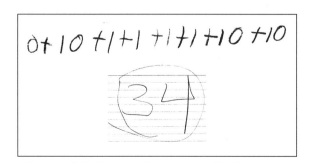

▲▲▲▲▲Figure 12–2 *Katya's problem.*

▲▲▲▲▲▲Figure 12–3 *Conner got to 50 in another way.*

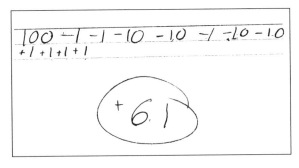

▲▲▲▲▲▲Figure 12–4 *Rachel shared a long problem.*

"That was a long problem, Rachel," I said. "Please read it again, a little slower, so everyone has the chance to think about it carefully." Rachel reread the problem slowly. A few hands went up. Rachel called on Andy.

"Seventy-one," Andy said.

"No, that's not it," Rachel replied.

"Maybe sixty," Allie said with uncertainty.

"No, that's not it either," Rachel said, giggling.

"It's sixty-one," Ramon said.

"That's it," Rachel said.

The students enjoyed the activity and seemed to be making some connections between the digits in numeric notation and what they represent in terms of tens and ones. Many more experiences would be needed, but most had a foundation on which to build and connect.

EXTENSIONS

1. Have students start somewhere else on the 0–99 chart. For example, start at 15 and figure out the moves needed to get to another number, such as 25, 28, 45, and so on. Choosing starting numbers and target numbers that are a multiple of ten apart (15 to 25 or 35, for example) gives children additional practice thinking about adding ten to a number.

2. A more difficult challenge would be to go from larger to smaller numbers, for example, from 37 to 24.

Questions and Discussion

▲▲▲

▲ *Why did you give the students a number like seventeen, for which there was a shorter way to reach than by adding one ten and seven ones?*

I chose the number seventeen as I didn't want students to become one-dimensional in their thinking. I wanted to give them a situation that would increase their flexibility in considering how numbers are composed. Also, this kind of thinking about numbers supports students' number sense when they are faced with a situation calling for rounding numbers. It helps students understand why seventeen is closer to twenty than it is to ten.

CHAPTER THIRTEEN
GUESS MY NUMBER

Overview

Instead of using concrete materials, *Guess My Number* engages students in comparing the sizes of numbers. Most children this age are able to count to one hundred (and beyond) and, given two numbers, tell which is greater and which is less. This game provides a way to reinforce children's familiarity with numbers.

Materials

▲ optional: rules for *Guess My Number*, 1 per student (see Blackline Masters)
▲ optional: 0–99 chart posted for children's reference, or copies of 0–99 chart for children who need it (see Blackline Masters)

Time

▲ one class period to introduce the game, then additional time for playing and discussion

Teaching Directions

1. Tell the students you are going to teach them a guessing game.

2. Choose a child to be your partner to demonstrate the game, or play the game with the entire class acting as your partner.

3. Pick a number from zero to ninety-nine and write it on a piece of paper. Do not let the children see the number you chose.

4. Ask your partner (or someone in the class) to guess what your number might be. Respond to the guess with a clue: "Your guess is greater than my number," or "Your guess is less than my number."

5. Continue until your partner has guessed your number.

6. You may want to play another game to be sure the children understand, or you may feel this isn't necessary.

7. Review the game by reading aloud the rules.

Teaching Notes

Most children this age are able to count to one hundred (and beyond) and, given two numbers, tell which is greater and which is less. Although these are important skills, they aren't necessarily indicators of children's understanding of the place value structure of numbers. Children usually learn the pattern of the sequence of numbers before they understand the meaning of the positions of the digits.

This activity gives students a context in which to use and interpret the vocabulary *greater* and *less* as they give clues to their partner about their partner's guess relative to their "mystery" number. Giving and interpreting clues reinforce children's understanding of numbers. Also, students must use logic to give clues to their partner and to make sense of the clues given to them.

Posting the 0–99 chart can help reinforce and support children whose understanding or confidence is weak. As an alternative to posting the 0–99 chart, make copies and distribute them to those children who would like them.

The Lesson

▲▲

The day before I planned to introduce *Guess My Number*, I gave Amelia and Molly a copy of the rules and asked them to try to figure out how to play the game from the directions on the sheet. I was fairly certain they would be successful and then could help me introduce the game to the class.

By the end of math time, Amelia and Molly said they felt confident that they understood the activity. "It's a good one," Molly said. "The kids will like the guessing." Molly often positioned herself in an adult-like way.

"Would you girls be interested in teach-

ing the rules to the rest of the class?" I asked. They were excited by the idea.

"When?" Amelia asked.

"How about tomorrow?" I replied.

The girls grabbed each other, jumping up and down.

"You'll need to prepare," I said, to calm them. "You have to be sure you know the rules and have a way to help the others learn them."

"We can practice during lunch," Amelia said. They returned to their seats. I began math class the next day by telling the children that Amelia and Molly were going to introduce *Guess My Number*. The girls came to the front of the room.

The girls were shy. "We're going to show you how to play *Guess My Number*," Molly said in a soft voice. Molly looked at Amelia and neither of them seemed to know what to do.

"Who will guess first?" I said, to help them.

"I will," Amelia said.

"OK," Molly said, coming to life a bit. "I pick a number and Amelia has to guess it."

"She gives me clues," Amelia added. "If my guess is too big, she says, 'Big,' and if it's too little, she says, 'Little.'" Amelia changed the language on the directions.

"Can you say 'higher' and 'lower'?" Tomo asked.

"No," Amelia said, quickly and definitively.

I decided to intervene. "I think that Tomo's idea is OK," I said, "as long as his clues make sense to his partner. Tomo's words mean the same. You could also say 'greater' or 'less.' "

The girls continued. "Where should I write the number?" Molly asked me.

I suggested that she do so on the board under the corner of a poster that was tacked above. "That way," I said, "your number will be hidden from Amelia after you write it."

Amelia covered her eyes while Molly wrote the number *86*. However, she reversed the 6 and some of the other students were confused.

"The six is backward," I said to her softly. She fixed it.

"I'm going to write my guesses on the board," Amelia said. "That's the job of the guesser." Amelia's first guess was eighty-nine. As she wrote the *8* on the board, there was a gasp from the class. When she wrote the *9*, the others sighed with relief.

"Big," Molly said.

Next, Amelia guessed fifty-seven, not at all helped by the reaction from the class. She wrote *57* to the left of 89 and left a good deal of space in between them.

"Small," Molly said.

Amelia's next guess was sixty-three, and she wrote it in between the 57 and the 89.

"Small," Molly said.

Amelia continued guessing, and the class joined Molly in giving the clues. I stopped Amelia when she guessed seventy-nine.

"Before you guess again," I said, "can you tell me what you know for sure?"

Amelia looked at the information on the board. She had written all of her guesses in order of size. "It's eighty."

"It doesn't have to be," Andrew called out. "It could be anywhere in the eighties."

"That's what I meant," Amelia said. She then guessed eighty-one, skipped to eighty-four, and worked her way up to eighty-six. Molly showed her the answer.

"This game is like Hot and Cold," Abby said.

During the presentation, Molly and Amelia were soft-spoken and a bit disorganized, and the rest of the class was a bit impatient. However, their introduction worked out fine in that the class understood how to play the game. The game was a popular one. Molly was right—the children enjoyed the guessing.

LINKING ASSESSMENT TO INSTRUCTION

As I observed the children playing *Guess My Number*, I focused on their systems for keeping track of their guesses and on their strategies for guessing. In this way, I was assessing their logical reasoning skills more than their understanding of place value.

When Amelia and Molly introduced the game, Amelia used a system for writing her guesses so that they were in numerical order. However, when I observed the children playing, I noticed that the children used a variety of record-keeping systems, some more useful than others.

Abby, for example, wrote the numbers in no particular order on her paper. As Seth, her partner, gave her responses, she wrote B or L above the numbers and put an X through them to show they were wrong. (See Figure 13–1.) When it was Seth's turn to guess, he attempted to write his guesses in numerical order, listing them vertically. (See Figure 13–2.) For his first game, he had difficulty spacing the numbers on the page and wound up with several lists of numbers. After several games, however, he was able to place them more efficiently. It was interesting to me to note that even after Abby and Seth had played half a dozen games, neither paid attention to the other's system; they both continued writing guesses in ways that made sense to them.

Colleen had a system, but it didn't help her with guessing. She numbered her guesses and listed them sequentially. Sometimes Colleen kept track of the clues she had received to zero in on the answer, but at other times she made seemingly random guesses that didn't give her any additional information. For example, after Colleen was given the clue that forty-five was too big, she guessed sixty-seven. Her partner, Corrine, used Colleen's numbering system for guesses, but I didn't notice her making redundant guesses. (See Figure 13–3.)

▲▲▲▲▲▲Figure 13–1 *Abby's system of recording was to write* B *or* L *over each number to indicate whether the guess was too big or too little.*

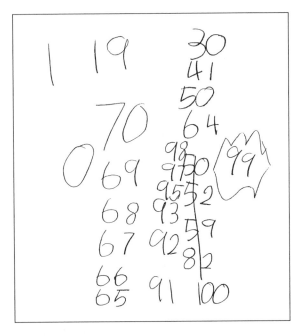

▲▲▲▲▲▲Figure 13–2 *Seth tried his numbers in order, but his system broke down as he made more guesses.*

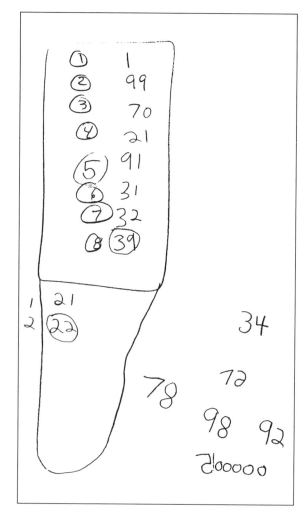

Corrine listed her guesses sequentially and numbered them.

A CLASS DISCUSSION ABOUT RECORD KEEPING

With about twenty minutes left, I began a discussion about the game. I was interested in having children explain their record-keeping methods. I didn't want to imply that some methods were better than others, but I did want to encourage children to choose a system that helped them keep track of their thinking. Also, I wanted children to see alternatives to the systems they were using so they would learn that there are different ways to record. My goal was to reinforce for children that they were to use methods that were useful and made sense to them.

"How are you keeping track of your guesses when you play?" I asked.

I called on Rudy. He explained his system, which was a variation of Seth's method of listing the numbers in order vertically. Rudy also explained how he chose numbers to guess. "I start with a number in the middle," he said, "and I write it in the middle of the paper. Then I have room to go up or down."

"What do you mean by a number in the middle?" I asked him.

"Like forty or fifty," he answered.

"So Rudy has a plan for making his first guess," I said. "A plan like that is called a strategy." I wrote the word *strategy* on the board. I planned to focus the children on strategies in a variety of ways throughout the year, and this was a good opportunity to introduce the word.

Maria raised her hand. "I like to start by guessing ninety-nine," she said.

"How come?" I asked. Maria just shrugged.

Sarah raised her hand. "I like to guess a big number, then a small number, like that," she said.

"Why do you do that?" I asked.

"I like it," she said. "It's like surrounding the number."

"What about other ways to record the numbers on your paper?" I asked.

Abby told how she wrote *B* or *L* above each guess. Then Teddy held up one of his papers to show how he crossed out numbers when they were wrong. "I don't cross them out a lot," he said, "because I still have to see them so I don't guess them again."

"I cross them out, too," Abby added.

Marina showed how she kept track of how many guesses her partner, Annie, made for each number. "It took her twenty-two guesses to guess fifty-six," she said.

"What's the fewest number of guesses she needed?" I asked.

"I got one hundred in only five," Annie said. Marina nodded her agreement.

I ended the discussion. I wasn't sure that the class discussion met my pedagogical goals, but I'm often not sure of the effect of my conversations with young children. I rely on later observations to provide evidence of the value of such a discussion.

Questions and Discussion

▲▲

▲ *One of the goals of the lesson was for children to gain experience using the vocabulary* **greater** *and* **less.** *In the lesson, many children used other words. How do you help children use correct mathematical language?*

One goal of mathematics instruction in general is to help children learn to use correct mathematical language when appropriate. It's common, however, for children to use words with which they are more comfortable. In *Guess My Number*, for example, children will often substitute "smaller," "littler," and "lower" for "less," and "bigger" and "higher" for "greater." Respond by continuing to use the preferred words. Teachers can best contribute to helping children become more familiar with correct language by modeling its usage.

CHAPTER FOURTEEN
RACE FOR $1.00

Overview

Pennies, dimes, and dollars offer a real-world application of our place value system. In this game, students roll dice to determine the number of pennies to take. When they have enough, they exchange pennies for dimes and dimes for one dollar. The goal is to get one dollar. Because the number of pennies and dimes is limited, students will find that it is necessary to exchange pennies for dimes, reinforcing the idea that ten pennies are equivalent to one dime.

Materials

▲ 1-quart zip-top baggies, each with 30 pennies, 20 dimes, and 2 play dollars, 1 baggie per pair of children (for play dollars, see Blackline Masters)
▲ dice, 2 per pair of children
▲ optional: rules for *Race for $1.00*, 1 per student (see Blackline Masters)
▲ optional: *The Go-Around Dollar*, by Barbara Johnston Adams (New York: Four Winds Press, 1992)

Time

▲ one class period to introduce the game, then additional time for playing

Teaching Directions

1. Show the class a baggie of money and describe its contents. Post the number of pennies, dimes, and dollars, and encourage children to check the contents of the baggie when they're finished playing.

2. Introduce the game by gathering the children and choosing one to play with you.

3. Give another child a copy of the rules and have him or her read them one at a time so that you and your partner can play.

Race for $1.00

You need:
a partner
a zip-top baggie with 30 pennies,
   20 dimes, and 2 play dollars
2 dice

Rules
1. Take turns. On your turn, roll the dice. The sum tells how many pennies to take.

2. Decide if you want to exchange. (10 pennies = 1 dime)

3. Give the dice to your partner. Then your partner follows Steps 1 and 2.

4. Play until one player has $1.00.

Notes
1. You may exchange only when you have the dice.

2. Watch to make sure you agree with your partner's moves.

---

4. Be sure to emphasize the two notes at the bottom of the directions. Setting a procedure for when children can exchange and stressing the importance of children monitoring each other's moves helps them stay engaged in talking about the game as they play.

5. As children play, circulate and observe. For an informal assessment, interrupt children and ask one or more questions: "How much money do you each have? If you put your money together, how much would you have? How much more would you need to have exactly one dollar?"

Teaching Notes

For a literary connection, read aloud to the class *The Go-Around Dollar*. In this book, Barbara Johnston Adams weaves a story about the travels of a single dollar with a collection of facts and anecdotes about the manufacture and use of dollar bills. In the story, Matt finds a dollar on his way home from school and uses it to buy shoelaces from Eric. Eric spends the dollar on bubble gum at the corner store, and Jennifer receives the dollar as change. The story traces the dollar bill until it winds up posted as the first dollar earned in a new store. Information on each page tells children about the paper used to make dollars, the special inks used, the symbols on the front and back, the length of time a dollar stays in circulation, and more.

One piece of work isn't sufficient for judging a child's understanding. A collection of evidence is necessary to compile an informative and accurate picture of a child's mathematical ability. From working with students in class, reading their written assignments, observing them at work, listening to their comments in class discussions, and talking with them individually, teachers can form a detailed impression of children's understanding. To form a complete picture of each child's understanding, I informally assess them throughout this lesson. I do this through observation and talking with students individually or in pairs. For less experienced children, change the game to *Race to $.25* or *Race to $.50*. Use dice that are numbered 1 to 3 or use one die that is numbered from 1 to 6. Using two dice numbered 1 to 3 will give students experience with the easier addition facts as well as the experience with tens and ones that comes with playing the game.

The Lesson

▲▲▲

Race for $1.00 was an easy game to teach and captured the children's interest because it used money. I showed the class one of the baggies of money. "For this game," I said, "you need a partner, two dice, and a baggie of money."

"How much is in there?" Andrew said.

"I haven't figured out the total amount in each baggie," I said, "but I know there are thirty pennies, twenty dimes, and two play dollars." I wrote this information on the board.

"Can we figure it out?" Andrew persisted. While Andrew and several other children were intrigued by the challenge of figuring out the amount of money in the baggie, others weren't interested in the problem. Also, some children could figure out the total without using the money, some would have to count the coins, and still others would have difficulty with or without money. This range in my class is, I think, typical of most second-grade classes. I wanted to respond to Andrew's interest while also respecting the diversity in the class.

"Yes, it would be fine for you to figure it out," I said. "But please don't do that right now. I'd like to teach you how to play the game first. Then when you get to work, you can choose to solve that problem first."

"Do we have to?" Timmy asked, nervous about this challenge.

"No, you don't have to figure out how much money there is in the baggie," I replied. "Your job will be to play the game I'm going to teach you now."

I gathered the students on the rug, asking them to sit in a circle so all could see as I modeled how to play the game. After the students were settled, I asked Maria to be my partner. "Would you like to go first?" I asked her.

"No," she said. "You go first."

I gave Teddy a copy of the directions. "Please read the first rule aloud," I said.

Teddy read, "Take turns. On your turn, roll the dice. The sum tells how many pennies to take." I rolled the dice, got a 5 and a 3, and took eight pennies.

"Now what?" I asked. "Please read the second rule."

Teddy read, "Decide if you want to exchange. Ten pennies equals one dime."

"I don't have enough pennies to exchange," I said. "Read the third and fourth rules."

"Give the dice to your partner. Then your partner follows Steps One and Two," Teddy read. "Play until one player has one dollar."

I gave the dice to Maria and she rolled a 1 and a 3. She groaned and took four pennies. I waited a moment and asked her to give me the dice.

"Remember," I told the class, "don't just take the dice. Wait until the other person hands them to you. Also, you need to watch to be sure you agree with the number of pennies your partner takes and that your partner exchanges correctly."

Maria handed me the dice and I rolled them. This time I rolled a 4 and a 2.

"You get six," Eli said.

I took six pennies and then said, "I have enough to exchange ten pennies for a dime. Watch, Maria, to be sure you agree." I counted out ten pennies, returned them to the baggie, and took a dime. "So now I have one dime and four pennies; that's fourteen cents." I handed the dice to Maria.

Maria rolled two 3s and took six pennies.

"How much do you have now?" I asked. Maria counted and found she had ten pennies.

"You can exchange," Sarah told her.

"Do I have to?" Maria asked, looking at me.

"No, you don't have to exchange right now," I said, "but eventually you will have to in order to work toward getting one dollar. Would you like to exchange now or wait?"

"I'll wait," Maria said.

"Then pass the dice to me," I said. Maria gave me the dice.

"So that's how you play," I said. I decided not to continue with the game. The rules for the game are simple, and I thought that most of the children were ready to play.

I said to the children, "Before you and your partner begin to play, I want to read the two notes at the bottom of the directions," I said. "They're important for you to know." The two notes direct the children to exchange only when they have the dice and to be sure to watch each other as they play.

"One more thing," I said. "When you're finished playing, check your baggie before you return it to the supplies shelf to be sure it has thirty pennies and twenty dimes."

The children returned to their seats and began to play.

LINKING ASSESSMENT TO INSTRUCTION

When I circulate and supervise during work time, I have several different kinds of questions I pose to children to challenge their thinking and to help me assess their skill with reasoning numerically. Sometimes I ask children how much money they would have altogether if they combined their coins. At other times, I ask them how much more they need to get to exactly one dollar, or how much more one has than the other.

Assessing Seth and Abby

I interrupted Seth and Abby and asked them to tell me how much money they each had.

"I have thirty-nine cents," Seth said. He knew how much he had without having to check. Abby, however, spread out her dimes and pennies to count. "I've got forty-six cents," she said.

"If you put your money together," I said, "how much would you have?" I was interested in seeing how the children would solve this problem, specifically if they would think about regrouping pennies into a dime.

Seth and Abby slid their coins closer together, being careful not to mix their piles. Seth came up with an answer first. "It's eighty-five cents," he said. He had counted the dimes to get seventy cents, then slid one of Abby's pennies over a bit (still keeping their piles separate) to combine with his nine pennies for another ten cents, and finally counted Abby's remaining five pennies.

Abby, however, counted the dimes to get seventy cents and then proceeded to count the pennies by ones to finish. "I got eighty-five cents," she also said.

"And if you put your money together," I then asked, "how much more would you need to have in order to have exactly one dollar?"

"I've got to get a piece of paper," Abby said, while Seth started counting on his fingers. Abby's strategy was to write the number *85* and underline it. "That's so I know where I started," she said. Then she continued writing the numerals up to 100.

While she was doing this, Seth got an answer. "It's fifteen," he said. "We need fifteen more cents."

"Let's see if Abby gets the same answer," I said. She had written all the numbers and was now counting them. Her concentration was impressive to me. "I got fifteen," she said. Both children seemed pleased. I left them to finish their game.

From this interaction, it seemed to me that Seth was more facile and confident with reasoning numerically. Abby was more cautious, being careful and methodical both in her counting and in her writing. This is the sort of information that helps me form mathematical profiles of my students.

Two days later, when Seth and Abby were playing the game again, I again interrupted them. "You're going to ask us how much we have altogether, aren't you?" Seth asked.

"Yes," I said. "How much do you have?" Abby had thirty cents and Seth had thirty-four cents. It was easy for them to figure out that they had sixty-four cents altogether. They both counted the dimes and then added on the pennies.

"What question do you think I'll ask next?" I said.

"How much more we need to get one dollar," they both answered, more or less in unison.

"Try to figure it out," I said, "and then come get me when you've both agreed on an answer." I left them. They each decided to use paper and pencil to solve the problem. Also, both of them used the method Abby had used the last time, writing *64*, underlining it, and then writing the numbers from 65 to 100. However, they got stuck when Abby got an answer of thirty-six cents and Seth got thirty-three cents. They were completely perplexed.

I looked at their papers and found Seth's error. "You left out some of the numbers in the nineties," I said. He corrected his error and then counted the numbers beginning with 65 and ending with 100, underlining each as he did so.

"How come you decided to use paper and pencil instead of counting like you did the other day?" I asked Seth.

"It was too far to count," he said. He paused for a moment and then added, "I think I should have counted."

"It's easy to make mistakes either way," I said. "I think it's a good idea to do a problem two ways to have a check, or to check with a partner, as you did with Abby." I left them to continue their game.

Even though Seth made a careless error when he tried Abby's method, I saw his decision as willingness to be flexible about his approaches to problems. He had displayed this flexibility regularly since the beginning of the year. Abby's method seemed to make sense for this problem, and he tried it. Abby, on the other hand, was more limited in the approaches she was willing to use. When she had a method that made sense to her, she continued to rely on it and wasn't interested in other ideas.

Assessing Teddy and Katy

I initiated a conversation with Teddy and Katy at the end of a game, just as Teddy had won. "I have a dollar and two cents," he said.

"How much money do you have, Katy?" I asked.

"I have ninety-five cents," she answered. "It was close."

"Can you figure out how much more Teddy has?" I asked.

In a moment, Teddy blurted out an answer. "I have seven more."

"Do you agree?" I asked Katy. She shrugged.

"Can you explain to Katy how you figured it out?" I asked Teddy.

"I counted," he said. "I did ninety-six, ninety-seven, ninety-eight, ninety-nine, one hundred, one hundred one, one hundred two." He kept track with his fingers. Katy seemed to understand.

"If you put your money together," I then asked, "would you have two dollars, more than two dollars, or less than two dollars?"

"More," Teddy answered. "No, less."

"Less," Katy said.

"Take some time and figure it out," I said.

This time it was Katy who offered an explanation. "If I take Teddy's extra two cents, that gives me ninety-seven cents," she said, "and that's not enough for an extra dollar."

Teddy was thinking while Katy answered. "We'd have a dollar and ninety-seven cents," he said.

"That's right," Katy replied.

"So you both agree," I said.

Teddy was quick numerically and confident in his ability. When he was interested in a problem, he generally stuck with it and worked until he had an answer that satisfied him. He never seemed to get ruffled or

be troubled when he made an error; he was curious and confident. Katy, on the other hand, was tentative about her math reasoning. She vacillated in her responses, sometimes being clear and other times confused, sometimes being willing and other times reticent. I felt she needed many more experiences to strengthen her understanding and build her confidence.

Assessing Molly and Amelia

When I interrupted Molly and Amelia, Molly had thirty-seven cents and Amelia had twenty-nine cents.

"How much do you have altogether?" I asked.

They looked at each other's coins, and, like Seth and Abby, they were reluctant to intermingle them.

"Look," Amelia said, "if you put the pennies together, you'd have enough to trade for a dime."

"But how many extras would there be?" Molly asked. Amelia began counting on her fingers while Molly was focusing on the money.

"I think it's sixteen cents," Amelia said.

"Wait a minute," Molly said. "I have to give you a penny and then you can get a dime and then I have six pennies left. So it's a dime and six extras."

"That's what I said," Amelia said.

"So how much do you have altogether, counting all your dimes and pennies?" I asked.

"Oh yeah," Molly said. They counted together and figured out they had sixty-six cents.

"I have one more question," I said. "How much ahead is Molly?"

"Ooh," Molly said, "that's hard."

"No, it isn't," Amelia said, and she counted on from twenty-nine to thirty-seven, using her fingers. "It's eight."

"Do you agree?" I asked Molly.

"I'm not sure," she said. "Wait a minute, let me see."

"You just have to count," Amelia said.

Molly sighed. "Let's just play," she said.

This conversation confirmed my previous observations of Amelia and Molly. Amelia calculated mentally easily, more easily than Molly and many of the children in the class. Molly felt more comfortable when she relied on some concrete material or story context. Also, Molly was a bit of a dreamer and her attention tended to wander when she felt overwhelmed by a problem.

I left the girls to continue their game.

Catherine and Hassan's Not-Enough-Pennies Problem

Catherine and Hassan ran into a problem with the money when they were playing *Race for $1.00* on another day. Some pennies were missing from the baggie. Children sometimes borrowed money from one baggie for another and forgot to return it. Hassan had three dimes and seven pennies; Catherine had two dimes and nine pennies. There were plenty of dimes left in their supply, but only seven pennies. Catherine rolled double 6s.

She came and got me. "What should I do?" she asked, almost wailing.

"What's the problem?" I said.

"I need to take twelve pennies and there aren't enough," she said.

"I told her what to do," Hassan interjected, "but she doesn't believe me."

"Can you tell me what Hassan's suggestion was?" I asked Catherine. She shook her head "no."

"What was your idea?" I asked Hassan.

"I told her just to take a dime and two pennies," he said, "because that makes twelve cents."

"I don't get it," Catherine said.

"How much money are you supposed to take?" I asked.

"I got two sixes," she said, "and that's twelve."

"Why do you think Hassan suggested taking a dime and two pennies?" I asked.

Catherine hesitated for a moment. Then she reached and took a dime and two pennies. She sat quietly for a moment and I just waited. Hassan was being very patient also, seeming somewhat intrigued with Catherine's pondering.

"OK," she said in a musing tone, fingering the coins, "a dime is ten cents and then you go eleven, twelve . . . Oh," she said, looking up and brightening. "It works. It's twelve cents."

"That's what I told you," Hassan said in a somewhat superior tone.

"Yes, you made a good suggestion," I said. "But an idea only seems like a good suggestion to someone else when it makes sense to him or her, too." I left the children to continue with the game.

When Catherine got confused, she was always quick to come to me for help, instead of stopping to think about the problem herself or seeking help from her partner or another classmate. Her number sense was weak, but her need seemed as much emotional as mathematical. I was working to help her learn to rely more on herself and her partner.

Assessing Marina and Annie

I interrupted Marina and Annie and asked, "Can you each tell me how much money you have?"

"I have fifty-one cents," Marina answered.

"Forty-seven, no, forty-eight cents," Annie said.

"So who has more so far?" I asked.

"She does," Annie said. Marina nodded.

"How much more?" I asked.

Marina immediately started to think about the problem. She closed her eyes and brought one hand up to use her fingers. She counted softly to herself, "Forty-nine, fifty, fifty-one." She did it again to check. Meanwhile, Annie screwed up her face. She seemed confused. She looked down at the coins and began rearranging them. She matched her dimes and Marina's dimes by arranging them into two columns and noticed that Marina had an extra dime.

"Is it ten cents?" Annie asked hesitantly.

"No," Marina said, "it's only three cents. Look, you go forty-nine, fifty, fifty-one." Marina used her fingers to illustrate her thinking.

"Oh, OK," Annie said.

I wasn't convinced Annie understood, as I knew her number sense was fairly weak. Marina, on the other hand, was confident about her math ability. She wasn't finished thinking about the money. "I think we have about one dollar together," she said.

"How do you know that?" I asked.

Marina reached for a pencil and paper. She wrote 48¢ and 51¢ and underneath wrote 50 + 49 = 99. "I put one from the fifty-one on the forty-eight so I have fifty and forty-nine," she explained, "and that makes ninety-nine. All we need is one more penny."

Annie watched and didn't comment. I feel that conversations like this one gave Annie models for thinking about numbers. I was careful, however, to avoid having Annie feel that she was deficient by not emphasizing the need for getting a correct answer quickly and by not praising Marina for her math ability.

I left the girls to continue with their game.

HOMEWORK

As an additional follow-up to this lesson, have children teach someone at home how to play *Race for $1.00*. Remind them that they will need thirty pennies, twenty dimes, and two dollars. You may want to duplicate play dollars and send them home.

Some children may not have dice at home. Show children a substitute. Demonstrate cutting twelve slips of paper, numbering two each from 1 to 6, putting them in a bag, and drawing two out. Add the numbers on the two slips of paper to determine how many pennies to take. Remind the students to replace the slips of paper back in the bag after each draw. You may also wish to send home a letter to parents explaining the value of the game.

Dear Parent,

Race for $1.00 is a game that provides experience with exchanging pennies for dimes, thus relating the 10s and 1s structure of our number system to the real-life example of money. Please play at least three games with your child.

As you play the game, stop from time to time and ask your child to count up how much money you each have and compare the amounts to see who has more. Together, figure out how much more one person has than the other.

EXTENSION

After the children have had some experience with the game, read *The Go-Around Dollar*, by Barbara Johnston Adams. After you've read the story aloud, leave the book out, so students who are interested can read it on their own. At a later time, if a child finds a particular tidbit of information especially interesting, invite him or her to share it with the class. Also, children might be interested in writing their own stories about the adventures of a different dollar bill.

Questions and Discussion

▲▲▲

▲ *Many of your children seem to count using their fingers. Why do you allow this?*

I see no problem with students using their fingers to keep track of their thinking, especially at this age. Fingers are handy manipulatives that are always readily available. The students I am more concerned about are those who don't know what to do. The students who use their fingers often know what to do to solve the problem, and they are simply using their fingers as a tool to help them find the solution. As a student gains experience and his or her confidence grows, the need to use fingers will lessen.

▲ *Do you think there is value in having students play both* **Race for $1.00** *and* **Cover a Flat** *(Chapter 15)? They are very similar activities.*

When children repeat activities or do similar activities that are of interest to them, they bring their prior experience to each new encounter. They are given the opportunity to cement their understanding and try other ideas to stretch their thinking. Ultimately students increase their confidence, deepen their understanding, and gain practice.

▲ *Is it OK to use play coins instead of real pennies and dimes?*

It is fine to use play coins, although I prefer to use real coins. Students gain experience and confidence counting money as the result of handling real coins while playing the game. If you choose to use play coins, it is important that they appear as realistic as possible.

▲ *Why don't you use nickels as well since children find it easier to group by fives?*

An important aspect of this game is to provide students with a real-world application of our place value system. Pennies, dimes, and dollars are real-world examples of our base ten number system. Nickels don't fit. Also, money is an excellent context for children to strengthen their skills in grouping by tens.

CHAPTER FIFTEEN
COVER A FLAT

Overview

Cover a Flat is similar to *Race for $1.00* but uses base ten blocks instead of money as a context for learning about the base ten number system. Base ten blocks offer a spatial model for thinking about place value that is particularly helpful for some children. The goal of the game is to completely cover a hundreds square, or flat, with tens rods. Children take turns rolling dice to find out how many unit cubes they can take. When they have enough units, they trade units for rods and rods for a flat. The game provides children concrete experience with regrouping.

Materials

▲ zip-top baggies (1 per pair of students), each with 30 unit cubes, 20 tens rods, and 2 hundreds squares (flats) (if you don't have flats, duplicate centimeter squares onto heavy paper and cut out 10-by-10-centimeter squares; see Blackline Masters)
▲ dice, 2 per pair of students
▲ optional: rules for *Cover a Flat*, 1 per student (see Blackline Masters)

Time

▲ one class period to introduce the game, then additional time for playing and discussion

Teaching Directions

1. Show the class a baggie and describe its contents. You may want to list the number of cubes and rods and encourage the children to check the contents when they're finished playing. (**Note:** If the children have not had experience with these materials, be sure to provide time for free exploration.)

2. Ask children how many unit cubes are needed to cover one flat. (With children, I use the term *flat* and *hundreds square* interchangeably.) Have all those who offer answers explain their reasoning. It most likely won't be obvious to all children that the flat has one hundred squares, but don't worry about this; children can still play and learn from their experience with the game.

3. Introduce the game by telling the students that the goal is to cover the hundreds square. Give a student a copy of the rules to read as two students play. Or, you may prefer to model the game with a student as your partner.

Cover a Flat

You need:
  a partner
  a zip-top baggie with 2 flats, 20 tens
    rods, and 30 unit cubes
  2 dice

Rules
1. Each player takes a flat.

2. Take turns. On your turn, roll the dice. The sum tells
    how many unit cubes to take. Place them on your
    flat.

3. Decide if you want to exchange 10 unit cubes for a
    tens rod.

4. Give the dice to your partner. Then your partner
    follows Steps 2 and 3.

5. Play until one player covers his or her flat with ten
    rods.

Notes
1. You may exchange only when you have the dice.

2. Watch to make sure you agree with your partner's
    moves.

---

4. As children play, circulate and observe. For an informal assessment, interrupt children and ask one or more questions: "Do you have enough blocks to cover a flat if you combined your blocks? Who has covered more squares? How many more? How many more blocks would the person with fewer blocks need so both would have the same amount?"

5. After students have had experience with this activity, try the assessment *How Much Is Covered?* (on page 155).

Teaching Notes

Race for $1.00 and *Cover a Flat* are essentially the same activity, just embedded in two different contexts. Making the exchanges in *Race for $1.00* requires that children understand the convention of our money system, that a dime is worth ten pennies and a dollar is worth ten dimes. With base ten blocks, children can actually physically compare blocks to verify that an exchange is valid. They can concretely show that ten units are equivalent to a long (or rod), and ten longs make a flat.

Doing both activities is valuable as students are given the opportunity to explore and deepen their understanding of the structure of our number system in different contexts.

The Lesson

▲▲

"I have a new game to share with you today," I began. "The idea of the game is to completely cover the flat with ten rods," I said as I showed the children a baggie in which I had put two flats, twenty tens rods, and about thirty unit cubes.

"Before I tell you any more about the game, I want to ask you a question," I continued. I held up a hundreds square and one unit cube and asked them how many cubes they thought would fit on the square.

Andrew knew immediately. "It's one hundred," he said.

"How do you know?" I asked.

"Because there's ten in a row," he said, "and ten rows, and that makes one hundred." Andrew was an extraordinary boy who announced to me one day that he was a "big number kind of kid." I had come to believe him.

"Any other ideas?" I said.

"You could count by tens," Amelia said. "Can I show?" I nodded, and Amelia came to the front of the room and counted by tens, running her finger down each row as she did so.

"Does anyone have a different way to figure?" I asked. There weren't any more volunteers. I wasn't convinced that all children knew that one hundred unit cubes would cover the flat, but I decided that they would have a chance to figure it out when they were playing the game and were close enough to a hundreds square to get their hands on it.

I then chose Jonathan and Eli to play the game at a table in front of the room and had Gwyn come up to read the rules.

"Read the rules step-by-step," I said, "so that Jonathan and Eli can follow them."

Gwyn began with the materials. "You need two flats, twenty tens rods, thirty unit cubes, and two dice," she read. I gave the boys the baggie of blocks and a pair of dice.

"Rule one," she continued, "Each player takes a flat. Rule two: Take turns."

She stopped before finishing reading the second rule and said to the boys, "You have to decide who goes first." Jonathan and Eli looked at each other. Neither of them was particularly competitive, and after a few moments, Eli said that he would go first. Jonathan nodded his agreement.

Gwyn continued to read, "On your turn, roll the dice. The sum tells how many unit cubes to take. Place them on your flat. Three: Decide if you want to exchange ten unit cubes for a tens rod. Four: Give the dice to your partner. Then your partner follows Steps Two and Three."

Eli rolled the dice. A 4 and a 5 came up and he counted the dots. "It's nine," he said.

"Do you agree, Jonathan?" I asked. Jonathan hadn't done the addition and looked over at the dice.

"Yes," he said, "you go five, then six, seven, eight, nine." He used his fingers when he counted.

"So what are you going to do, Eli?" I asked.

"Take nine cubes, Eli," Sarah said.

"I know," Eli said. He took nine unit cubes and lined them up on one row of the hundreds square.

"You can't exchange," Gwyn said, "because you don't have enough, so you have to give the dice to Jonathan."

"That's an important rule," I reinforced. "Your partner can't just take the dice. You have to hand the dice over to your partner when you're done with your turn."

Eli gave Jonathan the dice and he rolled them. He got a 2 and a 1. "That's only three," he complained and put three unit cubes on his flat.

"Now give Eli the dice," Gwyn instructed.

Eli rolled them, this time getting two 3s. "It's six," he said quickly. The doubles are always easy for children to remember.

"Do you agree, Jonathan?" I said, to reinforce that partners were supposed to pay attention to what each other was doing. Jonathan nodded. Eli added six unit cubes to his flat.

"You can exchange," Gwyn said.

"I know," Eli retorted, a bit annoyed that he was being rushed. He carefully counted ten unit cubes, not making use of the information that there were ten in one row of the hundreds square. He replaced them with a tens rod.

"Now give the dice to Jonathan," Gwyn directed.

"Wait a minute, Eli," I interrupted. "First, tell the class what you have on your flat right now."

"I've got a rod and five little ones," he said.

"Do you know how many little squares on your flat are covered up by the tens rod and the five unit cubes?" I asked.

"It's fifteen," he said.

"Raise your hand if you agree that Eli's blocks cover fifteen squares," I said to the class. More than half of the children raised their hands.

"Who can tell how they know?" I asked.

I called on Seth. "It's ten and five more, and that's fifteen," he said.

Leslie had another idea. She counted on from ten. "You can go ten and then eleven, twelve, thirteen, fourteen, fifteen," she said.

No other children had suggestions, so I asked Eli to pass the dice to Jonathan.

Jonathan rolled a 3 and a 4. He counted on his fingers and got seven. Eli was figuring in his head and the boys said "seven" at the same time. Jonathan reached for the unit cubes.

"You'll have just enough to exchange for a tens rod," Andrew said. Jonathan ignored him, however, and counted out seven unit cubes and placed them on his hundreds square. Then he counted all the unit cubes, found he had ten, removed them, and put one tens rod in their place.

I thought that this was sufficient to introduce the children to the game. I thanked Gwyn for helping with the directions. I reminded children about exchanging only when they had the dice and watching each other as they took their turns. I told Eli and Jonathan that they could continue their game or start another. They decided to finish the game and Eli rolled the dice.

LINKING ASSESSMENT TO INSTRUCTION

As I circulated, I looked for opportunities to assess individual children's understandings and asked different questions, depending on what I already knew about the children and where they were in the game. For example, sometimes I'd ask children if they had enough blocks to cover a flat if they combined all the blocks each of them had. Sometimes I asked children to tell how many squares they each had covered and compare the amounts, figuring out how many more squares one had covered than the other. This sort of problem wasn't too difficult when the game was close and both had the same number of tens rods, as it was easy to compare visually. (If done numerically, no regrouping would be needed.) Sometimes I phrased the question differently and asked children to figure how many more blocks the person with fewer would need so both of them would have the same number of squares covered on their flats. Usually I did this because making a numerical comparison seemed too difficult for the children.

Assessing Nick and Hassan

Nick and Hassan were almost halfway through a game when I interrupted them. Nick had five tens rods and three unit cubes on his flat; Hassan had four tens rods and eight unit cubes on his. I asked them, "Do you have enough blocks to cover a flat if you put both of your blocks together?"

"I don't think so," Nick said.

"How do you know?" I asked.

"I just guessed," he said.

"How could you figure it out?" I asked.

"There are almost enough tens rods," Hassan said. While Nick and I were talking, he had counted their tens rods. "There's nine," he continued. "I think we'll have enough."

Nick got interested. "Oh yeah," he said, "maybe we can get another rod." He began counting their unit cubes.

"It works!" Hassan was pleased. "We'd have one more extra little one."

"How many squares have you covered so far on your flat, Nick?" I asked.

"Fifty-three," he said.

"And you?" I asked Hassan.

"Forty-eight," he answered.

"So fifty-three plus forty-eight is a whole flat plus one extra. How much is that?" I asked.

"What do you mean?" Nick asked.

"I know," Hassan said. "There's a hundred on the flat, and then one more, so it's one hundred one."

"Oh yeah," Nick said.

"So fifty-three plus forty-eight is one hundred one," I said. "Do you think you'd get that answer if you pressed 'fifty-three + forty-eight' on the calculator?" I am always looking for ways that children can use calculators to confirm their thinking. Also, I wanted to help the boys see the connection between our number system and the game.

Each boy reached for a calculator and tried it. They were still clumsy with calculators and often pushed buttons incorrectly. Nick got 101 and Hassan's display showed 5348.

"Try it again," I said to Hassan, "and be sure to press the plus sign."

"Here, I'll show you," Nick said, reaching to grab Hassan's calculator. Hassan held his calculator out of Nick's reach.

"No," he said, "I want to do it." Nick cleared his own calculator and did the problem again. This time, both boys got 101. They returned to their game.

Assessing Molly and Amelia; Teddy and Catherine

When I interrupted Molly and Amelia, Molly had three tens rods and two cubes, while Amelia had three tens rods and seven cubes. It was easy for the girls to tell me how many squares they had each covered, and that Amelia was ahead by five cubes.

However, when I interrupted Teddy and Catherine, they weren't able to figure out how many more squares Catherine had covered. Teddy had twenty-seven squares covered and Catherine had thirty-four.

"Teddy has more little ones," Catherine said, "but I have another rod."

"I could get another rod," Teddy said.

"But then you'd be ahead," Catherine answered.

I made a suggestion. "Suppose you got some more unit cubes, Teddy, so you could exchange for a tens rod, and still have four left over to match Catherine."

Teddy and Catherine looked at their flats and were silent. After a moment, Teddy became animated. "I know," he said, "I could roll a ten and get a rod, and Catherine could roll a three and get more cubes. Then we'd match." So much for my suggestion.

Assessing Leslie and Jason

I interrupted Leslie and Jason and asked, "Who has covered more squares so far?" They looked at each other's flats and agreed that Jason had more. He had two tens rods and three unit cubes; Leslie had one rod and seven cubes.

"How many more?" I asked.

"That's hard," Jason said.

"Do you know how many squares you've covered?" I asked.

"I've got twenty-three," he said.

"And I covered seventeen," Leslie said.

"So how many more would have to be put on Leslie's flat so it matched Jason's?" I asked.

"I need to put on one more rod and take off some cubes," she said. "I'd have to take off four little blocks."

I'm always surprised when children have a different way of thinking about a situation than I do. Leslie made sense of the situation in a way that hadn't occurred to me but seemed logical. Her response was a reminder to me not to hold a preconceived notion of what I'd like a child's response to be, but to be curious about what he or she might say.

I probed with another question. "What do you need to roll, Leslie, so you'd get the blocks you need to match Jason?"

She was stumped. Her answer of putting on one more tens rod and taking off four cubes didn't help her with my question.

"Ooh, look," Jason said, "if you got a six it would work. Then, you'd be up to me." He was looking at their hundreds squares and suddenly had seen a new way to think about the problem.

I squelched my thought about probing further as I felt Leslie's and Jason's attention drifting. I was eager for the children to connect their concrete experience to numerical reasoning, but I knew this wasn't the right time. I left the children to continue their game.

EXTENSION

Another way to give children experience with the base ten number system using concrete materials is to link it to metric measurement. Using the same rules as *Race for $1.00* and *Cover a Flat*, students can play *Make a Meter*. In this game, students use unit cubes, tens rods, and a meter stick. Be sure to use 1-centimeter cubes and rods that are 10 centimeters long. Students roll two dice and find the sum to determine the number of units to take. They place the units on top of a meter stick. Players exchange units for tens rods. The winner is the first player to cover the meter stick with ten rods.

Questions and Discussion

▲▲▲

▲ **Race for $1.00, Cover a Flat,** *and* **Make a Meter** *are really the same game played with three different materials. Why are they presented as three different activities?*

The structure is the same, but the use of different materials allows children to see the same idea in three different ways. This increases the chances that more students will understand the mathematics and provides students with the opportunity to deepen their understanding. Because the rules are the same, students are confident about what to do, but the variety of materials keeps them interested and, therefore, learning.

▲ *My students have not had much experience using base ten blocks. I'm afraid that they will play with the blocks rather than use them for their intended purpose in this lesson. What do you suggest?*

Allowing students time to explore anytime a new material is introduced is time well spent. This exploration time provides students with the opportunity to find out about the materials, especially if you give them some specific ideas to explore. When they explore base ten blocks, for example, asking students to find out how many cubes it takes to make a rod is an appropriate way to focus their attention. Near the end of the exploration time, give students a one-minute warning. This gives students a chance to finish what they were doing and prevents the feeling of interruption.

▲ *Once you have introduced this game and students have played it, what else would you do with it?*

Once the students have played the game and had the opportunity to discuss it, I make it available as a menu or choice activity that they can return to. This way, students continue to play and strengthen their understanding through experience and practice. Whenever possible, as students have additional opportunities to play, I like to interact and pose problems, as in the vignette, giving them practice with computation and me insights into how their understanding is developing.

ASSESSMENTS

Overview

This section suggests six assessments, five of which are intended to take students a short time to complete, generally ten to fifteen minutes. The sixth is an individual student interview. The individual student interviews are based on three questions and are designed to reveal what students do and do not understand about place value. You can ask the three questions in one sitting or in three separate interviews. *Numbers on the 0–99 Chart, Catherine's Problem*, and *How Much Is Covered?* involve children in using place value knowledge to solve addition problems with two-digit numbers; you can repeat these assessments by changing the numbers involved. *How Many 10s?* asks children to interpret base ten notation to determine how many tens and ones are in fifty-eight. *How Many Ways to Make 36?* asks children to think of as many ways as they can to make thirty-six using tens and ones. All the assessments with the exception of the individual interviews relate directly to lessons in this book.

For other suggestions about assessing children's understanding and skills, read the "Linking Assessment to Instruction" sections for the following lessons: *Dollar Signs*, the *Five-Tower Game, Guess My Number, Race for $1.00*, and *Cover a Flat*.

Teaching Notes

Assessing student understanding through writing gives teachers insights into what students have and have not learned. For students, writing assignments provide opportunities to reflect on their learning, solidify their thinking, raise questions, reinforce new ideas, and review older ideas. I typically give students writing assignments at least once per week.

Class discussions are important to the writing process. A discussion before writing provides students ideas to consider and include in their writing. This can be especially helpful when children's learning is new and fragile. Leading a discussion after students write gives them the chance to share their own thinking while considering the ideas of others. These discussions help students become flexible thinkers.

When students are working on writing assignments, I circulate throughout the class, offering assistance. When students need help, I begin either by asking them to explain their ideas to me or asking them questions to spark their thinking. After I listen to students' explanations, I suggest that they begin by writing down the exact words they spoke. I sometimes tell a student to make her thoughts go from her brain, past her mouth, down her arm, and out her pencil onto the paper.

This assessment section also has suggestions for individual interviews. One-on-one interviews, while the least practical for classroom teachers, are the most effective for revealing a child's understanding. Although it's not possible during classroom instruction to conduct individual interviews for all students, interviewing even a few students can help hone teachers' skills at questioning children during regular lessons. For these interviews, choosing children who represent a range of experience and understanding is useful for getting a sense of the breadth of reactions and responses students will have about place value.

When conducting individual interviews, it's important to suggest, prod, push, question, and encourage. When students give responses, ask them to explain their thinking: "Why do you think that?" "Why does that make sense to you?" "Can you explain that?" If children change their minds at any time, probe their thinking: "Why does your new idea make sense?" "How come you changed your thinking?" If children give an incorrect response, present them with contradictory information and ask them to reconsider their thinking in light of the new information.

However, it's also important to avoid leading the children and directing them to think in any particular way. The goal for individual interviews is the same as for all lessons and assessments: to have children express their own ideas and explain their understanding in ways that make sense to them. At all times, the focus should be on finding out how they think and reason.

INDIVIDUAL INTERVIEWS

Following are questions that are useful for finding out what students know and don't know about place value during a ten- to fifteen-minute interview.

1. The Relationship Between Numbers and Groups of Tens and Ones

Give a child a cup with twenty-four tiles or beans and direct him or her to put the objects into groups of ten. Ask: "How many groups of ten and how many extras are there?" Then ask: "How many are there in all?" Finally, ask the child to write the number.

All students should be able to put the tiles or beans into groups of ten and report the number of groups and extras. However, students' responses to telling the total number of tiles or beans will differ. Those children who fully understand place value will know immediately that there are twenty-four beans or tiles; those whose understanding is partial or fragile may have to combine the tens and add on the extras; some children will have to count the tiles or beans one by one.

2. The Significance of the Positions of Digits in Numbers

Present a problem that gives insights into a child's number sense. If this is a separate interview, begin by having the child count out twenty-four tiles. Ask: "Suppose I didn't want twenty-four tiles but only sixteen. Take some away so that only sixteen are left." Subtraction is hard for primary children. While some children can figure out how many tiles to remove, others will need to count out sixteen tiles and discard the rest.

Then ask the child to write the numeral for sixteen. Then point to the 6 in the numeral and ask: "Can you show with the tiles what the six means?" Then point to the 1 and ask: "Can you show with the tiles what the one means?" Children who understand place value show six tiles for the 6 and then explain that the 1 represents the remaining ten tiles. However, if children show, as is typical with second graders, that the 1 means one tile, probe further: "If these six tiles stand for the six and this one tile is the one, then where do the rest of the tiles belong?" This prompt is designed to present students with a contradiction and to provide another way to interpret their understanding.

3. Solving an Addition Problem

Give an addition problem that again allows you to check on a child's understanding of the meaning of the digits in a number. If this is a new interview, begin by having the child first count out sixteen tiles. Ask: "Suppose you took twenty-five more tiles. How would you figure out how many you would have altogether?" Children who understand place value will have some way of using their information about tens and ones to solve the problem. If the problem is too difficult, children will respond that they have to get tiles and count them or will count on their fingers. If so, change the problem to a simpler one that requires less counting: "If you add five more tiles onto the sixteen, how many will you have?"

Most children will count on from sixteen to twenty-one using tiles, on their fingers, or in their heads; some will take five tiles and count them all, starting with one. When children answer either problem, have them verify their calculation with the tiles. If they were incorrect, they'll have the chance to deal with the inconsistency between their idea and what the tiles show.

Then ask: "If you put all those tiles into groups of ten, how many groups would you have? Would there be any extras?" Children who understand place value will be able to give the information easily; children whose understanding is partial or fragile may be able to answer the question after thinking about the numbers and doing some figuring; some children will have no idea of the answer and no way to think about the question.

If you'd like, have children write the number and ask the same questions recommended previously for the number sixteen, having them interpret the meaning of the digits in the numeral. Some children can apply the structure of tens and ones to the meaning of the digits in numbers twenty and larger, while the structure doesn't make sense for numbers in the teens.

Numbers on the 0–99 Chart

PROMPT

We had 39 numbers on the chart yesterday and we added 12 more today. How many numbers are on the chart now?

The problem described draws on the lesson *The 0–99 Chart* in Chapter 2. Students are asked to add two two-digit numbers with regrouping to figure out how many numbers are on the chart.

Relating the problem to their experience in the lesson *The 0–99 Chart* provides a context that is familiar to students. In this way, the problem is not an isolated exercise but one that connects to their classroom learning. To introduce the assessment, I removed the 0–99 chart from the wall, turned it around, and replaced it, so the children could no longer see the numbers. "We had thirty-nine numbers on the chart after yesterday's class," I said, "and we added twelve more numbers today. How many numbers are on the chart now?" I wrote this information on the board as I described the problem.

I explained to the students that I turned the chart around because I wanted to see how they would solve the problem if they couldn't count the cards. I also explained to the students that I wanted them to work individually and to use words, numbers, and pictures to show their solutions so I could better understand their thinking. I told the students they could use any materials that would help them solve the problem.

For this assessment, do not worry whether the children have been taught the standard procedure for adding with regrouping. The goal here isn't to test children's proficiency with the standard algorithm but rather to test their ability to think and reason mathematically. When children are faced with the problem of combining numbers that require regrouping, and when they haven't been taught the standard procedure for "carrying," they must resort to their own resources. Their search to make sense of the problem and the methods they use to add can provide insights into their understanding of place value and their ability to make use of the tens and ones structure of our number system.

Figures 1 through 4 show how several students approached this problem.

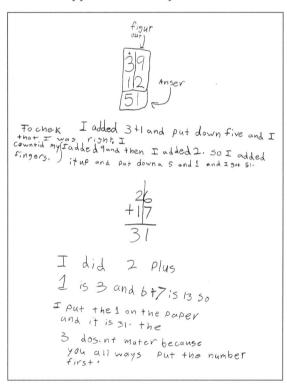

▲▲▲▲▲▲**Figure 1** *Marina's paper showed her consistent use of an incorrect algorithm.*

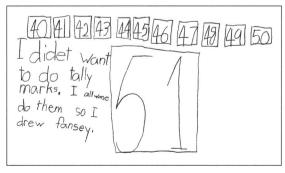

▲▲▲▲▲▲**Figure 2** *Seth solved the problem by counting on from 39.*

▲▲▲▲▲▲Figure 3   *Rudy's solution showed his understanding of place value.*

▲▲▲▲▲▲Figure 4   *Grace could use the standard algorithm, but when asked to explain the meaning of the "little 1," she didn't know.*

Catherine's Problem

PROMPT

Catherine has two piles of lentils, one with 49 lentils, the other with 17. How many lentils does Catherine have altogether?

Catherine's Problem is similar to the *Numbers on the 0–99 Chart* assessment, as it also presents children with an addition problem that requires regrouping. In this problem, the children are to add forty-nine and seventeen. Giving addition problems at different times is valuable for getting information from students to compare with previous assessments.

This problem came from a situation that occurred when Catherine was working on *Fill the Cube*. (See the "Extensions" section on page 57.) She was stumped by the problem of figuring out the total number of lentils she had in two piles, one with forty-nine lentils and the other with seventeen. The next day, I took the opportunity to present the problem to the class. I had children solve it individually so that I could use their papers to assess the class in general and individual students as well.

Clearly, this same situation will not occur in your classroom. Another might arise that suggests an addition problem to present to your students. If not, consider telling your students the story about Catherine's problem and asking them to solve it. As long as they've had experience with *Fill the Cube*, Catherine's experience will be familiar to them.

Figures 5 through 10 show how some students solved this problem.

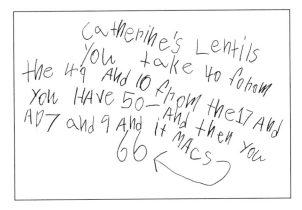

▲▲▲▲▲▲**Figure 5** *Teddy used 10s and 1s to do the adding.*

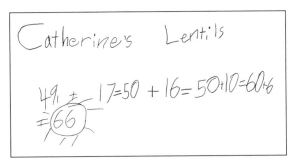

▲▲▲▲▲▲**Figure 6** *Even though Molly didn't use words, I accepted her paper because the numbers communicated her thinking clearly.*

▲▲▲▲▲▲**Figure 7** *Catherine drew 17 tally marks and counted.*

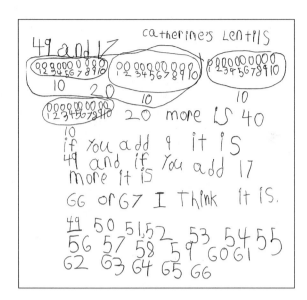

49 and 17   catherines Lentils

10   20   10   10

20 more is 40
if you add 9 it is
49 and if you add 17
more it is
66 or 67 I think it is.

49 50 51,52 53 54 55
56 57 58 59 60 61
62 63 64 65 66

▲▲▲▲▲▲**Figure 8** *Eli showed a mix of using 10s and 1s and counting on.*

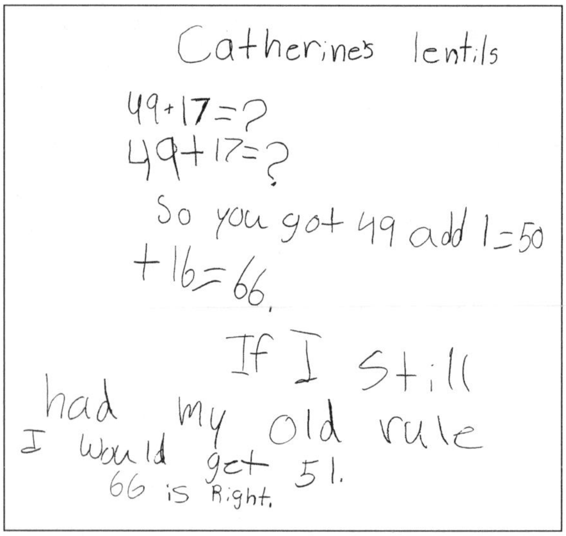

Catherines lentils

49 + 17 = ?
49 + 17 = ?
So you got 49 add 1 = 50
+ 16 = 66.

If I still
had my old rule
I would get 51.
66 is Right.

▲▲▲▲▲▲**Figure 9** *Marina made a terrific breakthrough.*

Catherine's Lentils.

49   50 51 52 53 54 55 56
        1 2 3 4 5 6
57 58 59 60 61 62 63 64
8 9 10 11 12 13 14 15
65 66
16 17

▲▲▲▲▲▲**Figure 10** *Seth counted on, the method he trusted most for adding.*

How Many 10s?

PROMPT

How many 10s in 58? How many 1s? Show how you know.

In this assessment, children are asked to report the number of tens and ones there are in fifty-eight and explain why their answer makes sense. The number fifty-eight was chosen because the assessment followed the *Counting Fish* lesson (Chapter 5) and used the number of cubes the children had counted. However, the assessment can be done with any number.

The children's explanations of the number of tens and ones are extremely important. Children can learn the pattern that, in a two-digit number, the first digit tells the number of tens and the second tells the number of ones. However, being able to recognize that pattern isn't necessarily an indicator that a child understands the meaning of the pattern. The key to a child's understanding of the place value structure of our number system is that the tens digit tells how many groups of ten there are, while the ones digit is a count of individual objects.

Also, note that on the previous day, the class discussed the number of tens and extras there were in fifty-eight. Therefore, figuring out the number of tens and ones isn't an issue in this assessment. Rather, the point is for the children to explain the answer. The emphasis for the children is on making sense of the situation and finding a way to convince others. Whether the children know the number of tens and ones or have to figure it out, their reasoning process is what is most important for revealing their understanding.

To support the children in their writing efforts, I wrote the following on the board:

There are ___ 10s in 58 and ___ extras.
I think this because _____ .

Note: This assessment can also be conducted at the end of the unit to assess the change and growth in children.

Some approaches children took to solving this problem are shown in Figures 11 through 15.

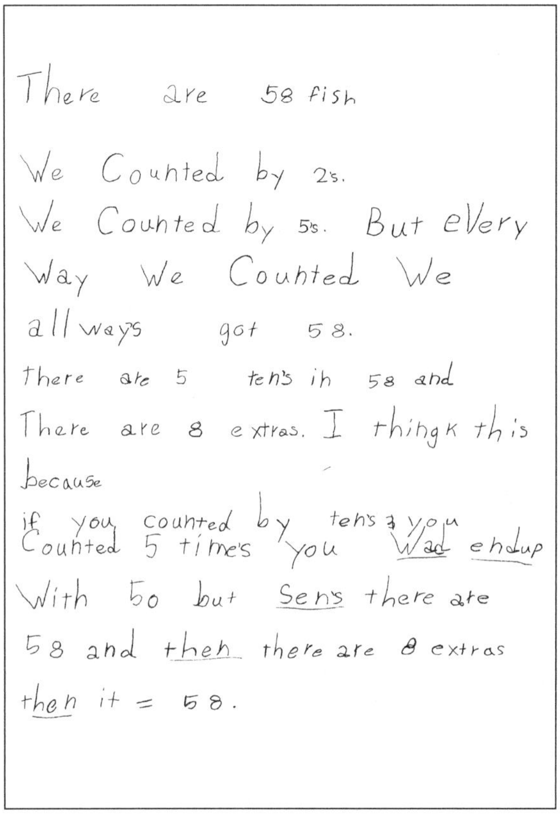

▲▲▲▲▲▲**Figure 11** *Amelia was a prolific writer and enjoyed explaining her math discoveries.*

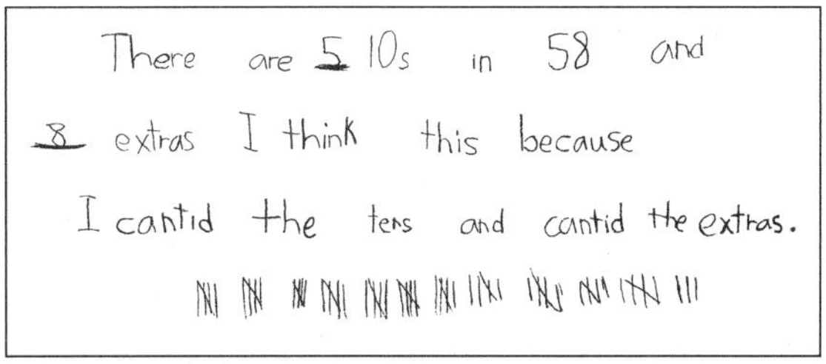

▲▲▲▲▲▲**Figure 12** *Jonathan resorted to drawing tallies, his preferred method for making sense of numbers.*

there are _ 10s in 58 and extras. I think this because There are 5 10s and 8 are left.

then will be 8 mor Left so It will be that eKws 20

1 10 10

al the 2 10S-eX Ws =40 10 110 If you add won mor 10 it eKws 50 and

▲▲▲▲▲▲Figure 13 *Eli's work revealed his math thinking but showed the need for more work on his writing.*

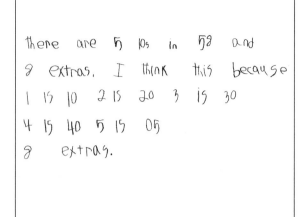

there are 5 10s in 58 and 8 extras. I think this because 1 15 10 2 15 20 3 is 30 4 15 40 5 15 05 8 extras.

▲▲▲▲▲▲Figure 14 *Hassan's math understanding surpassed his ability to communicate in writing.*

There are 6 tens and 8 ones

10, 20, 30, 40, 50, 51, 52, 53, 54, 55, 56, 57, 58,

There are 6 nines and 4 ones

▲▲▲▲▲▲Figure 15 *After figuring out how many 10s and 1s there were in 58, Andrew figured out how many 9s and 1s there were.*

How Much Is Covered?

PROMPT

Two children were playing Cover a Flat. *One had covered 28 squares on her hundreds square; the other had covered 35 squares. If they put all of their blocks together on one flat, how many squares would they cover?*

This assessment draws on children's experience with *Cover a Flat* (Chapter 15). For this assessment, I had children work in pairs, as it's not necessary for all assessments to be done individually. Having children work in pairs on an assignment provides the additional opportunity to listen to their conversations while they talk about the problem they're solving.

Explain the problem and write the following on the board:

One child covered 28 squares.

One child covered 35 squares.

Give children directions for working on the problem: "First, tell each other the problem and make sure you both understand it.

Then talk about how you could solve it. Finally, solve the problem and explain your thinking on paper. If you each have different methods, you should write about both of them." To remind the students of the directions, write the following on the board:

1. *Tell.*
2. *Talk.*
3. *Write.*

Figures 16 through 18 are examples of the students' work.

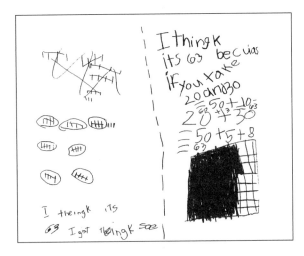

▲▲▲▲▲▲Figure 17 *Gwyn explained how she solved the problem numerically and also made a drawing to illustrate her solution. Jonathan, however, used tally marks and didn't indicate how they helped him arrive at the answer.*

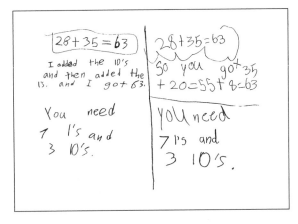

▲▲▲▲▲▲Figure 18 *Marina and Leslie both used 10s and 1s but expressed their reasoning in different ways. They also figured out how many more were needed to cover one flat entirely.*

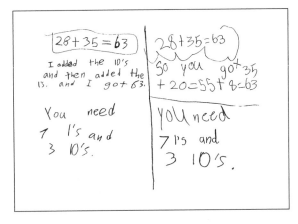

▲▲▲▲▲▲Figure 16 *Nick and Abby showed their different ways of solving the problem.*

How Many Ways to Make 36?

PROMPT

Show as many ways as you can to make 36 using 1s and 10s.

Before I gave the students this assessment, they had explored *Target Numbers* (Chapter 12) and had played the game of *Tens and Ones* (Chapter 11). I was interested in knowing if students were able to think about numbers flexibly and if they could use the structure of the base ten number system to represent numbers. Figures 19 through 21 demonstrate the span of student responses.

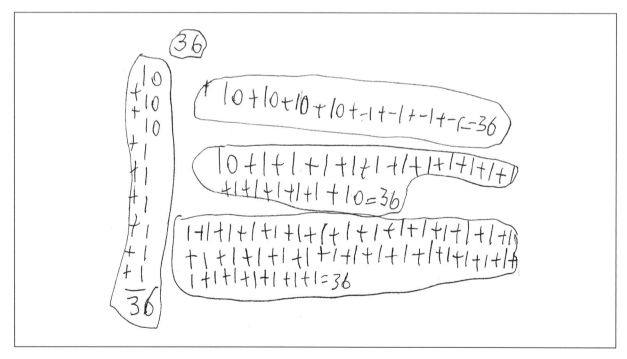

▲▲▲▲▲▲Figure 19   *Andy used a die to help him think about ways to make 36.*

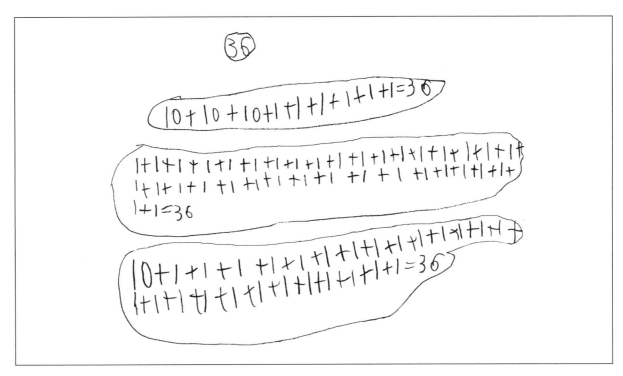

▲▲▲▲▲▲Figure 20   *Samuel persisted until he successfully found three ways to show 36.*

36

0 +|+|+|+|/+|+|/ +|+|+| +|+ +|+|+|+|+/+|+|+|+
|+|+|+|+|+|+|+ |+|+|+|+|+|+|+|=36 |+|+|/+|+|+|+|+
(2)0 +|0 +|+|+|+|+|=36   (3)+|0
                                 +|0
                                 +|0
                                 +|0
(4) |0 +|0 +|0 +|0 -|-|-|-|=36   +|0
(5)+|0 (6)+| +|0
    +|0   +|0   +|0
    +|0   +|0   +|0
    +|0   +|0   +|0
    +|0   +|0 36   -|0
    +|0   +|0   -|0
    +|0   -|0   -|0
    +|0   -|0   +|
    36   -|0   36

BLACKLINE MASTERS

0–99 Chart

0	1	2	3	4	5	6	7	8	9
10	11	12	13	14	15	16	17	18	19
20	21	22	23	24	25	26	27	28	29
30	31	32	33	34	35	36	37	38	39
40	41	42	43	44	45	46	47	48	49
50	51	52	53	54	55	56	57	58	59
60	61	62	63	64	65	66	67	68	69
70	71	72	73	74	75	76	77	78	79
80	81	82	83	84	85	86	87	88	89
90	91	92	93	94	95	96	97	98	99

0–99 Patterns

0	1	2	3	4	5	6	7	8	9
10	11	12	13	14	15	16	17	18	19
20	21	22	23	24	25	26	27	28	29
30	31	32	33	34	35	36	37	38	39
40	41	42	43	44	45	46	47	48	49
50	51	52	53	54	55	56	57	58	59
60	61	62	63	64	65	66	67	68	69
70	71	72	73	74	75	76	77	78	79
80	81	82	83	84	85	86	87	88	89
90	91	92	93	94	95	96	97	98	99

Five-Tower Game

You need:
  a partner
  about 100 cubes
  2 dice

Rules
1. Take turns. On your turn, roll the dice. The sum tells the number of cubes to take. Snap them into a tower.

2. When you're done, pass the dice to your partner. Then your partner follows Steps 1 and 2.

3. Do this until you each have five towers.

4. Each player makes a long train with his or her five towers. Count your cubes in two different ways.

5. Compare your trains to see who has more and who has less. Figure out how many more cubes are in the longer train.

6. Record.

Make a Shape Sample

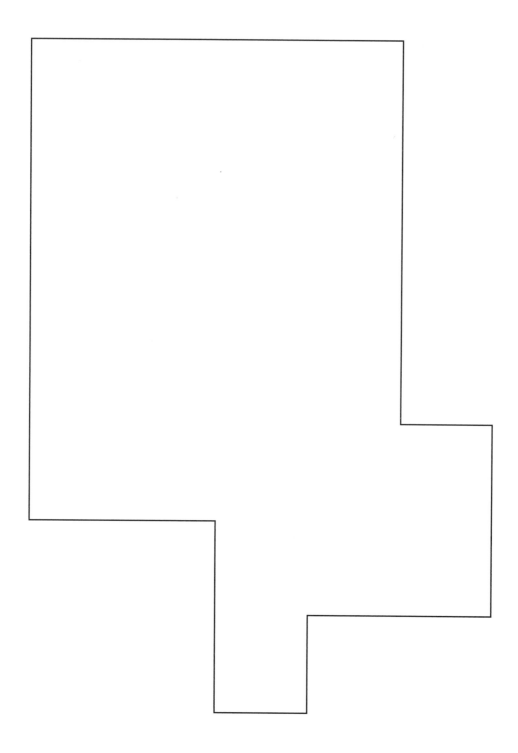

 From *Lessons for Introducing Place Value, Grade 2* by Maryann Wickett and Marilyn Burns. © 2002 Math Solutions Publications

Make a Shape

You need:
   color tiles

Rules
1. Draw a shape. You want to be able to cover the inside with 35 tiles.

2. Test by covering the inside of the shape with color tiles. Use 10 tiles of one color, then 10 of another, and so on, until it's covered.

3. Count the color tiles.

4. Record the number of tiles inside your shape.

5. Repeat the activity: draw, test, count, record.

From *Lessons for Introducing Place Value, Grade 2* by Maryann Wickett and Marilyn Burns. © 2002 Math Solutions Publications

1–100 Chart

1	2	3	4	5	6	7	8	9	10
11	12	13	14	15	16	17	18	19	20
21	22	23	24	25	26	27	28	29	30
31	32	33	34	35	36	37	38	39	40
41	42	43	44	45	46	47	48	49	50
51	52	53	54	55	56	57	58	59	60
61	62	63	64	65	66	67	68	69	70
71	72	73	74	75	76	77	78	79	80
81	82	83	84	85	86	87	88	89	90
91	92	93	94	95	96	97	98	99	100

The Game of Hippety Hop

You need:
  a partner
  a 1–100 chart
  1 game marker
  1 set of number cards

Rules
1. Draw a score chart and write your names at the top of the columns.

Maritza	Kasey

2. Place the marker above the top row of the 1–100 chart.

3. Player 1 draws a card and hops by ones, tens, and/or hundreds to reach the target number in as few hops as possible. Both players must agree on the number of hops. Player 1 records the number of hops in his or her column on the score sheet.

4. Player 2 follows Steps 2 and 3.

5. Continue until each player has drawn five numbers.

6. Both players figure their total hops. The player with the fewest number of hops for all five numbers wins the game.

The Game of Tens and Ones
Record Sheet

Name

From *Lessons for Introducing Place Value, Grade 2* by Maryann Wickett and Marilyn Burns. © 2002 Math Solutions Publications

The Game of Tens and Ones

You need:
   a partner
   2 0–99 charts
   2 markers
   1 die with faces labeled +10, +10, +10, –10,
      +1, –1

Rules
1. Each player places a marker on the zero on his or her own 0–99 chart. Players take turns rolling the die.

2. Player 1 rolls the die and moves a marker according to the roll on his or her own 0–99 chart.

3. Player 1 checks that Player 2 agrees and then hands the die to Player 2.

4. Player 2 follows the same steps as Player 1, using his or her own chart.

5. The winner is the first player to move his or her marker to 99. To win, a player must land on 99 exactly. For example, if a player lands on 90 and rolls a +10 on the next turn, the player must pass, as there are only nine boxes from 90 to 99. Players may not move their markers past 99 and off the chart.

Guess My Number

You need:
   a partner

Rules
1. Player 1 picks a number from 0 to 99 and writes it down.

2. Player 2 makes a guess and writes it down.

3. Player 1 gives a clue:

    "Your guess is greater than my number."
    or
    "Your guess is less than my number."

4. Continue playing until Player 2 guesses the number.

5. Switch jobs and play again.

 From *Lessons for Introducing Place Value, Grade 2* by Maryann Wickett and Marilyn Burns. © 2002 Math Solutions Publications

Race for $1.00

You need:
    a partner
    a zip-top baggie with 30 pennies, 20 dimes,
      and 2 play dollars
    2 dice

Rules
1. Take turns. On your turn, roll the dice. The sum tells how many pennies to take.

2. Decide if you want to exchange. (10 pennies = 1 dime)

3. Give the dice to your partner. Then your partner follows Steps 1 and 2.

4. Play until one player has $1.00.

Notes
1. You may exchange only when you have the dice.

2. Watch to make sure you agree with your partner's moves.

 From *Lessons for Introducing Place Value, Grade 2* by Maryann Wickett and Marilyn Burns. © 2002 Math Solutions Publications

Cover a Flat

You need:
    a partner
    a zip-top baggie with 2 flats, 20 tens rods, and
      30 unit cubes
    2 dice

Rules
1. Each player takes a flat.

2. Take turns. On your turn, roll the dice. The sum tells how many unit cubes to take. Place them on your flat.

3. Decide if you want to exchange 10 unit cubes for a tens rod.

4. Give the dice to your partner. Then your partner follows Steps 2 and 3.

5. Play until one player covers his or her flat with ten rods.

Notes
1. You may exchange only when you have the dice.

2. Watch to make sure you agree with your partner's moves.

 From *Lessons for Introducing Place Value, Grade 2* by Maryann Wickett and Marilyn Burns. © 2002 Math Solutions Publications

INDEX